Passage to Spiritual Power

Its Many Gifts Are Yours Should You Choose – Joy, Peace, Love

Adonia E. Wylie

Monastère Publishing

Revised second edition copyright © 2025 Adonia E. Wylie
First published 2008 as *Power: Our evolutionary path to the Divine Creative Field*

Adonia E. Wylie asserts her moral right to be identified as the author of this work.

All rights reserved. No part of this publication may be reproduced or transmitted in any form or by any means, electronic or mechanical, including photocopying, recording or information storage and retrieval systems, without permission in writing from the copyright holder.

Published by Monastère Publishing
Contact: monastere.publishing@gmail.com

A catalogue record for this book is available from the National Library of New Zealand.

ISBN 978-0-473-72967-7 (paperback)
ISBN 978-0-473-72968-4 (EPUB)

Contents

Author's Note	ix
Introduction	xi
1. THE SCIENTIFIC FRONTIER	1
2. RELIGIONS OF THE WORLD	26
Taoisim	31
Buddhism	35
Hinduism	42
Judaism	48
Christianity	53
Islam	58
3. SOUL	63
4. KNOW THYSELF	81
5. EVOLUTION	100
6. LOVE	121
7. FEAR	145
8. FREE WILL	164
9. TRUST AND FAITH	183
10. THE GOLDEN STRANDS	200
11. THE PHYSICAL BODY	222
12. THE EMOTIONAL BODY	230
13. THE MENTAL BODY	248
14. PASSAGE TO SPIRITUAL POWER WITH ALL ITS MANY GIFTS	270
Addendum: The Physical Body	293
About the Author	313

When I was young and free and my imagination had no limits, I dreamed of changing the world. As I grew older and wiser, I discovered the world would not change, so I shortened my sights somewhat and decided to change only my country. But it too seemed immovable.

As I grew into my twilight years, in one last desperate attempt, I settled for changing only my family, those closest to me, but alas, they would have none of it; and now, as I lay on my deathbed, I suddenly realise: if I had only changed myself first. Then by example, I might have changed my family; from their inspiration and encouragement I would then have been able to better my country, and who knows… I may even have changed the world.

— Attributed to a 10th century Anglican bishop

*We are all embedded
within a highly intelligent interactive field.
If we are wise, we will choose to interact with it.*

*This book is dedicated with love and gratitude to all my teachers,
past and present and in all realms, who have walked with me for a
time upon my path.*

Author's Note

One may read this book from cover to cover, or dip into it wherever, as you choose. Your intuition will direct you to the answers to questions you may have asked of the Divine. Therefore, use as you choose, there are no rules. God Bless.

Introduction

> By love they know me in Truth,
> Who I am, and what I am,
> And when he knows me in truth
> He enters into my Being.
>
> — *Bhagavad Gita 18–55*

How do we arrive at the point whereby words such as these hold for us real meaning? How do we come to not only understand, but also to see and to experience the vision and oneness of all? How do we begin to have faith in the Truth, and how do we learn not only to rest in the One but above all to love with a oneness of love the source of all?

Right now, all the above is difficult, if not impossible, as we have lost our way. We have become separated and disconnected from the real and the whole and have become fascinated and therefore focused upon the glamour of the illusory, the unreal. We have lost contact with the core of our being, our Soul, and therefore we have lost contact with the Divine Spiritual Reality, because it is only through our attention, interaction and recognition of our Divine Soul that we may approach and realise the Divine Ineffable Reality.

How did we lose our way? How did we first take such a wrong turning and arrive where we are today, immersed in separation with all its consequent confusion, ills and mental ill health? Many people including Pope John Paul II date this wrong turn to the philosophies of Isaac Newton and René Descartes some three hundred years ago with their fixed material worldview. As Pope John Paul II wrote in his book *Memory and Identity*, "Descartes' famous statement "Cogito ergo sum" ("I think therefore I am") radically changed philosophical thought: not only did it change the direction of philosophy, but also it abandoned what philosophy had been up to that point in time. Man was now the sum total of everything, and God was reduced to an element within human consciousness; God was no longer the ultimate explanation of the human. The God of revelation had ceased to exist as the God of the philosophers. All that remained was the idea of God, a topic for free exploration by human thought".

Descartes established the idea that nothing could be believed to be true unless one could prove it. As our understanding of the vast system in which we live is so pitifully small, therefore so also is our ability to prove reality. Thus what we believe to be true is such a dim and often incorrect minute fragment of the whole that we live for the most part in deluded darkness. We have lost our way. This is in part because, incredible as it may seem, we are in the 21st century living our lives based upon the 17th century understanding of Isaac Newton. In a Newtonian world, all was fixed, a mechanical, material universe of separation, a universe where time was an absolute and space was structured according to the known/agreed laws of motion. From Newton onwards our understanding of the universe changed, and a great divide appeared between the realms of the spirit/immaterial and that of the material/physical. Church and state/science moved ever more apart – until now. Now there is recognition that we have taken a wrong turn. If we wish to move forward, the right path must again be found.

Introduction

The path back to the Real, back to our Soul, back to the source – the Divine, is the path of Love, Peace, Joy and Spiritual Power.

The real meaning of Power is anything that flows from the Divine Creative source of all. The "I Am", the "God" of the above passages is the ultimate Power of all. Divine spiritual power is an all-encompassing, complete in itself, vital, potent and above all healing Power of infinite creative source and love. Divine Spiritual Power brings authority over all things temporal as it is omnipotent, omnipresent, omniscient, infinite and undying. Should we choose to seek, understand, and gain Divine Spiritual Power, we are choosing to seek knowledge of and loving unity with not only the "I Am" – "God", but ourselves.

In finding our way back to the right path, it is necessary to consider more realms than merely the manifested one, that which we can touch and see: we must also look at the un-manifested realms. We would be doomed to failure should we seek only in the manifested realm, as the source of all comes from the higher planes of consciousness. The manifested portion/realm represents such a minuscule proportion of the whole that we cannot arrive at the truth, or indeed any sort of clear and whole picture at all, if we wholly reside in and examine only that realm. The "Divine", the "One", is primarily found and understood outside of this space-time continuum. On the other hand, perhaps it is more accurate to say; the Divine appears more obscure, harder to find in the material realms, as we, when dwelling in this realm, are so easily confused by the distracting material aspects. Therefore, it is to other realms we need to travel if we are to find our way back to the right path.

I need also to mention here the use I have made of particular words. Language is always rather inadequate when talking about or describing aspects outside the realms of the five senses, so please bear with me. When I use the word "God" (simply means all that is good), and "he" in that context, I am not implying any gender nor am I putting forward any particular religious thought by using the word

God. It is just a convenient word to indicate the Supreme Consciousness, the Unified Field, the Unified Field of Love, the Divine Creative Field, the Creator, Allah, Yahweh or what you will. I have also used extensively the word "soul": again, it is convenient because most people have an understanding of what is meant by this word but spirit, divine essence, integral undying energetic core and so on could also be used.

This book s a simple guide back to the right path, back to ourselves and a fully conscious empowering relationship with the Divine Creator. It is the path back to healing not only ourselves but also all on the planet at this time. I may sometimes appear to stray into the regions of what many may label as weird, or New Age stuff, and some may not want to be caught reading such material. To those readers I say: before we go too far along the path of closed minds, suspend disbelief for the moment and remember that "There are more things in heaven and earth, Horatio, than are dreamt of in your philosophy." (Shakespeare, *Hamlet*)

Chapter 1
The Scientific Frontier

The real voyage of discovery consists not in seeking new landscapes, but in having new eyes.

— *Marcel Proust*

Before embarking on a conscious journey to full loving spiritual unity, there are some fundamental things we must first understand. This epic journey, which started from the moment of our non-physical creation, has been evolving through time and space for aeons unbeknown to us, as for the most part we are still relatively unconscious. To evolve successfully, to become fully conscious, aligned and spiritual light beings of high spin and infinite Love, Peace and Joy, there are certain things we must first do. In order to start we will need a basic understanding of the fundamental underlying systems and laws of the environment in which we reside. Currently we have two major views of the multiverse available to us. One is the left-brain scientific point of view, which itself can be broken down into two primary aspects, classical science and quantum physics. The other is the more right-brain view held by the many and varied religions.

The world as viewed today by current scientific thought is vastly different from the one seen in previously held world-views. Classical science began by examining the phenomenal world of that which is evidenced by the senses. This world was a three-dimensional one with only height, length and breadth. As science evolved, so did our understanding of the world around us and it became clear that further dimensions were required if we were to more fully understand it. With time and then space-time being added to our dimensions, a greater, more holistic picture began to emerge. Newton and Einstein, the fathers of our modern scientific thought, proposed many theories that are now being displaced by the more recent theories of quantum physics. These are like the many branches of a tree: they cover many different areas and are sometimes in conflict one with one other as new frontiers are being crossed all the time. One could say the entire field is in a continual state of groundbreaking discovery, with new theories often being discarded in full or in part with unprecedented rapidity. However, it is important to understand we do not have all the answers yet, although large pieces of the picture are starting to appear. Within all these new cutting-edge discoveries there are emerging some constants linking all. It is in the detail that dispute is arising – the detail is often overthrown by later discoveries, but the underlying ground is remaining. These fundamental constants are giving us a vastly different view of the multiverse than hitherto imagined.

When we examine some of the fundamental precepts of quantum physics, it becomes clear that the path the scientists have taken is bringing them to the place the mystics of various religions have occupied for thousands of years. Is theology about to become a branch of physics, or is physics about to become a branch of theology? It does not matter. What matters and is exciting is that they are no longer in opposition but appear to agree. With this agreement we are getting a more accurate vision of ourselves and of our place in the multiverse.

Over seventy years ago, the birth of quantum physics brought into question the Newtonian mechanistic principles. The idea of a fixed, solid world of separate parts independent from mind and spirit was shown to be untenable. Yet in so many ways in so many areas of our lives, we still think and live as though the Newtonian principles are fact. We are slow to change and this slowness is causing us many fundamental problems. Some of the trouble we are in today started with Descartes. Before his statement "Cogito ergo sum" – "I think therefore I am" all philosophical thought and theology were linked and the Divine was the ground and source of our being. Suddenly the Divine was displaced by the "I" which now enjoyed priority, with the result that science became the realm only of pure thought (left-brain logical, separated, rigid, analytical stuff). Our world was split asunder into the two domains of matter and everything else, which included all the things we do not understand. "I" and "matter" ruled the day.

Einstein slightly changed the fixed world of Newton, starting in 1905 when he coined the phrase "space-time continuum", saying they were not two separate things but one: time may speed up or slow down, while space may expand or shrink. In other words, this was the overturning of the fixed rigidity of Newton's theories. Einstein said, "Nature shows us only the tail of the lion, but I do not doubt that the lion belongs to it even though he cannot at once reveal himself because of his enormous size." The tail is what we see in nature and the four fundamental forces of gravity, electromagnetism and the strong and weak nuclear forces describe this. The lion, it is hoped, is the ultimate theory that will unify them all in one simple elegant equation. Einstein knew he was seeing and understanding only a small part of the lion. However, even though he spent the last thirty years of his life in a fruitless quest for the fabled Unified Field Theory, he gave us this very accurate image of where the scientists were at that time.

The main problem was that the first force, gravity/time, had been described and understood by Einstein's General Theory of Relativity. The other three had been described and supposedly understood by quantum theory, but the two could not be united. The scientists were looking for an overall theory that would explain everything but, until recently, they were unable to bring together all they thought they knew into a simple elegant whole. Glimpses of greater parts of the lion enabled them to make educated guesses (left-brain) as to the whole lion, often combined with an educated guess is an intuitive leap (right-brain). With these two at play, the Divine Reality began to reveal itself.

> I never came upon any of my discoveries through the process of rational thinking.
>
> — *Albert Einstein*

It appears that Einstein was using both hemispheres of his brain in his search for truth. Indeed, to gain greater understanding we must employ the whole being rather than the favoured bits, i.e. our left-brain or merely aspects of the whole. If Einstein functioned in this manner, it is probably a good approach for us all to employ. If we attempt to approach the mysteries of the whole solely via the left-brain, we are guaranteed to fail as it is impossible to arrive at the gnosis (knowledge of spiritual mysteries) solely through this aspect of the brain. The path of the mystics coupled with our left-brain will ensure success. The problem for us in our modern, scientific, separated and materialist world is that we find the ways of the mystics unacceptable. Our energetic, dominant left-brain cannot always validate the mystics' intuitive leaps, so it interferes and deletes all unacceptable information as nonsense, and we thus continue in our limiting ignorance.

All of science agrees on one basic tenet: the only stuff appearing to exist in the entire multiverse is energy. There is nothing else but energy, absolutely nothing else! (they have recently discovered Dark Matter and Black Holes, but these are only different aspects of energy). One cannot create energy and one cannot destroy energy. All that one can do is to change its form. Theories regarding the particular forms energy takes have changed with time and further research. It was once thought that energy could be in particle form and then become a wave, then a particle again, but this view has changed. Electrons were once thought of as particles spinning around an atom much like a miniature solar system, but now it is believed the electron is smeared throughout the whole of space as a quantum wave, which only collapses as a particle into our physical space-time when a conscious observer observes it. It seems for a particle to appear in our space-time dimension a necessary part of the process is the involvement of a conscious observer. In other words, consciousness – human beings are participating in the creation of our own physical reality. Without the conscious observer, the particle remains as part of the quantum soup outside our space-time dimension. It was also found that when a wave collapses it is not possible to predict where the particle will end up: it may materialise hundreds or thousands of miles away, but when it does arrive, it arrives at that place in zero time. In other words, it bypasses both space and time.

Einstein and many other scientists, together with every major spiritual tradition on Earth, believe that the multiverse is composed of a single contiguous unified field of energy, sometimes referred to as Ether, Zero Point, Background Energy or Implicate Order ("implicate" means enfolded i.e. invisible, as opposed to the manifested world, which is "explicate", unfolded i.e. visible). When the quantum wave in the implicate realm collapses, it unfolds into the explicate realms and becomes part of the physical realm we are so familiar with. While we inhabit the explicate or unfolded realm of this particular space-time dimension, our day-to-day conscious mind is completely unaware of the implicate realms and all within them. However, some think that our conscious mind has two levels and that we are possessed of a higher mind that is aware of and may inhabit all realms outside of this particular space-time dimension.

David Bohm, one of the great physicists of the twentieth century, wrote that "ultimately the entire universe with all its particles, including those constituting human beings, their laboratories, observing instruments etc., has to be understood as a single undivided whole, in which analysis into separately and independently existent parts, has no fundamental status". In other words, it is pointless to examine the universe as though there was such a thing as separation – it is a single, contiguous whole. Bohm went on to say that "seemingly all separate objects, entities, structures and events in the visible world were only temporarily seemingly separate and that all were derived from a deeper order of unbroken wholeness". He gave the example of a stream whose ever-changing patterns of ripples, splashes and waves have no independent existence: they only for the moment give the appearance of such and quickly vanish back into the stream which is the underlying contiguous whole. The transitory life of each wave implies only a relative independence or free will within the overall order and control of the stream. Bohm described the whole universe as a kind of giant flowing hologram. He held the view that each tiny part of the explicate order contained within it all the information of the implicate order (this is the basic theory behind holography). Therefore, the entire universe is held or contained within each single particle that makes up our being and everything else. We are in reality a universe of universes. There are worlds within worlds within worlds in which the total order is contained in each region of space and time.

Bohm saw reality as a sort of projection from the higher dimension, higher vibratory levels of reality with the apparent stability and solidity of objects and entities being generated by a ceaseless process of coming into being and then dissolving back into the implicate order, much as a wave arises and dissolves back into the stream. Higher orders organise the lower ones, which in turn affect the higher, so we have a seemingly intelligent organiser (as apparently haphazard movements of individual electrons manage to produce highly organised overall effects) and cause and effect at work ceaselessly. More importantly, it appears to be a process of continual refinement. Energy in its ceaseless cyclic activity follows a spiral pathway, resulting in an overall higher resonance and thus greater unfolding, so this is an evolutionary process. There is no such thing as separation; all idea of separation is an illusion. We live in and are part of a fluid and intelligently ordered energy field. This field is also a highly interactive field in which information is passed faster than the speed of light, because in a non-local world, where all is "one"

The Scientific Frontier

instantaneous communication is the norm. We can all choose to consciously interact with this field. We all have all the equipment needed to do this, Einstein's theory of relativity where nothing can travel faster than the speed of light is overturned. This interactive process of infinite intelligent refinement is seemingly directed to a particular end. We are not alone, as there is no such thing as separation, and we are evolving toward an intelligently designed endpoint. What is even more remarkable is that each one of us is unique, indeed it is being proposed that every single thing in creation is unique, so we have individuation within oneness. Think about that for a moment.

Another great scientist of the twentieth century, Max Planck, said, "There is no matter as such!" All matter originates and exists only by virtue of a force which brings particles of an atom to vibration and holds this most minute solar system of the atom together. We must assume behind this force the existence of a conscious and intelligent Mind. This Mind is the matrix of all matter.

With this new vision of the multiverse scientists are now beginning to understand that the Darwinian view – "Survival of the Fittest", is quite incorrect. The more they look, the more it becomes apparent that co-operation, not competition is the key. In other words, for us to survive we must learn how to co-operate in relationship with all that is, and communication is of course an essential aspect of that.

To encapsulate, if we go to the level below atoms to the sub-atomic to elementary particles, we find some very strange properties indeed:

- Everything is connected to everything else.
- A particle appears to be possessed of intelligence and memory, and this intelligence is shared through this universal interconnectedness.
- Particles that are far apart (i.e. non-local) are able to communicate with each other in an instantaneous manner that is not yet fully understood.

- Particles can be in more than one place at a time. This ability appears to be a fundamental property of the fabric of the universe.
- An observer in the act of observation changes the activity of the particle/wave – the particle does not exist in the physical world until the observer observes it and the act of observation freezes and changes its motion. By merely trying to measure a part of a particular experiment, the experiment will not repeat itself but will change with this action on the part of the experimenter: focusing on what is happening changes the outcome. With the most fleeting thought passing through the mind of the experimenter, the outcome of the experiment is altered.
- We appear to be co-creators, as our participation is essential to some of the processes.
- Underlying all, we find a highly intelligent pattern or information that is the basic fabric of consciousness.
- Underlying all, we find a highly intelligent pattern or information that is the basic fabric of the multiverse.

All of this led Einstein to say once, "I am not sure the moon is still there when I turn my head." In other words, maybe our physical world exists only when we look at it, or interact with it. The computer program in our being translates the quantum energy field into pictures – you could say "virtual reality" for us – and when we are not looking, or if the program is changed, it is just a field of conscious intelligence again.

Ether or background energy was discussed and written about back in the nineteenth century and it was known about in quantum science for quite some time, but for some reason it was largely ignored. Now it is back in focus. This field of energy has some amazing properties: it measures at zero degrees Kelvin, the absolute lowest possible known temperature, equal to minus 273 degrees Celsius. According to Newtonian principles, at this temperature all molecular and atomic life would cease, but instead what was found was a seething mass of energy. This energy field is extremely dense and some scientists are starting to look to it as an infinite ever-renewable source of energy. It has been calculated that a cup of zero-point energy is enough to bring all the oceans of the world to boiling point. There is a continuous flow of energy from this background field into our physical, manifested world and back again into the background field. Particles and photons appear to jump into existence only to disappear again; some appear so unstable they are labelled virtual particles. Together with all this particle activity, it appears we also have wave activity. Within this field sometimes there are waves, at other times particles; so in quantum physics we ended up with something called wave-particle duality. Once again, all that has changed and it is becoming universally accepted that there are only waves in this sea of ether or background energy, with matter being the focal point of a vibration in the field. Now we are getting into really exciting stuff. The key words here are "focal point of a vibration" which could be focused attention, focused energy – sound, words, numbers, music – creating matter out of the waves of the sea of background energy.

In the 1980s, something quite dramatic happened in the world of the physicists. Some of them realised that the subatomic particles such as electrons may not be particles at all, but tiny vibrating strings. Suddenly we had something called Superstring Theory, a radical departure based on the idea of tiny strings vibrating in ten-dimensional space-time. It is proposed that subatomic particles are nothing more than different resonances of the vibrating superstrings in the same way that different musical notes emanate from the different modes of vibration of a violin string. The forces between the charged particles for example, are the harmonies of the strings – so the universe is a symphony of vibrating strings. Physicists found that in order to see the whole picture clearly and to make all their complex calculations work out correctly they had to move onto higher ground into "hyperspace". Leaping to higher dimensions can also help to clarify the laws of nature: in 1915 Einstein changed completely our notion of gravity by leaping to the extra dimension of time; in 1919

Theodor Kaluza added a fifth dimension and in so doing made all the equations to do with space-time and electromagnetism work.

When the strings move in ten-dimensional space-time they warp the space-time surrounding them in precisely the way predicted by general relativity. By moving to the eleventh dimension, string theory simply and elegantly unified the quantum theory of particles and general relativity. Better still, gravity is not an inconvenient add-on, as String Theory requires gravity. Therefore, the universe is starting to look as though it is not only a purposeful, coherent, intelligent web or membrane, it is also a symphony. Sound and its vibrations are a key here. When physicists examined the eleventh dimension, they found some very strange properties indeed. Space-time starts to behave in quite different ways from what was first thought possible, and current theories postulate that everything is actually happening simultaneously past, present and future all at once – or, if you like, there is no past, present or future, just the one present unified, connected, musical field encompassing all. What is certain is that the linear view we have of the multiverse is certainly incorrect. Are we multi-dimensional beings who dwell in multiple realms, interconnected to all that is? In the words of physicist Michio Kaku who named this theory M Theory – for Membrane, Multiverse or Magic, "For the first time we can see the outline of the lion and it is magnificent. One day we will hear it roar."

This idea of multiple realms and time being an illusion because all events are happening simultaneously is gaining ground. In our personal virtual reality that we create moment by moment, "out there" is an illusion. Time does not exist as it is we who are doing the moving through the eternal reality of consciousness. It has been postulated that we may exist in more than one virtual reality at a time, with our higher consciousness arranging and directing the lower one. It appears that events are laid out in a pre-arranged pattern that we have not yet reached, but when we do we may change slightly: in one reality we may take a particular job, in another we may not. In this way, we may experience all possibilities simultaneously. It sounds like a great and interesting game, does it not? This idea explains precognition, remote viewing, life after death and a host of other things that have been puzzling scientists and searchers after truth for a long time.

Chaos Theory has some interesting aspects that help us to understand the whole. Chaos in Greek mythology is the cosmic force, the formless void or great deep of primordial matter out of which all is created – the raw material, if you like, out of which all is fashioned. Chaos Theory is so-called because the systems that it describes seemed to be disordered. The analogy used was that the flapping of a single butterfly's wing today produces a tiny change in the atmosphere; over time, what the atmosphere does, diverges from what it would have done if the butterfly had not flapped its wings; and because of this, a tornado that would have devastated a part of the world maybe now does not, or maybe one that was not going to happen now does. This phenomenon is known as "sensitive dependence on initial conditions", and means that just a small change in the initial conditions can drastically change the long-term behaviour of a system. This shows us the interdependence and interconnectedness of all things. Consequently, the name of this theory is somewhat of a misnomer as Chaos Theory shows us the underlying interconnectedness of all things. It is really about finding the underlying order in apparently random data. The process can best be described as a system that is continually making order out of apparent chaos. Driven by the outward thrust of the formless void in its need to organise and attracted by the perfect symmetry of the Divine Implicate Order, we could say Chaos Theory is a view of evolution in action. With this view, the Second Law of Thermodynamics, which states that all order will eventually decay into disorder, is overthrown. The driving thrust of the universe is to move from chaos to order, into ever-increasing realms of refinement. This is now believed to be the all-pervading action. It is now proposed by a number of scientists that individual but not separated systems, linked and interacting through the background field, are evolving according to an underlying plan/law or pattern. Therefore, individuation within oneness.

Another field of study that is revealing new and exciting knowledge is that of so-called life after death phenomena. Scientists have discovered that at the ceasing of metabolic action (death) the information or pattern of the consciousness (religions would call it the soul) leaks out into the universe at large – but rather than dissipating, it hangs together. This phenomenon is called quantum entanglement or quantum coherence. It is by this mechanism, scientists are beginning to believe, that we continue to exist, or consciousness and memory remains intact and functioning, outside the physical body after death.

Many studies are being carried out with schizophrenics, epileptics and people who have experienced a near-death experience (NDE). It is postulated that immediately before physical death, the brain triggers the release of a cocktail of chemicals. This creates an electrical storm throughout the energy field of the being, which has the effect of catapulting in a spiral motion, the integral underlying and intrinsic field or soul, out of this time-space continuum and into another. Exiting rapidly in a spiral motion would create the effect so many people report from NDEs of moving through a tunnel with light at the end. It is in this way, scientists theorise, that we survive bodily death.

Another theory which is harder to comprehend involves the idea of multiple realities. Scientists postulate that our inherent programming creates a virtual reality of our surroundings and everything in it, and that this reality is individual. In other words, each of us is living in our own individual virtual reality. This reality is linked, as all is linked within the system, so that at the point of so-called death we appear to die to others linked to our virtual reality – we drop out of their picture, so to speak – but we remain in our own. We continue on, often unaware at first that anything has happened at all.

Within all these different theories an essential picture is beginning to emerge: it is becoming increasingly certain that memory/consciousness and individual but not separated energy fields or souls continue on after physical death.

It was once thought the only places memory was stored in the body was in the brain and immune system. This was found not to be so. Each cell in our body stores memory and, what is more, each cell of our body is possessed of intelligence. We are each of us a field of intelligence and stored memories within the larger fields of intelligence and stored memories of the multiverse. Therefore, there is a great deal more going on in our bodies in an intelligent way than was first thought. Each cell is able to communicate instantaneously with another and non-locally, with information shared around faster than the speed of light. Memories from both this life and the lives of our ancestors are stored within our bodies and are accessible and affect our bodies and our lives each moment in ways that heretofore were unthinkable.

We are beginning to get a picture of a purposeful intelligent interconnected field or web in which memory information and consciousness are held. I have thought for some time that the World Wide Web (WWW) is a reflection of the way things really are. If we use the WWW as an analogy, we will have no difficulty imagining the multiverse as an immense, electrical, purposeful and energetic web with all information, memory, consciousness, programming or patterning being stored and shared. The WWW contains knowledge, information and an integral interconnectedness and as such is a source of information and power: it is a small and imperfect reflection that man has created of the unified field that Einstein believed existed, and which is now being proven a reality. Good and evil, positive and negative are also held within this web.

Let us now look at what Japanese author Masaru Emoto discovered. Remembering a lesson at school that no two snowflakes were the same, just as no two fingerprints are the same, he embarked on a study of water and its properties. Basing his study on the belief that all in the known multiverse is energy resonating at particular and different rates, Emoto set out to see what would happen if water were subjected to different resonances, i.e. music, words, emotions and pictures. After exposing the water to positive and negative stimuli he then froze it until it produced crystals, which he photographed. The results were astonishing. He says he made the following extraordinary discoveries: water seemed possessed of intelligence and memory; it was interactive; and it responded to words, pictures, emotions and music. In addition, he found it was impossible to get beautiful and harmonious crystals to form from polluted water or some city tap water from around the world. It appeared that negative emotions, negative words or pollution formed either ugly distorted crystals or no crystals at all. Curiously, Emoto also found that ignoring the water he was testing caused a greater negative response than sending negative emotions or words towards it. The formation of the most beautiful and perfect crystals appeared after exposing the water to the words "love" and "gratitude". Love linked with gratitude appeared to ramp up the power of love in that the crystals thus formed were of greater intricacy and enhanced perfection than the crystals formed from exposure to love alone. Water exposed to different music formed different crystals: heavy metal music resulted in ugly, ill-formed crystals – no surprise there. The more beautiful and harmonious the music, the more positive the words, the more beautiful were the crystals that formed.

We know that our physical bodies are comprised mostly of water, which is one of the greatest conductors of energy and is extremely sensitive to electromagnetic fields. As the sun, moon and other planets change positions in the heavens, these changes are reflected in chemical reactions that use water as a base. Water, as Emoto discovered, has an electromagnetic memory which enables it to remember different charges or resonances and polarisations for long periods. It is no accident that all our electromagnetic fields and memory programs are embedded in a water bag (the body) as water is the perfect medium for us to manifest in the physical. Water is the chosen medium through which life manifests in this space-time continuum, as water is perfectly suited in all aspects for the task.

In similar vein, the Russian biophysicist Pjotr Garjajev found while studying the human genome that it was possible to reprogram the human DNA simply by using words with the correct resonant frequencies. In other words, using human speech with the words modulated to the resonant frequencies, scientists could simply reprogram the human genome. Are we getting into the realms of magic and spells here? Emoto was doing with water what Garjajev was doing with human DNA.

To conclude, thoughts, emotions, words, music, sound – all resonances whether positive or negative – interact with and affect the surrounding environment and everything in it. In some instances, the effects are noticeable but in all cases an effect is created with subsequently everything affected; maybe we are merely unable to consciously register it.

Other research similar to the two examples above now confirm that our emotions and thoughts affect our daily lives – in particular our health – in profound and sometimes alarming ways. Negative emotions or thoughts may degrade our immune system and thereby cause disease and death; positive emotions and thoughts enhance our health and well-being and assist longevity. Many scientists now look upon our DNA as a biological computer, with all the cells in our body able to store memory and communicate with each other; this has even been observed if the cells are removed from the body and taken some distance away (even great distances); i.e. our cells are able to communicate non-locally with each other.

With all this new information we should start to rethink many things, not the least being blood transfusions and organ transplants. Disturbing information is coming from research undertaken with organ transplant patients, who often show marked personality changes or even physical body changes – a recent young transplant patient's blood group changed from O negative to O positive (the donor's group) after receiving donor organs, which with all we now know about the human body and the world around us is not surprising. Indeed, it would be surprising if this were not the case. It is often only our current deep state of unconsciousness that allows us to engage in these practices and not observe the results. In our ignorance, we do not consider the possible irreparable damage done to our intrinsic being – our soul field – in our attempts to increase our physical longevity at all costs. Without conscious awareness and holistic vision, we are unable to see the true results of our actions. We should also include here Cell Phone use, Wi-Fi, Cell Phone Towers and anything else that is an unnatural energy field likely to interact, block and otherwise disturb our natural Divine field.

Now we need briefly to go back in time to the ancient science of Sacred Geometry and the Platonic Solids, as scientists are taking a fresh look at these ancient arts. The Egyptians, Sumerians, Hebrews and the ancient Greeks all possessed this ancient knowledge and wisdom. Sacred Geometry was thus termed as it was believed that if one understood this science fully one would understand how the universe and all of life was created. The Platonic solids are named after Plato who wrote in the fourth century BC that these five three-dimensional forms – cube, tetrahedron, octahedron, dodecahedron and icosahedron – are the basic building blocks of matter.

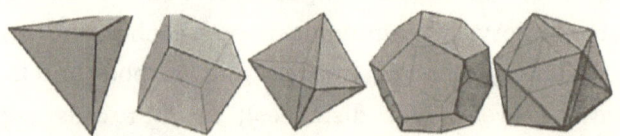

Tetrahedron, Cube, Octahedron, Dodecahedron, Icosahedron

The Freemasons' symbol is a carpenter's square and a compass, which are all the tools needed to practise Sacred Geometry: this implies that the early secret societies of Freemasonry were about understanding and practising the ancient, powerful and (after the rise of the Catholic Church) secret wisdom. If we go back to "there is only energy" and the explicate realm coming into existence via the focal point of a vibration in the background field, there must be some system whereby matter is held in form. It is now postulated that the Genesis story is in fact an allegory for the process of creation whereby resonance forms a focal point in the background field and thus energy moves from the implicate realm to the explicate realm and is then held in the explicate realm by particular and purposeful arrangements of spheres and platonic solids.

Genesis pattern

The Genesis pattern is one of the most important patterns in sacred geometry. This pattern, formed by seven interconnecting spheres, is believed to be the pattern for the origin of life; hence, it took seven days to create life. The pattern also perfectly contains a pair of tetrahedrons, which together create a familiar sacred symbol – the Star of David, which is the Jewish symbol of sacred life.

The resonance of particular words, numbers and sound, form different patterns – Platonic Solids – for the controlled movement of energy in the background field and matter is thus formed by the progression and nesting of the platonic solids. Platonic Solids will nest perfectly inside a sphere and inside each other infinitely. Infinitely repetitive patterns that keep a constant ratio even though their size may change are called fractals and are how holograms are constructed, as each piece is an exact replica of the whole. Scientists are now beginning to believe that these particular shapes are formed by harmonious wave cycles that follow the Golden Mean ratio so here again with the Platonic Solids, we have sound being the origin of manifested physical matter and Platonic Solids being the vehicle, pattern or law that holds the wave in place. The Hindu/Buddhist beginning word or vibration was believed to be Om and/or Hu. The Bible has this to say:

> In the beginning was the Word, and the Word was with God, and the Word was God.
>
> —*John 1:1*

It looks as though the universe is one great glorious and harmonious symphony, with sound being integral to the system. There are currently many theories regarding how matter is formed from the surrounding field, and integral to them all is the Torus. We know that energy in the multiverse moves in a spiral motion, the most efficient way. We also know that spirals are a fundamental pattern or law of the multiverse. What is more, these spirals correspond in all cases to the Golden Mean ratio. Matter when formed to the Golden Mean ratio is in perfect and sublime proportion and it is this perfection of proportion that is reflected throughout all the natural world from the seemingly simple to the most complex. All of life is built upon this one essential blueprint: our own DNA helixes are a case in point. We have seen that waves form in the background field when conscious observation or resonance plays upon it, but it is thought that what is initially formed are vortices spiraling upwards out of the background field. Whenever there is resonance, there follows a particular field which shapes energy initially into a toroidal form.

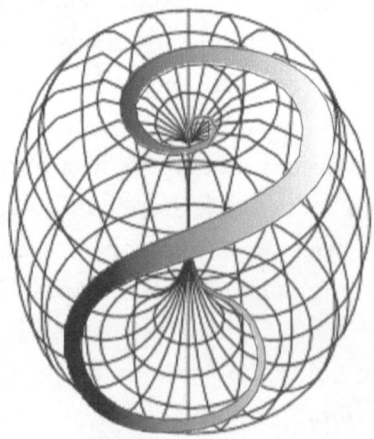

Phi spiral on the doughnut's surface

Imagine a small tornado: these vortices are natural flow forms for all energy and if you imagine one vortex spiraling up, with another reversed and joined in the middle, we get a double vortex. This spiral corresponds to the Golden Mean ratio and can be perfectly described by a set of Phi or Golden Mean spirals.

When these spirals circle round the torus, they meet and interfere; as a result of this interference, two new additional spirals will be created that will again have wavelengths that are in the Golden Mean ratio, therefore the interference will be non-destructive and will simply result in more harmonics in the series ad infinitum. Whereas destructive interference is the norm in spiral or wave interference, the only exception in nature is when waves interfere with Golden Mean wavelengths. In other words, the spiral can re-enter itself around the doughnut shape without destroying itself.

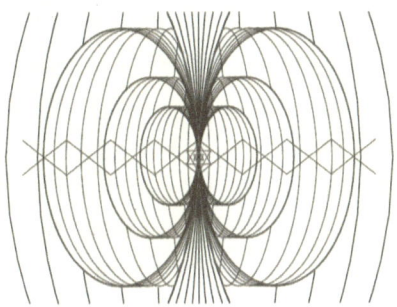

Phi spirals in nested doughnuts

It is now thought that the Phi spiral is the only possible way for the universe to nest and become self-organising. This is how stable matter is formed from the ether or Zero Point field as a form of pure wave interference. The Golden Mean spirals of the doughnut shape eventually spiral into a perfect zero still point in the nucleus of the vortex that coincides with the nucleus of the atom. A primary still point of toroidal flow is to be found within each of us, and it is to this point that all meditation techniques are directed. It is further believed the implosion of these golden waves into the torus is the origin of gravity.

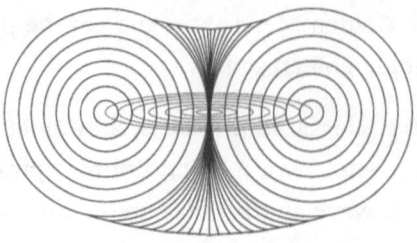

Toroidal flow

We find many times in religious writings a passage saying something like, "In between the inward breath of God and the outward breath of God lies the great secret." Is this possibly telling us about the movement of energy flowing up the spiraling vortex, cascading over the sides, sucked in again and up through the middle, much as we breathe in and out? During the moment of time that the breath is inside the funnel of the two vortexes, change/evolution occurs. It is also a simple diagram of the multiverse expanding from the source to return again to the source, and this is now believed to be the overall residing action of energy. If we look at the Big Bang theory which postulates that the universe came into existence with one explosive event, the result of which was energy being flung ever outwards, the movement we still have today, and if we were also to postulate that it was in fact a toroidal flow event that happened as this action is found throughout the multiverse (with the Big Bang we are merely working in larger scale), then the idea assumes greater sense and clarity. If this is the case as many scientists theorize, the universe will begin to contract at some time in the future, because when our universe reaches the outermost edge of its particular torus energy form, all will begin to move back towards the centre to then enter again in the eternal process of refinement towards perfection. All is in a continual process of infinite creation, spiraling towards refinement and perfection and this appears to be the underlying action and law throughout the multiverse.

The Platonic solids and the spirals of the torus, the Golden Mean ratio is to be found throughout the universe. Scientists have now measured the field generated from the spinning vortex – toroidal flow energy field of the Heart Chaka (Sanskrit word for wheel) located at a point between the two breasts, when in the moment of loving and this field was found to be coherent, unified, and harmonious and cascaded to the Golden Mean proportions. In other words, the frequency of love corresponds to the Golden Mean. It is now postulated that as the multiverse appears to be formed of energy patterns that correspond to the Golden Mean with the same resonance as love, and as these patterns are also fractal – the very warp and weft of the multiverse is infinitely Creative Love. The universe, from its largest planets and suns to the smallest atom and us, is constructed the same way and operates under the same underlying patterns/laws, the ground of which is the resonance of love. The heart chakra is the primary focal point for the unified coherent field of love to inflow from the Divine and outflow from us all.

To recap: creation is triggered by sound/focused intent, which forms a concentrated energy spiral in the background field which then becomes a continual process of unfolding of all the fields involved. This then is held in individual but not separate form, by a process we do not yet fully comprehend. It is thought that the continual unfolding of the Divine creative process is able to continue and progress only with ongoing focused intent – mind, which may be inherent or in the form of a plan or pattern – religions would call this God. For the process to complete, alignment is key: any misalignment causes distortion, so the process is no longer to the Golden Mean, is not fractal and the continual unfolding process degrades or halts. The ultimate goal of creation is now thought to be the complete and perfect unfolding of all the energy fields involved – aligned, coherent, harmonised = perfect spin = higher resolution = the resonance of perfect creative love. With all this information pouring in, many scientists are now coming to the conclusion that the universe is self-aware, which means that everything within the universe is self-aware. All the atoms, rocks, stars and planets – everything is self-aware, everything is sentient. This will not be news to the indigenous people who have always believed the whole of creation was aware and interactive and, as such, sacred and should therefore be honoured and protected. If everything is alive and interactive, then consciousness must play a large role in the scheme of things.

Masaru Emoto has this to say: "Traditionally speaking, anyone who says that consciousness has an effect on the physical world risks certain ostracism for being unscientific. However, science has progressed to a point where the failure to understand consciousness and the mind limits our understanding of much of the world around us." What was thought impossible only a few years ago is starting to look extremely feasible today. Our view of the world around us is destined to change even more radically in the near future and our current age will look as ignorant and dark as the Dark Ages do to us today. It all makes one begin to agree with the Buddhists who say that all of life on this physical plane of existence is an illusion.

So where are we now after all the above?

- There is one intelligent unified field of energy, the ground out of which everything is formed and this field is interactive.
- Everything is connected. There is no such thing as separation or isolation, nothing existing or functioning independently in a vacuum on its own. There is individuation, but no separation within oneness.
- Sound or focused attention appears to be an integral aspect in the creation process.
- We appear to construct our own virtual reality, a reality that also has time as an artificial construct.
- Everything – every thought, every word, every action, every sound within the unified field because there is no separation – has an effect upon the entire field.
- Consciousness appears to have the ability to survive the so-called death of the physical containment.

- There is a coherent intelligence and memory or pattern that is held in all things within the unified field.
- There appears to be multiple verses rather than a uni verse.
- There appears to be a continual evolutionary process of refinement at play.

Einstein told us in the theory of General Relativity that energy, matter and space-time are all particular arrangements working on the tiniest of scales. All the forgoing theories have common threads running through them that agree with the fundamental philosophies of many of the great religions (as we will see in the next chapter). All seem to agree upon a vital unified field of interconnectedness where memory and intelligence (consciousness) play a fundamental role as part of the inherent plan or pattern of the field. The idea that anything at all can be separate from anything else is an illusion. The logical conclusion is that our every thought, our every word and action, will affect the field and everything within it. This is a sobering and exciting idea. There are other realms of reality beside our current material one and there appears to be a constantly evolving action towards ever-increasing refinement (higher vibratory rate) of all within the field. This must naturally include our most vital core aspect our soul, as it engages with all else in an evolutionary journey towards ever-greater consciousness and refinement. Therefore death, as we currently understand, it is a lie and an illusion.

It now appears that we can become conscious co-creators in relationship with the all-pervading intelligence of the field. Initially, our power is as limited as a wave upon a stream, but to understand the stream, to consciously interact with it, to consciously create and steer ourselves within it, is not only possible – it is also reasonable to presume that this is what we are destined to do. Any action within the stream that raises the vibratory rate locally will affect and assist the whole to move to higher spin and therefore greater refinement. With greater consciousness and therefore wisdom, we can actively participate in our own evolutionary journey, thereby ensuring our success. Through writings of the ancient mystics, myths, legends and the Bible stories, we hear about what seem to us today impossible stories of miracles and feats. Is it not possible those stories are true? Is it not possible that the ancients possessed accurate knowledge of the multiverse and the laws that underwrite it and armed with this knowledge and aligned with these laws, were able to create these so-called miracles?

> In 1987, Pope John Paul II commissioned the Vatican Observatory in Castel Gandolfo to investigate the relationship between religion and modern science at the highest intellectual level; a series of scholarly conferences have taken place there since. In 2000, they explored quantum mechanics in keen detail, elucidating how God might act within the scope of natural laws, as up-to-date science discerns them. The results are fascinating, and, although incomplete, they undermine pet theories such as the claim that all religion is superstition, or results from a superficial state of mind brought about by a gene.
>
> — *Daily Telegraph*

If Pope John Paul II decided it was worth his while to look at quantum mechanics in relation to religion, I am sure it is worth our while also. In the light of new knowledge, scientists are discovering that what was first thought of as fact, as concrete and certain, is now certainly incorrect. A case in point on a relatively simple level is that our soil teems with around a hundred times more species than previously thought. A thimbleful of soil contains at least one million bacterial species, rather than just the ten thousand that has been the accepted view up until now. The implications of this one new discovery have been described as staggering and it is said we need new mathematical methods in order to understand the vast diversity of life. In another recent case, scientists studying the human genome believed that the entire complement resided in only 1.5 per cent of a cell's DNA, prompting some in their arrogant ignorance to dismiss the other 98.5 per cent as junk. Now they have found that "junk" DNA is not junk at all but is crucial to life: it appears to be the cell's "operating system" which runs the genes.

A favourite recent discovery of mine is the following; when a male mouse meets the object of his desire, he sings her a love song. Using computer analysis scientists have been able to establish that the sounds the mice make are more than mere random sounds – they are full-blooded love ballads. For sounds to qualify as a song there have to be distinct categories of sound instead of just one sound made repeatedly. Trials with forty-five different mice revealed that each male mouse sang a slightly different tune.

Another example is a recent study on how starlings are able to fly in formation, remain in a cohesive group and regroup quickly again even after an attack. Existing models and theories on how this were done have now been shown to be incorrect. In a flock of 3,000 birds, each starling constantly kept track of seven others irrespective of their distance. An interaction based upon the number of neighbours, rather than their distance implies rather complex cognitive capabilities in birds. The birds are smarter than we thought.

These two delightful examples only go to show that all within the multiverse is communicating in an intelligent and meaningful way with all else: it is just that for the most part we are blind and deaf. These examples bring us to the understanding that we do not know everything and that a great deal of what we think we know is wrong. We need to understand that the testimony of science is essentially the testimony of our left-brain and our five senses within this explicate realm of matter. The so-called hard facts and logic of science rest upon the eye, ear, nose, tongue and touch of mankind and it is only when we make a leap of intuitive understanding, the right-brain, into those other realms that Einstein referred to that we begin to get a glimmer of the truth of reality This is why it is important to keep an open and enquiring mind at all times. With an open mind, we will find that in fact we know very little at all. With this knowledge of our ignorance comes a great humility, which is all we need to move forward.

Chapter 2
Religions of the World

This body Arjuna, is called the field. He who knows this is called the knower of the field.
Know that I am the knower in all the fields of my creation: and that the wisdom which sees the field and the knower of the field is true wisdom.
Hear from me briefly, what the field is and how it is, what its changes are and whence each one comes; who is the knower and what is his power.

— *Bhagavad Gita 13:1–3*

What are the essential fundamental beliefs of some of the world's major religions and do they show unity of thought and divine direction? Are religious beliefs in conflict with scientific theories? If we look for a moment at this passage from the Bhagavad Gita, it reminds us of the intelligent interactive unified field of the scientists. Unfortunately, when examining many ancient belief systems, we find very often that integral parts of their teachings have been lost over time. This was because it was considered dangerous in the extreme to reveal powerful divine wisdom to the profane. The keeping of spiritual knowledge as arcane (secret) was also possibly for temporal reasons, as spiritual knowledge is power and power was kept for the so-called sacred, powerful few. Spiritual power was always, until our present unenlightened age, inextricably linked with temporal power. In our modern western society, we have discarded all notions of spiritual power as mere illusion. However, as we saw in the last chapter, our modern view of the multiverse is starting to look as though it is itself the illusion. We have now reached a point in our evolution where we are required to take something of a leap in order to survive and we are moving into a time where sacred and hidden knowledge of the past is coming back to us. This knowledge, previously allowed only to a select few, is now regarded as the birthright of all humankind. Indeed, it is considered imperative that all are now possessed of an understanding of this ancient, sacred and powerful information. We should understand that it is impossible to abuse this power as by the slightest act of even thinking of abusing it, one loses it, so there is no need to fear it. We do, however, have to approach the attaining of spiritual wisdom and power with great respect and humility.

If we look at all the major religions, we will not find any great essential difference between them. It is true they bear different names, their language may be different, and they are often enormously different in the detail, but their essential messages are all the same. The three religions of Judaism, Christianity, and Islam have been in conflict for centuries, even though both Christianity and Islam have their roots in Judaism and all three are technically monotheistic. This violent and bloody argument is essentially about who was the true messenger from God. The Jews believe he has not arrived yet, the Christians say it was Jesus and the Muslims say it was Muhammad. As silly arguments go, this would have to be the greatest. The Muslims recognise Jesus as a great spiritual teacher but say there is only one deity – the One God – and therefore Jesus was not his son. To the Christians this is as blasphemous as it is to the Muslims to say Jesus is the son of God. Even within Christianity itself, we have had terrible conflicts with one arm of the Church pitted against another. There are the Catholics who give greater prominence to Mary, the mother of Jesus, versus the Anglican Church, which does not. Catholics and Protestants have been fighting out their differences ever since the Church split into different sects, of which there are now many. So today we have Jews and Christians, Muslims and Jews, Christians and Muslims, Christians and Christians (Catholic and Protestant), and Muslims and Muslims (Sunni and Shia) waging war on each other in the name of God. All the arguing that organised religions indulge in is foolish in the extreme, but we must bear in mind that religions are man-made constructs and are therefore imperfect. If we look behind the differences and do not engage in the arguments but find the essential messages and wisdom that is in them all, we will be on the right path.

Chapter One was composed primarily of left-brain analytical theories, ideas and discoveries. Now we need to switch hemispheres somewhat and move more into the right-brain as this is the area of the brain through which the line of prophets, mystics and messiahs throughout the ages received their information. This was through "divine inspiration" which is direct contact with the Divine Creative Field or God, or direct contact with an elevated being that is itself directly linking to God. The information arrives fully formed, is always positive in content, for the good of humankind and all else, and often arrives without explanations or footnotes: as a result, human interpretation may cause grievous errors to be made. The messages received through contact with the Divine are very similar in content whether received many thousands of years ago or a relatively short two thousand years ago. No matter when received or by whom, they all carry the same essential information: the same golden threads run throughout. Because it has never happened to you, do not make the mistake of thinking it is not possible or it will never happen to you. All conscious beings may receive information in this manner, but some of us have not yet acquired the skills. If with knowledge, wisdom, understanding and love of the Divine we approach this method of communication, then we will find it possible.

According to the dictionary, the word "God" means "Superhuman being, worshipped as having power over nature and human fortunes, a deity of heaven". There are many words for God: the Taoist word "Tao" which means the way, the stream of life or Ch'i, the audible stream of all that is; "Brahman/Vishnu – the Supreme One" of the Hindus; the Jewish "Yahweh" meaning the One God; "God" the Christian Anglo adaptation of good, meaning all that is good; the Muslim "Allah" which means the God; "Anami" meaning the Nameless One; "Adonai" meaning Lord; and Hu, the natural sound name for God. These are all different words for the same thing, depending who you are or where you come from, and there are many more. In this book, we will use the word God or the Divine Creative Field. Here we will look briefly at six major religions – Taoism, Buddhism, Hinduism, Christianity, Judaism and Islam – dealing with their primary, original beliefs rather than all the many additional teachings on social mores, ethics, sects, sub-sects and splits that all have spawned over time. The eastern religions of Taoism, Buddhism, Hinduism and Islam have always had as an integral part of their belief system a unified world view. Spirituality is woven into daily life; man, mind, matter, nature, religion, science and all else is the warp and weft of a unified cosmic tapestry. All are just aspects of an integral, unified whole. The following are the essential core beliefs:

- There is one God alone, out of which all has sprung; he merely has different messengers bringing this information at different times to different races.
- Everything having sprung from this one source is a unity, connected to everything else; there is no such thing as separation. God is omnipresent, immanent, omnipotent, and transcendent.
- We are all possessed of a divine immortal soul – a fragment or spark of the One God.
- As we are immortal, we live on after physical death, at which time we go to other realms, multiverses, paradise etc., or return here.

- We are all in the process of becoming more God-like, or that is the intention.

As we look at some of the philosophies of the mystical realms, of the right-brain, we will also find talk of unified fields, streams, patterns and sound symphonies and we will start with the Tao, which means the way, the stream of life or Ch'i, the audible stream of all that is.

Taoisim

> The Tao
> Gives birth to the one:
> The One
> Gives birth to the two;
> The Two
> Gives birth to the three –
> The Three give birth to every living thing.
> All things are held in Yin, and carry Yang:
> And they are held together in the
> Ch'i of teeming energy
>
> — *Tao Te Ching*

This could very easily be a description of creation using the Platonic solids model. In almost all mystical writings, we come across the "three", the trinity bringing forth life.

The origins of Taoism are lost in the mists of time, but it is believed that the original source was the *I Ching* – the Book of Changes. Another source of Taoist wisdom is the *Tao Te Ching*, reputedly written by Lao Tzu, although this is in doubt and more probably it is a collection of texts spanning more than eight hundred years which were committed to paper some four hundred years after Lao Tzu lived. Taoism is composed of many strands: the main body emerged a few hundred years BC but one of the strands, shamanism, is eight thousand or more years old. With shamanism as one of the strands of Taoism, we naturally find the sage or mystic – one who seeks by contemplation and self-surrender to obtain union with or absorption into the Deity. (Self-surrender is a key concept here.)

> They grace things without possessing them,
> They benefit everything but ask for nothing back,
> They give themselves into everything without seeking control.
> This is the essence of the original intention.
>
> *— Tao Te Ching*

A Taoist master believes in the one supreme, the Tao, which cannot be represented in an image. The Tao is viewed as a stream of energy – an audible sound current, a stream in which all are interconnected and in which all live, move and have their being. The Tao surrounds everyone (so it is more like a field than a stream) and one must listen to it to find enlightenment. The Tao is the natural order of all things and the study of nature helps us to understand this. The Tao is the force that flows through the multiverse of parallel realities, so to a Taoist there is no such thing as separation. For the Taoist master, the only thing that exists in the multiverse is energy – the Tao, the existence of all other phenomena, are merely manifestations of that energy, energy that is governed by universal laws. The Taoist master studies how energy behaves given a certain set of circumstances. This study takes the form of contemplation, meditation or introspection in silence, as it is only in silence that one can hear. It is considered that hearing the sound of the energy in all its patterns is important in understanding the patterns and the laws underlying them. Taoism records the knowledge that many parallel realities exist, and a mystic or sage is one who is able to access these other realms of reality or dimensions. A sage may enter these other realms in order to bring back advice, wisdom and prophecy. Over the past many hundreds of years, these have come to overlay the essential original beliefs, assisting people to live peacefully and constructively together, and also advising them how best to attain their evolutionary goal of oneness with the Tao.

In Taoism, everything is understood to be sentient. It is the eternal, creative reality in which we are all immortal souls striving for greater perfection, therefore we are all engaged in an evolutionary process in which we have eternal life. This striving for evolutionary advancement/perfection is considered to be the reason for each life. A common symbol of Taoism is the one above showing the energies of positive and negative, masculine and feminine, Yin and Yang, in balance and equal. It represents the balance of opposing forces to be found throughout the universe. This perfect balance signifies the unified field, the Divine Creative Field or God and a state of oneness. The Taoist master aspires to achieve this state of oneness, as when the master's field is the same as the Tao or God, then he becomes at one with the Tao. This is considered the ultimate accomplishment, as in this state of being one knows all, one sees all, one is all, and perfect balance, joy and peace become a reality. The Taoist master not only strives for this individual state of oneness but also works towards the balance of oneness for the world. The eternal struggle we all engage in with the diversions/illusions of the lower vibratory physical realms of matter is the constant subject of discourse within Taoist literature. The illusion of matter is considered to be the main obstruction to the attainment of perfection. A great disciple of Lao Tzu had this to say:

> The perfect man employs his mind as a mirror. It grasps nothing; it refuses nothing. It receives but doesn't keep. Thus he can triumph over matter, without injury to himself.
>
> — *Disciple of Lao Tzu*

In other words, we must not allow ourselves to become too closely entwined in matter, deluded by it, as it will keep us from attaining our evolutionary goal of perfection. Be in this world, but not of it: this is the art of Wu Wei, which is action without apparent action.

The Taoist view of the multiverse has more in common with David Bohm's view than it does with our Western view of our physical universe being a solid fixed reality of separate parts, where some are sentient and some are not. The audible stream is constantly changing, creating and moving, and if one is to live successfully, the Taoist idea is that one should come to understand the characteristics of this stream, to see and hear it as it truly is and to practise the art of Wu Wei – flowing with it.

> Without going anywhere, you can know the whole
>   world, you can know the ways of Heaven.
> You see: the further away you go, the less you know...
>   The sage does not need to travel around: Why?
> Because he can still understand. He sees without
>   needing "to see",
> He never does anything, and yet it all happens.

We will find as we go that the universe is full of such paradoxes: that is what makes it all such fun. To practise the art of Wu Wei successfully, one must be a conscious and fully integrated being, must be in balance, calm, attuned to all that is, able to understand, see and hear all that is and to then move (quite possibly without physical movement) with the Tao to accomplish one's purpose. As the Tao flows impartially throughout the multiverse, so humankind should also function, disavowing all action of personal will. When we are a fully integrated, aligned being, our will, will quite naturally be the will of the Tao. If we are able to comprehend the Tao in all its glory, we will never fear anything in this life, nor will we fear death and beyond.

> *Oneness generates everything: When the sage rules in the*
>   *light of it, He rules everything.*
> *A wise man never tries to break up the Whole.*

Buddhism

> All beings are primarily Buddhas
> Like water and ice.
> There is no ice apart from water;
> There are no Buddhas apart from beings.
> Not knowing how close the Truth is to them
> Beings seek for it afar – what a pity!
>
> — *Hakuin, Song of Meditation*

Buddhism is one of the fastest-growing belief systems today, partly because it appeals to the educated person. With Buddhism, we are not asked to believe what appears to our left-brain to be illogical or impossible myths and stories. So what is Buddhism essentially about?

It is similar to Taoism in some of its views of the multiverse. Buddha reputedly sought enlightenment and accordingly he sat under a Bodhi tree meditating or in contemplation while suffering extreme austerities, and it was when he was approaching extinction that he gained the enlightenment he so sorely sought. We can see from Buddha's descriptions of reality that he without doubt achieved an altered state and managed to pass from this space-time continuum and into another, where he saw all, understood all and in this understanding merged with all. Buddha's vision of reality again has more in common with David Bohm's view of reality than much else. Without a doubt, Buddha saw the whole lion, even if only momentarily, and as a result he was very clear about the illusory and transitory nature of the material world with all its suffering. He taught at length about the dangers of becoming caught up in the unreal material world as though it had substance and was real.

> Thus, shall you think of all this fleeting world:
> A star at dawn, a bubble in a stream;
> A flash of lightning in a summer cloud,
> A flickering lamp, a phantom, and a dream.
>
> — *The Diamond Sutra*

Buddha clearly saw the interconnectedness of all things. If we are to perceive the multiverse as Buddha did, as a non-material intelligent energy soup, then it must be one body and therefore interconnected. Buddha saw this sea of energy as appearing to be in an eternal state of flux – of conditions, causes and effects and with this sea of energy infused with an essential intelligence and pattern which, while appearing to change, was actually constant and changeless.

> Buddha is not a physical body, but it is enlightenment. A body may be thought of as a receptacle; then if this receptacle is filled with enlightenment, it may be called Buddha. Therefore, if anyone is attached to the physical body of Buddha and laments his disappearance, he will be unable to see the true Buddha. In reality, the true nature of all things transcends the discrimination of appearance and disappearance, of coming and going, of good and evil. All things are substance-less and perfectly homogenous (consisting of parts all of the same kind).
>
> — *II The Appearance of Buddha – The Teachings of Buddha*

For Buddhists, Buddha was an enlightened being who taught of the one universal, timeless, changing and changeless entity, and they view the illusory material world as cyclical: a cycle or wheel of birth, pain, suffering, death and rebirth. They believe in a constant cycle of coming into being, living then dying to be reborn again. They call this process reincarnation, which is the belief that the immortal soul or the Coherent Energy Package merely slips off its lower vibrating coat of materiality at the point we call death. It then moves into another realm until it re-clothes itself with a coat of lower vibrating energy/matter upon re-entering this space-time continuum. The soul then once again resides in this physical realm in another turn of the endless wheel in the hope or search for enlightenment.

The aim of devout Buddhists – and it sounds very sensible to me – is to get off this endless cyclical, unconscious way of being in order to evolve to a higher vibratory plane of existence. Therefore, they strive for less suffering, discord and disharmony and for greater peace, harmony and joy. They see a spiral as the exit point from the wheel, and it could be that the initial circle they describe is merely the first turn of a spiral. Spirals come in two forms, the Archimedes spiral, which is regularly spaced, and the logarithmic spiral, where the distance between the turns increases geometrically as one moves away from the centre. If it is a logarithmic spiral we are talking about here, as one increases spin rate one would then move further along the spiral in decreasing spirals, with increased compression, increased spin and subsequent power. The Buddhist philosophy maintains that in order to move onto this spiral we must accomplish among other things the art of balance and non-attachment to the material world, together with what amounts to the art of Wu Wei. This makes sense, as if you are trying to move away from something, it does not help if you are attached to it. To move away therefore, we must let go and "let God", or practise Wu Wei and go with the natural flow form of energy or, in the Judeo-Christian belief system, adopt "Not my will, but Thine", i.e. the self-surrender of the mystics.

Once we have managed to get on the spiral, we may in the early stages still slip back onto the wheel. If we do not move forward with enough power, if we are not extremely mindful, conscious and diligent, we may thus fall back. After a certain point, it is considered no longer possible to fall back into the initial wheel and our path onwards on the spiral is assured, although the rate of progress is individual. The Buddhists have a curious saying for such gentle peaceful people who teach "do no harm" and this is, "If you should meet Buddha on the road to enlightenment, kill him." This means that we are never to stop and worship at the feet of anyone along the way, as it will delay or halt our progress. Progress along the spiral path towards the sacred goal of enlightenment is considered to be the only reason for life on this plane.

Buddhism is very particular when it comes to describing the many other multiverses that exist. It also has detailed teachings on how to die successfully, even to the point of telling us the position we must lie in to facilitate and ease the soul energy field flow at the point of physical death and beyond.

One of the most helpful and useful aspects of Buddhism is the emphasis placed upon balance in all things, the Yin and the Yang of it all. As Buddha was obviously aware of the underlying patterns, unity and rhythm in the multiverse, he realised that the balance of opposing forces was an integral part of the process of alignment and hence further enlightenment in this particular space-time continuum. It is impossible to, at will, achieve a state of high spin if one's energy field is inclined to be either more positive or more negative – out of balance. A perfect balance between the two poles is required in order to slip out of this space-time continuum; hence, the path of the Middle Way has a major place in Buddhist philosophies and practices. The Middle Way is essentially a very logical, sensible and doable path. If we were to think about all the facets of our life and if we were to just employ the belief system of balance in all things – not too much of this, not too much of that – many aspects of our life would instantly be a great deal better. Taken to its conclusion, the Middle Way is the art of consciously functioning in perfect balance between all things, centred, observing, focused and holding a non-judgmental position while employing the high art of non-attachment to outcomes, balanced perfectly between the physical and the spiritual – Heaven and Earth we align, harmonise and cohere all our fields. With our primary focus on other realms of higher vibratory rate, on causes rather than effects, we walk the tightrope, falling neither to left nor right. Because Buddha saw the world as ephemeral, the quantum soup in a constant state of becoming and ceasing, he taught that to become attached to anything material was entirely unreasonable and illogical and that the practice of attachment could only bring pain and misery. We have our being in a moving stream or field of energy and to become attached to something is to try to become static. Not only are we trying to stand still, we are also trying to keep a wave in place, trying to keep it in existence when the underlying law/pattern is that it should fall back into the energy soup. With the practice of attachment, we give ourselves an impossible task that can only lead to pain and anguish. One of the most profound teachings of Buddha is that we should accept without resistance the natural order of all things, as it is our resistance against the natural order that causes us pain, not the event itself. With attachment we are fighting a battle that cannot be won, endeavouring to go against the natural order of the Divine Creative Field – how could this not end in suffering and pain?

The precepts of the Middle Way and non-attachment are central to Buddhism, and one must first understand these clearly in order to follow the Buddhist's Noble Eightfold Path to enlightenment. The practice of non-attachment does not mean we do not participate in life in a full and meaningful way; it does not mean we may not be ambitious or have close personal relations for example, but it does mean that the way to a peaceful, rational, fulfilled life is to understand the essential nature of all. With understanding, we may then choose to do or be as we will, but we choose our path without attachment to the outcome. This is another way of saying that we are allowing God to have the final say, rather than our own will and desires. This way of being, once perfected, will result in us being immensely more joyful, peaceful, loving and powerful. This essential message is echoed in all the many religious belief systems, and it is one of the hardest of all the practices to accomplish. However, in order to attain great spiritual power, it is essential that we first must give up all desire for power and control. This is a classic example of those wonderful paradoxes that lie along the path to spiritual enlightenment and power and make the journey so much fun, for to gain great spiritual power one must first relinquish all desires in that regard. Buddhism, in common with other religious belief systems, has many teachings on how to more perfectly live in society. The Noble Eightfold Path covers all desired behaviour, together with being the intended initial steps towards enlightenment. They are simple and elegant and cover pretty much all one needs to start on any spiritual journey. The eight instructions are less perhaps from their time than the Ten Commandments, and have usefulness and power in any era:

1. **Right View.** Unless you are looking in the right direction with the right viewpoint, little will be accomplished of worth.
2. **Right Thought.** Our thoughts are powerful creative forces, for good or ill.
3. **Right Speech.** The sound and outgoing energy of our thoughts, again for good or ill, are powerful and reinforce and create where we are spiritually.
4. **Right Concentration.** Without concentration or focus, Right View, Right Thought etc will accomplish little.
5. **Right Effort.** Without the effort, little will happen at all on any front.
6. **Right Behaviour** and
7. **Right Livelihood.** Together with thought and speech, these are natural outpourings from the Right View, with concentration and effort.
8. **Right Mindfulness.** Just how conscious are you in all you do?

Buddhists believe that if we do no harm at all to anyone or anything, then we have lived well. At the current stage of our evolutionary journey, this is a very hard thing to do, as quite apart from intentional harm many times we may quite unconsciously do harm, which is why we need to be mindful or conscious at all times.

Buddhists also list Five Hindrances to spiritual enlightenment: sense desire; ill-will; restlessness and anxiety; sloth and torpor; and doubt and indecision. With sense desire we become enmeshed in the physical desires of the flesh and thus are distracted from our true purpose. With ill-will we generate negative, low vibratory energy – the opposite of what we should be seeking to do. Restlessness and anxiety make it impossible to be aligned and harmonious: a higher vibratory rate is impossible to achieve and so travel to the divine realms that Buddha experienced is also impossible. With sloth and torpor, no effort on any evolutionary front will be made. Doubt and indecision will have much the same effect, since without faith and belief nothing is possible.

> Both life and death arise from the mind and exist within the mind.
> Hence, when the mind that concerns itself with life and death passes on,
> the world of life and death passes with it.
> An unenlightened mind rises from a mind that is bewildered by its own world of delusion.
> If we learn that there is no world of delusion outside the mind,
> the bewildered mind becomes clear;
> and because we cease to create impure surroundings, we attain Enlightenment.
>
> — *Theory of Mind – Teaching of Buddha*

Hinduism

> Everything rests on Me as pearls strung on a thread.
> I am the original fragrance of the earth.
> I am the taste in the water.
> I am the heat in the fire and the sound in space.
> I am the light of the sun and the moon and the life of all.
>
> — *Bhagavad Gita 7:7–9*

Hinduism derives its teachings from many venerable sacred texts. Prime among them is the *Bhagavad Gita* ("The Song Celestial"). The entire belief system may be summed up in a few short words: "Ekam sat vipra bahudha vadanti" ("That which exists is one; sages call it by various names"). Like the Tao, the origins of Hinduism are lost in the mists of time and these words were possibly written ten thousand years ago or more, and they have run through all Indian philosophy like a golden thread.

Hinduism teaches not only that there is unity in the Supreme One, but unity among men and in all life. In fact all that lives is One life, One in origin and One in essence: there is no separation. It is in that One that all things live, move and have their being.

One of the names of the One is Brahman, which means the one causal entity beyond time and space that is both immanent and transcendent. A messenger or prophet of Brahman is Krishna, who is regarded as a deity or avatar (one who has deliberately descended into the material realms with a particular mission in mind). An avatar is the same in essence as Brahman, as is also an Atman or soul. Messengers or prophets and souls are all comprised of the same as the Brahman/Vishnu or God – all are one and the same. To the casual observer Hindus appear to have a bewildering array of gods, but these are simply representations of different aspects of the One Supreme. Representing the One in this way created an easily understandable series of images for people who often could not read or write. These clear pictorial aids were an attempt to bring down to the Earth plane ineffable realities to assist the people to a greater understanding so that they each could then come to know, understand, love and seek the Supreme One.

Hinduism's many sacred writings cover spiritual realities, the evolutionary path to enlightenment, and ethics – how best to live and warnings of what happens if one does not live ethically. One great body of sacred texts is called the *Upanishads*: much of it has been irrevocably lost over time, but what remains is of great value. The *Upanishads* are to a Hindu what the New Testament is to a Christian. There are also the *Vedas,* which comprise four great works: *Rig Veda, Yajur Veda, Sama Veda* and *Atharva Veda.* The *Vedas* teach that the whole of creation is a projection – Brahman projects itself into all form and substance, exactly the way a hologram works in that each facet of creation contains the whole within it. All is the product of the One, which put simply is the projection of the cosmic mind, the Mahat. This manifests all in the material explicate realm by projection, and thus is inherent in all forms and manifestation. From stone to intellect, all is the product of one substance, Akash. Any differences lie solely in the greater or lesser degree of manifestation. As there is but one substance at the substratum of all things in the material universe, so there is but one primary force from which all other forces are derived, and this is called Prana. Prana acting upon Akash produces all forms.

"Akash" is derived from the Sanskrit word "Akasha" which means ether. "Prana" means breath: it is the life force and is considered to be the mother of thought and mind. Therefore, mind initiates and projects the breath which, acting upon the ether, creates all. Many texts relate that the sound/vibration of the word "Om" was the initiating action in creation, and in fact sound plays a major role in Hinduism as Shabd, a Sanskrit word meaning sound current, the esoteric essence of God, is fundamental to the belief system. This sound current vibrates in all creation and is considered to be so radiant, so indescribably glorious, that once immersed in it, the soul loses all interest in things of the material plane as they pale in comparison and interest beside Shabd. Once contacted, Shabd is thereafter the only true reality.

Much has been added to the *Vedas* over the great ages of their existence: it is a vast body of work containing one hundred thousand *shoklas,* or couplets: fourteen thousand of these deal with spiritual aspects, while eighty-six thousand are about problems on the physical plane. The *Vedas* also include the ancient spiritual practice of yoga, which in its full and original form teaches non-attachment to illusory material things. Attachment to the material is considered to be the road to pain and grief, as is non-acceptance of events or resistance to what is. The texts also dwell on the need for balance, the middle way; indeed equilibrium is called yoga, which is considered to be one of the primary paths to enlightenment. So, the middle way is a key to enlightenment. Yoga attempts to impart an understanding that all is impermanent except the immortal soul, as Hinduism incorporates belief in the transmigration of souls. This is the constant returning of the immortal soul to the physical plane (as described before in the section on Buddhism). Yoga in its pure form is a powerful and practical spiritual practice which will lead to enlightenment. Unfortunately, some essential aspects have become lost over time, possibly as a safety device as it has until recently been the accepted wisdom in all ancient spiritual teachings that knowledge is revealed only when the student reaches each particular level. Regrettably, if we say the word "yoga" to most people today they think of a system of exercise that merely keeps the body balanced, relaxed and in good shape. This is an erosion of a once great practice.

The *Bhagavad Gita* is a clear and profoundly wise little book, it has much to say that will elucidate and is well worth reading:

> The contacts of matter, giving heat and cold, pleasure and pain – they come and go; they are impermanent. Arise above them.
>
> — *Bhagavad Gita 2:11*

> Set your heart upon your work, but never on its reward. Work not for a reward, but never cease to do your work.
>
> Do your work in the peace of the divine, free from selfish desires; don't be moved in success or failure.
>
> Dwelling in the divine is an evenness of mind, a peace that is ever the same.
>
> *— Bhagavad Gita 18:23–26*

The *Gita* clearly points out the results of a descent into materiality:

> When a man dwells on the pleasures of sense, attraction for them arises in him.
>
> From attraction arises desire, the lust of possession, and this leads to passion, to anger.
>
> From passion comes confusion of mind, then loss of remembrance, the forgetting of duty. From this loss comes the ruin of reason, and the ruin of reason leads man to destruction.
>
> *— Bhagavad Gita 2:62–63*

Together with the positive benefits to be gained by eschewing materiality:

> But the soul that moves in the world of the senses and yet keeps the senses in harmony free from attraction and aversion, finds rest in quietness.
>
> In this quietness falls down the burden of all her sorrows, for when the heart has found quietness, wisdom has also found peace.
>
> There is no wisdom for a man without harmony, and without harmony there is no contemplation. Without contemplation, there cannot be peace, and without peace can there be joy?

(Harmony – agreement pre-established between body and soul before their creation – *Concise Oxford Dictionary*)

— *Bhagavad Gita 2:64–66*

Hindus believe in the transmigration of immortal souls – there are many passages in all the great body of works that relate this belief. There are some conflicting texts with regard to immortality, as we shall see, but here the *Gita* is clear regarding the immortality and transmigration of the soul:

Interwoven in creation, the Spirit is beyond destruction. No one can bring to an end the Spirit which is everlasting.

— *Bhagavad Gita 2:17*

As a man leaves an old garment and puts on one that is new, the Spirit leaves his mortal body and then puts on one that is new.

— *Bhagavad Gita 2:22*

Beyond the power of sword and fire, beyond the power of waters and winds, the Spirit is everlasting, omnipresent, never-changing, never-moving, ever one.

— *Bhagavad Gita 2:24*

Hinduism has a vast cosmology – the many realms or levels the soul may visit or reside in is a complex and detailed subject.

Work done without faith is nothing: sacrifice, gift, or self-harmony done without faith are nothing, both in this world and in the world to come.

— *Bhagavad Gita 17:28*

A man attains perfection when his work is worship of God, from whom all things come and who is in all. When a man has his reason in freedom from bondage, and his soul is in harmony, beyond desires, then renunciation leads him to a region supreme which is beyond earthly action.

— *Bhagavad Gita 18:46, 49*

Here again we see the essential unity in all three Eastern religions, the belief in one entity with all of creation emanating from the one essential substance and with sound being an integral part of creation. We also have the belief in parallel or other realities to which the immortal soul in its evolutionary journey may travel. Now let us move on to the more recent religions where the language is quite different but the fundamental belief systems are the same.

Judaism

> How many are the things You have made, O Lord; You have made them all with wisdom; the Earth is full of your creation.
>
> *— Psalm 104*

Jews, Christians and Muslims all recognise the same origin, Abraham, and essentially all three religions have as their base the ancient texts of the Jews which are the *Torah*, the *Kabbalah* and related works. The *Torah* consists of the first five books of their whole teachings which are called the Tanakh. The first five books are *Genesis, Exodus, Leviticus, Numbers* and *Deuteronomy,* which are also the first five books of the Christian Bible. A great deal of the teachings of Judaism are to do with the laws or ethics for living within a society in a constructive and law-abiding manner. They include laws regarding health, diet, dress and general behaviour, and most had very sound reasons behind them when created. The *Kabbalah* or Book of Creation is well worth studying as it incorporates sacred geometry, numerology, astrology and knowledge of other realms (multiverses) besides this one. The word Torah means "teaching – instruction or especially law" and the word Kabbalah derived from the Hebrew – kabal means "to receive", so the Torah and the Kabbalah are the received teaching or law of Judaism.

Judaism is the belief in the One God, an immanent God. God revealed himself to the people of Israel and disclosed his name, as to disclose one's name is to make oneself known to others. The sacred and mysterious name of God was revealed as YHWH ("I Am He Who Is, I Am Who Am or I Am Who I Am"). This is at once a name revealed and a refusal of a name, and hence it expresses God as infinitely above everything that we can understand – God is ineffable and yet he is close to us. A personal God. This God has many other names: Jehovah, En Soph (the Infinite One), Yahweh (the One God). This overarching, omnipotent master creator is too indescribable for a likeness to be created. Indeed, it is blasphemous to try. God is unitary: he cannot be called a cause as this would imply another thing and there is only one. The messenger or prophet of this One God was Moses, who received as a direct communication from the One God the Ten Commandments together with other spiritual wisdom and illumination. These simple commandments are absolutes for any society to positively and harmoniously cohere and evolve.

There are two accounts of creation in *Genesis:* first, the initial creation of the universe, and second, the creation of Adam. The *Kabbalah* relates that God did not actually create the world but created the ingredients according to an original plan that would then allow the world to develop all matter along with space and time:

> God allowed the universe to develop by itself, re-newing His creation each seven thousand Divine Years, or 2.5 billion earthly years. All the laws of nature and the properties of matter had been fixed for all time, as it is written.
>
> *— Sefer Yetzirah, The Book Of Creation*

> He hath also stablished them for ever and ever: He hath made a decree, which shall not pass away.
>
> *— Psalm 148:6*

As God was the creator of all, omnipotent and of infinite power, he was also to be greatly respected and feared:

> The fear of the Lord is the beginning of wisdom: a good understanding have all they that do his commandments: his praise endureth for ever.
>
> *— Psalm 111:10*

The potential anger of God is mentioned a great deal throughout the texts as this one Supreme Being ruled heaven and earth and was all.

The texts stress that the fear of God is the beginning of wisdom, but the use of the translated word "fear" here is not quite correct as what is being stressed is that one should respect and revere God and seek to know him, because with knowledge of God will come wisdom. With wisdom will come the ability to evolve to greater goodness – at which time:

> I believe I will gaze upon the Lord in the land of the living.
>
> *— Psalm 27:13*

The living are those who choose immortal life through relationship with God wherein they may ascend to higher realms – heaven, which is too wonderful to describe:

> Never has the ear heard it, no eye has seen it, other than God: That which he will do for those who hope in him.
>
> *— Isaiah 64:4*

Some might argue that the belief in the transmigration of souls is buried deep within Judaism. That aside, there is certainly a belief in the soul being able to travel to other realms beside this one. Some argue that it is not possible to believe in reincarnation and heaven at the same time as they contradict each other. However, Judaism as with most of the major religions has a belief in levels, or varying degrees of realms, to which the soul may travel. It is not impossible that the two beliefs, reincarnation and heaven, may not contradict each other but instead complement each other perfectly, in that the soul moves through the evolutionary process of reincarnation, followed by ascension to a perfect realm (heaven) once a particular level of evolution has been reached.

Judaism has much to say about the soul, describing three major aspects of it: the Vital Soul, the Spirit and the Innermost Soul. The three are seen as one within the other, but each has its separate abode within the one and a further five aspects are described from this whole.

> Believe not that man consists solely of flesh, skin and veins. The real part of man is his soul, and the things just mentioned are only outward coverings. They are only veils, not the real man. When a man departs this life, he divests himself of all the veils which cover him.
>
> — *Zohar: The Book Of Splendour*

The *Torah*, like the Old Testament, appears on the surface to be a collection of simple historical stories as both are written in a quite obscure manner with a great deal being lost in translation. Until we understand the underlying pattern of the multiverse, a great deal of the wisdom in both books may not make much sense. Once we have gained a greater understanding, all becomes a lot clearer. As we have seen, some of this obscurity may be to a degree deliberate. Here again with Judaism we have the belief in One, One entity from which all manifests and while individuality is apparent at the sub strata of all, separation and multiplicity are not possible as we cannot even have cause and effect because that implies two and there is only one. Within this one, there are other realms the soul may travel to on its immortal journey.

Jesus's initial spiritual belief system was Judaism; much later, some would have it, he also studied in the Eastern Mystery schools and there does appear to be a great deal of evidence for this in his teachings. The great divide from Judaism to the creation of a new religion, Christianity, came about because the Hebrews had long prophesied that a Messiah (a liberator of oppressed peoples) would come at a particular and critical point in their history. When Jesus was proclaimed the Messiah, many Hebrews refused to accept this. A great part of this resistance came from the hierarchy of Judaism itself, as spiritual and temporal power were wielded together and a new spiritual leader was a great threat indeed. If the new Messiah really was the liberator of oppressed peoples, then he was also a great threat to the Roman occupiers, and so he was crucified at the relative beginning of his ministry. The main body of Judaism is still waiting for its Messiah; the breakaway group evolved into the Christian belief system as we know it today.

Christianity

> This is my commandment,
> That ye love one another,
> as I have loved you.
>
> *—John 15:12*

Christianity has one belief that sets it somewhat apart from the other faiths discussed here. This is the one that so greatly incenses others of different faiths – the belief that Jesus was the son of God and that he entered this physical realm as a willing sacrificial victim in order that all of humanity could redeem their fundamental and original state of sin. This idea of sacrifice came from the old Judaic system of sacrifice handed down from time immemorial. It is believed that sacrifice started as a method of attempting to cheat karmic debt, or "As ye sow, so shall ye reap", which as we will see is one of the natural laws underwriting the multiverse. The idea was that instead of paying for one's own sins, one offered a blood sacrifice which God would accept instead. In other words, this was a naive attempt to cheat or deceive God. This belief could also preclude one from calling Christianity a monotheistic belief system, as Jesus is worshipped as a God in his own right instead of merely a messenger from God.

Christianity itself is a blend of ancient belief systems. Sacrifice, virgin birth, crucifixion and rising from the dead are all found in many other religions such as the cult of Mithras, Krishna, Prometheus, Adonis, Zoroaster and more. Many Christian rites and festivals were derived from and overlay the Mithraic, Druidic and other pagan rites and festivals. Easter, for example, is at the time of an important pagan festival linked to the cycles of the moon, which is why it moves from year to year; many ancient gods celebrated their birthdays on 25 December. The politically expedient interweaving of the many and various belief systems that is Christianity was created in order to effect some sort of cohesion thereby making it possible to establish temporal power over all. The emperor Constantine is considered the main architect of the Christian religion: drawing all the threads together into a cohesive whole he created a powerful belief system that endures to this day. This is not to denigrate the essential messages that Jesus preached, which have the same golden threads running throughout common to all the major religions. Indeed, without these golden threads it is unlikely any belief system could or would survive for long. The longevity and the similarity of all should alone make one pause for thought. Without essential truth, no belief system/religion would long outlive its source. All the other belief systems we have looked at so far include love as part of their fabric – indeed, the love of one another and of God is considered in all to be an essential aspect of the whole. However, with Jesus we find the primary focus is clearly placed upon the act of loving and the power of love. One could say that Jesus's entire ministry was essentially about love. As we have seen, love is the warp and weft of the multiverse so Jesus knew exactly what he was talking about when he said:

> Thou shalt love the lord thy God with all thy heart and with all thy soul, and with all thy mind. This is the first and great commandment and the second is like unto it, thou shalt love thy neighbour as thyself. On these two commandments hang all the law and the prophets.
>
> *— Matthew 22:37–40*

If we are to hold in our minds the vision of the one perfect Unified Field of the Divine Creator, or God, which we are evolving towards, then that first commandment is not only very simple and clear but also makes perfect sense. As if, we were to hold our entire focus – utilising our heart, soul and mind – on the one thing we are wishing to move towards and become, then we may be guaranteed to accomplish it. If we love God with the whole of our being, we will become like that which we are focusing upon. Our energy fields will move to align, cohere and agree with the Divine Creative Field, resulting in a higher rate of spin and refinement of all our fields.

The second great commandment also makes perfect sense and ensures that we are working in loving relationship and co-operation in a holistic manner with all. If we love everyone as we love ourselves and as we love God – again, it would be impossible that we would not accelerate our evolution and in doing so would raise the vibration of the entire field, which would of course include all of life and the planet. If we are focused in this way it would be impossible to wreak harm either upon ourselves, each other or the planet. This is why the whole of the law hangs upon these two simple commandments. The simplicity and completeness of the message is astounding. It is also clear from the instruction "to love your neighbour as yourself" that Jesus regarded "All as One" without separation and as this was a fundamental belief of the Eastern Mystery Schools this is not surprising.

Note: today, many of us do not love ourselves. Loving ourselves is an essential part of the process of loving God and our neighbours.

Another well-known statement attributed to Jesus that has caused much misunderstanding and trouble is the following:

> I am the way, the truth and the life: no man cometh unto the Father, but by me.
>
> —*John 14:6*

Many Christians take this passage to mean that unless you are a Christian you will not be able to make contact with God; that the only path to God is through the worship of Jesus. Now this patently is a silly interpretation, as it would mean that before two thousand years ago it was not possible for any spiritual evolution to take place. If we look again at the passage, it more logically should say, "I am the way, the truth and the life: man cometh to the Father by me." A great spiritual teacher as Jesus undoubtedly was could teach, guide and show the way to God. Without a great spiritual teacher of high vibration who is in constant direct contact with the Divine, finding the way and then walking it can be difficult. All of us are able to contact the Divine when we know how, all of us can follow the directions of respective religions or teachings, but we need to understand there is not just the one path. A Hindu may approach God as simply as a Christian or a Muslim. There are as many paths to God as there are people; we just need to know how to find our own path and, more important, how to walk it.

Another powerful and important aspect to Jesus' teachings is that he stressed the immanence of the kingdom of heaven. He taught that God was inherent in all things, in particular that God was to be found within each one of us:

> Know ye not that ye are the temple of God, and that the Spirit of God dwelleth in you?
>
> *— 1 Corinthians 3:16*

This teaching again has its roots in the East and was not popular with the priests of Judaism. Indeed the idea of going within in a search for God is not approved of in many circles today, as this takes power away from the high offices of religion and gives it back to each individual where it belongs. However, as we will see, going within is the individual and only path we can take if we are to contact God.

Because Christianity has its roots in Judaism, we have the belief in one God, a Supreme Being who is creator of all. We then diverge into something more resembling the passage at the beginning of the Tao: "The one gives birth to the Two; the Two gives birth to the Three." We have here God, Jesus the Son of God and something called the Holy Ghost. You could ask ten different Christians who or what is the Holy Ghost and receive ten different answers. Some believe the Aramaic word that has ended up as "ghost", if correctly translated, means the feminine principle. It is quite possible that the early misogynist Church fathers changed the ancient belief system of Father-Mother, Positive-Negative to this obscure entity which can then be interpreted to mean the essence or all-pervading spirit of God. In any event, we have ended up with the trinity. Two arising out of the One Supreme at the beginning of creation is a common theme running throughout many belief systems. Three is the beginning of the tetrahedron in three-dimensional form, which is a sacred geometrical device and one of the Platonic solids. However, as the Judaic and other monotheistic belief systems are at the base, we must presume we have belief in One Supreme, with the messenger Jesus and the Holy Spirit being aspects arising from the One Supreme as in the Tao and indeed as the Catholic Catechism states – "the Father, Son and the Holy Spirit; three persons indeed, but one essence, substance or nature entirely simple". With Christianity, the soul is believed to live on after physical death when it may travel to other realms, of which there are primarily four: we have the choice of hell, purgatory, limbo or heaven, and we have only the one life to get it right. We have a very tight window of opportunity in which to evolve to the highest degree. Jesus left us a great legacy in that he attempted to simplify a very complex process, reducing the path to the Divine to one simple commandment that we love God and love one another. With this one commandment in place, there was no need for reincarnation – if we could follow this one commandment; we would ascend directly to the highest vibratory realm from this one life. One could say that Jesus was the greatest optimist.

Islam

> Allah is the First and the Last, and the Outward and the Inward; and He is Knower of all things.
>
> — *Qur'an – Surah LVII-3*

Islam is essentially the revelations received by Muhammad from Allah. Islam is the belief in the absolute Oneness of God: there is no God but God. Islam diverges slightly in its belief system in that although Muslims believe in the One God Allah, which literally means al-ilah – The God; this God is not only immanent but is also transcendent. Emphasis is placed upon the two different states of being of God: Allah is not only to be found out of this space-time continuum but is also to be found and approached through devotion and worship within this space-time continuum. Because God is both immanent and transcendent, beyond the power of mere humankind to envisage and describe, it is considered blasphemous, arrogant and lacking respect to even try to depict God in any way. Therefore Islam, like Judaism, has no representations of Allah and its mosques are beautiful and simple, empty spaces adorned only with religious tracts and infinitely repeating geometrical designs.

Muslims take their enormous respect for God into all aspects of their lives. No devout Muslim would attempt to create a perfect artefact, as to create something that is perfect is considered to be an insult to God. They will deliberately weave an imperfection in a rug, for example, to ensure they are not in danger of insulting God. This constant mindfulness of humility in relation to Allah is an integral and important aspect of the belief system.

Belief in Islam is based on six main factors: belief in God; the divine decree; his angels; his messengers; the Day of Judgement; and the revelations which were recorded in the Qur'an (literally "recitation"). A principal feature of Islam is that Muslims do not use the intermediary of a priest in their worship. The Five Pillars of Islam provide structure and guidance: *shahada,* testimony of faith; *salat,* prayer; *zakat,* the giving of alms; *sawm,* fasting; and *hajj,* pilgrimage to Mecca.

Each belief system we have looked at so far has chosen to place greater emphasis on different aspects of the whole: one or two essential messages became the highlight, the focus. If we are to succeed in our quest for spiritual power and unity with the Divine, it is helpful if we put all these separate primary focus points together, because then we start to see a glowing, holistic picture of sublime beauty. Islam has as its core an essential aspect without which any practitioner on the evolutionary spiritual path cannot succeed. The word Islam simply means "submission". The entire belief system could be summed up in this one short word, Islam – submission to the One Supreme God. Muslims view the universe as law-governed and everything in it follows the course that has been ordained for it by the One God.

Within this law-governed universe there is purpose; each creation has purpose according to Divine Intent. The belief in the immanence of God is consciously entwined throughout Muslims' daily lives – nothing, not even the smallest act, may take place unless Allah first either allows it or actively instigates it. Because of this, many Muslims believe that their life path is mapped out in its smallest detail before birth; they believe that their free will is limited by the overriding will of Allah. The powerful all-pervasive intent and law of Allah governs all that comprises the multiverse, from the tiniest specks of dust to the magnificent galaxies in the highest heavens. Islam holds that the material world is the creation of the One God and all was created with the vibration of the creative word, "Be" or "Hu" (depending whom you speak to). The *Qur'an,* the holy book of Islam, states that this act of creation took six days, however Allah's days are like thousands of years and so the act of creation is an unfolding, evolutionary process. This belief of creation coming about through sound is a common thread running through many belief systems: sound/resonance or a word (which of course is also sound/resonance), "Be", "Hu", "Om" or "in the beginning was the word", play the primary role in the act of creation.

The *Qur'an* not only encompasses many teachings on ethics and morality, but also places enormous emphasis on care of the natural world, which is considered a holy trust given by Allah to humankind. It states that the natural world is Allah's creation and therefore belongs to Allah. We are merely stewards or trustees on behalf of Allah. If we desecrate nature, we have by implication desecrated Allah. If one loves and respects Allah then one naturally loves and respects all. The *Qur'an* refers in many places to multiple realms:

> He who created seven heavens one above another; no want of proportion will you see in the creation of Allah. Look again, do you see any flaw?
>
> — *Qur'an 67:3*
>
> The seven heavens and the Earth and all beings therein declare His glory.
>
> — *Qur'an 17:44*

Again we have the belief in multiple realms to which the immortal soul may travel depending upon the activities of said soul while on Earth.

The same golden threads we have seen before run throughout Islam. These, together with the purity of Islam, coupled with the essential simplicity of its teachings and the fully conscious interweaving of spirituality with daily life, have ensured its longevity and success.

As we can see, there are many paths to enlightenment. One teacher speaking in a particular way may make sense to you; another, even though from the same culture, may not. If one accepts that an interactive intelligent creator is trying to make contact with us, trying to teach us about its existence and the meaning of ours, how is he to do this? We are all so different. Not only do we speak different languages, we think differently, act differently and nations are culturally quite different one from the other. With genetic encoding, we are discovering that men and women are quite different one from the other. Is it possible that just one prophet, one messenger would have succeeded, one who came in a specific time and for a short time at that? It does not sound a very rational way of going about things – so why not many prophets, many Messiahs? On examination they all appear to have come with the same message. Does it matter the name of the prophet? Is not the message the integral thing?

So there we have it. Over-simplification, you may say, but in essence that is what all the fighting and bloodshed has been about. Why can't we all just settle down and let each have their different ways and names, versions of events etc, as long as the essential teachings are there? All this other stuff is just peripheral. We know that temporal power and money are unfortunately part of any man-made religion, hence the clinging onto "My structure is the right one, mine is the best, all the others are wrong!" If we could just let go for a moment and find the middle way, look at the truth which is inherent in them all, then we may finally see the big picture, or as much as we will be able to see from our current limited vantage point.

What is vitally important is that we should be living with a holistic vision. The whole picture should be part of our daily lives, not merely the manifested physical aspect, which is of necessity of the lowest vibration. If we are to evolve successfully, if we are to become whole, aligned and coherent divine beings of high spin, light and power, then we must start to incorporate into our daily lives all aspects possessed of a higher vibration. At the present time, we appear globally to be going in the opposite direction – the lower the vibratory emanation, the more attraction it appears to exert over us and thus the greater level of mental ill health, depression and clouded vision so many are suffering from. We need to ask ourselves why this is? We are on a path of involution rather than evolution, which should be a cause for concern for us all.

As we can see now, the six religions discussed here have as their primary beliefs those scientific fundamentals described in Chapter 1, Science and Theology are moving ever closer together. The path to enlightenment, successful evolution and spiritual power and importantly greater Love, Joy and Peace is individual and unique. The important thing is that we should each start on the path – and to do this we need to recognise, align with and employ the powers of our own soul.

Chapter 3
Soul

There are two ways, the one of life, the other of death; but between the two, there is a great difference.

— Catholic Catechism, 1696

As so many spiritual texts relate that each individual journey to the Divine starts from within, because that is where the spirit of the Divine dwells, is there a particular focal point – vehicle that we need to first understand?

There is, of course. Scientists call this particular focal point a "quantum coherent field of energy"; religions call it the "soul". So the first question is, "Do we actually have one of those to begin with?" As we saw in Chapter One, scientists are starting to think we do because after death, or the ceasing of metabolic action, the essential "you" leaks out into the universe at large but does not dissipate. It is not lost or destroyed, but rather it hangs together in a phenomenon called quantum coherence. Many slightly different pathways and processes are postulated regarding our exit journey from the bag of water – our physical body manifestation – at the point of death. All the major religions, as we saw in Chapter Two, make many references to the immortal soul they say we each possess. (I will refer always to the coherent energy field/eternal divine presence within as the soul. If you prefer some other title, substitute it throughout this book should it make the meaning clearer or better for you in any way.) The *Gita*, eloquent as always, has this to say about the soul:

> Invisible before birth are all beings and after death invisible again. They are seen between two unseens. Why in this truth find sorrow?
>
> The spirit that is in all beings is immortal in them all: for the death of what cannot die, cease thou to sorrow.
>
> *— Bhagavad Gita 2:28, 30*

In other words, upon death, the soul moves from the explicate realm to the implicate, seen to unseen, visible to invisible. It has recently been postulated that what happens at the critical point of the process we call death is that the soul moves out of this particular time-space continuum, which necessitates leaving the lower vibratory mass of the physical behind. In moving from this time-space continuum, the soul naturally becomes invisible to most (but not all) of us and so we presume it has ceased to exist.

Some will answer, "Yes, but are we able to prove concretely that we have a soul?" It is, I think, even more difficult to prove we do not have a soul than to prove we do. The absolute concrete evidence either way is lacking. However, informed opinion is now weighted slightly more in favour of us having a soul than not. If we are to presume we have a soul (it is more accurate to say, "If we are souls", but in this world of separation we will continue) what is its function, how may we use it, get to know it, interact with it, align with it, take ownership of it – and if we do, what may happen?

The *Concise Oxford Dictionary* defines "soul" as "the immaterial part of man". The Latin for soul is anima (feminine) or animus (masculine), meaning essence, which is the underlying phenomena or absolute being; so the soul is the intangible, incorporeal complete aspect of the being.

If our soul is immaterial we may not see it or touch it. If we undergo an operation the surgeon will not be able to locate it, although physicists appear now to have contacted and described it in a very limited way. The fact that we may not contact our soul in the normal ways we contact everything else in the phenomenal world is not a reason to suppose it does not exist. Again, if we think in terms of energy only, all sorts of things previously thought to be impossible will start to appear more sensible, logical, positive and possible than previously held points of view. If all of creation sprang from the focused attention/resonance/sound of God, then we may presume that all in the multiverse is imbued with this divine energy, as the Divine Creative Field appears to be the creative, vivifying element and organiser of all. If all beings have a soul, a spark of the divine igniting them, it is reasonable to assume that all beings in the multiverse are engaged in the continual process of evolution driven by the fire within and the spiral thrust without to ever more coherent, complete and higher vibratory realms of existence. A belief in a divine soul is a belief in the process of evolution and the process of refinement to completeness and perfection.

As we have seen, the entire multiverse consists of one thing only: energy. With all in a constant state of ebb and flow, waxing and waning, growing and depleting; with seeming birth, life and death as fundamentals within the system. The whole is held within a spiral flow towards ever-greater refinement. Any apparent state of static stability is an illusion. Objects, and I use the word loosely appear to be static only because the inherent energy is moving at a slower rate or vibration than comparative objects. The higher the rate of vibration, the less static they appear and over a certain point of vibratory rate, some so-called objects will not be visible to our naked eye at all (although some people, animals or insects may still see them). The lower the vibratory rate, the more dense objects appear to be – we are able to see them clearly and they then often appear to be solid, immoveable. For the most part, we are more comfortable with things that appear to be fixed, solid and reliable, as most of us are uncomfortable with the notion of change and impermanence. It frightens us.

Now the curious thing is that in this landscape of impermanence, if one is in conscious relationship with one's own soul; the soul will be the one and only aspect that is in any way permanent and stable. The soul will be the one aspect that we may seek out, cling on to and through interaction with it find peace, joy constant love, stability and assurance; no matter what else is going on. This essential Divine aspect of ourselves (once we are consciously able to interact with it) always radiates calm, peace and assurance that is not to be found anywhere else in this material plane of existence. The most curious thing about all this is that this one rock we each possess in the vast ocean of the seething flux of the multiverse, this one entity that we can always depend upon we can neither see nor touch nor as yet wholly intellectually prove exists. Yet it is the source of all assurance, all wisdom, all peace, joy and love. Until we come to have direct knowledge, relationship and understanding of our own soul i.e. conscious loving interaction with our soul, we will remain stuck, almost wholly immersed in the physical and therefore in all meaningful ways separated from the source of all. This renders us effectively blind, deaf and unconscious, which leads to mental ill health, depression and often in extremis suicide.

> I am the beginning and the middle and the end of all that is. Of all knowledge I am the knowledge of the Soul. Of the many paths of reason I am the one that leads to Truth.
>
> Of sounds I am the first sound, A; of compounds, I am coordination. I am time, never-ending time. I am the Creator who sees all.
>
> — *Bhagavad Gita 10:32–33*

Many great men have attempted to find where in the body the soul resides. Plato held that the soul was located in the brain and that the brain and the spinal cord linked were the servants of the soul. Strato placed the soul in the forefront of the brain between the eyebrows. Hippocrates, Herophilus, the Arabian philosophers and many others also placed the seat of the soul in the brain. The Jewish Sefer Yetzirah describes the soul as having five parts, "three of which directly affect the mind – Nefesh, Ruach and Neshamah, the other two Chayah and Yechidah are called envelopments which cannot enter the mind. These two are eternally linked to the field of nothingness". If we move to Eastern mysticism, we will find the heart considered to be the home of the soul. In actuality, the location of the soul is in a different place with different beings at different times. If we were to look at a more fully aligned spiritual being, such as Jesus or Buddha, we would see their soul and their physical and other bodies as an immense coherent energy field, with the field of the soul radiating out from the centre, enveloping and extending far beyond the physical body. The field of a highly evolved soul is large and the physical body in fact resides in the soul field, not the other way round. For most of us, though, at this point in our evolutionary spiral, the energy field of the soul in this space-time continuum, is tiny, closed off and barely emits any field at all. The electrical energy produced from such a field is so minute as to be almost or completely undetectable. In other words, there is very little or no light emanating from the soul. In addition, as the soul in this state has little or no power, the physical being, the lower vibratory mass, may have assumed power over it and without conscious intervention this state of affairs will build. If the being is functioning in ways that are completely in opposition to the qualities inherent in the energy field of the soul, then the soul moves for its own protection as far as possible from the point of influence. This is misalignment. A being functioning with a closed off, weak and misaligned soul is on an involutionary path to greater negativity, unhappiness and ever weaker soul emanations. From here it becomes increasingly hard to turn the situation around. In the language of religion, we are now on the road to hell. If this state of affairs is further complicated by the breakdown of the physical body (which will in these circumstances inevitably happen) as a result of incorrect thoughts, words, deeds and possibly together with the ingestion of drugs or alcohol, we are making it even less likely the situation can be retrieved. Should we happen to die while in this condition we are in deep trouble.

There are many conflicting spiritual texts regarding the soul. Some passages appear to imply that everyone is possessed of a divine soul that is immortal and therefore unable to perish. Other passages speak quite clearly about the possible destruction of the soul, saying it is possible to kill or obliterate one's soul and that should we do such a thing we no longer have the possibility of further evolution and of course are no longer immortal. The *Bhagavad Gita* has this to say on the subject:

> The virtues of heaven are for liberation but the sins of hell are the chains of the soul.
>
> There are two natures in this world; the one is of heaven, the other of hell. The heavenly nature has been explained; hear now the evil of hell.
>
> Evil men know not what should be done or what should not be done. Purity is not in their hearts, nor good conduct, nor truth. They say: "This world has no truth, no moral foundation, no God. There is no law of creation: what is the cause of birth but lust?"
>
> Firm in this belief, these men of dead souls, of truly little intelligence, undertake their work of evil: they are the enemies of this fair world, working for its destruction.
>
> — *Bhagavad Gita 16:5–9*

The passages continue relating the many negative states of mind and acts man engages in until we come to:

> Three are the gates to this hell, the death of the soul: the gate of lust, the gate of wrath and the gate of greed. Let a man shun the three.
>
> — *Bhagavad Gita 16:21*

Christian texts in general teach that the "soul is immortal", because the soul is God's creation and therefore, we cannot destroy it. A priest will tell you only God may destroy his own creation. However, buried deep in Catholic scripture we find that should we choose to turn away from or deny the existence of God, then, we run the risk of destroying our soul. If we believe that in this whole glorious web of creation, we only exist at all through the creative power and intent of the Divine Creative Field/God as all the evidence is telling us, and if we were then to choose through the gift of our free will to deny "God", we are in reality denying our very own existence. Disbelief in God; is in fact disbelief in the reality of ourselves. If we proceed with a fundamental belief in nothing, in a negation of divine life, so we slowly but inexorably begin to destroy ourselves. The result can only then be our eternal separation from the Divine, and if we are eternally separated from the Divine which is life and which gave us life, then that which gave us life through the agency of our divine soul will ultimately cease to be available to us. Our divine soul is extinguished as we have chosen death over life.

> This state of definitive self-exclusion from communion with God and the blessed is called "hell". Jesus often speaks of "Gehenna," of the unquenchable fire, reserved for those who to the end of their lives refuse to believe and be converted, where both soul and body can be lost.
>
> The chief punishment of hell is eternal separation from God, in whom alone man can possess the life and happiness for which he was created and for which he longs.
>
> — *Catholic Catechism IV Hell 1033–1034*

> And fear not them which kill the body, but are not able to kill the soul: but rather fear him which is able to destroy both soul and body in hell.
>
> — *St. Matthew 10:28*

We may conclude from those passages that hell is actually the death of the soul. And death of the soul is eternal separation from God, because without our divine spark – our soul; communication and interaction with the Divine – the inflow of Divine life-giving energy – is impossible. Should we choose to deny the Divine inherent in all, choose not to believe in life, then we place our feet upon a path of involution towards lower vibration, lack of light and therefore life. Destruction of the soul may be caused by a belief in anything that is a negation of the Divine Creative Field.

We would be wise to presume it is as possible to destroy one's soul, as it is possible to destroy one's physical body. If the original spark of the Divine Creative Field is heavily overlaid and fractured with energies that are in direct opposition to its divine original inherent qualities, then the original spark may become extinguished if enough pressure is brought to bear. We have the free will to do this, as we shall see. Presumably the soul may under certain conditions fall back into the original warp and weft from whence it was formed, thereby losing the gift of creation, immortality and therefore all possible future evolution. With this in mind, to address the health of one's soul as assiduously, or more so, than one does the health of one's physical body is the only wise course of action. Our language is sprinkled with references to the soul. We use phrases indiscriminately without thinking about their possible greater meaning. For example, how many times have you heard, "I am beside myself, I am not myself, I am fractured, I am in pieces, I am losing it"? These are all very descriptive phrases of an instinctive sensing of a misalignment of the soul or of a general incoherence in all the fields. Often what is being felt and strongly registered is a fracturing within the entire multi-layered field. If we were to pay attention at these times and subsequently alter our thoughts, words or deeds, awareness such as this would assist to alter fundamentally the coherence or lack of in all the many layered fields that is you.

Very few of us are even remotely coherent and unified fields. Most of us are living in a state of extreme misalignment: we are not integrated and aligned with our soul and its positive evolutionary energies. If we go back to "all is energy", the soul has a higher rate of spin than the physical body, which is why it is invisible. Our visible physical body is vibrating at one rate and our soul at another higher rate. These two are rarely in accord and alignment; ideally, they should be, as the pinnacle of evolution may only be reached when they are. In almost everyone the soul is apart from the physical body. As we think in linear terms, let's say it is to one side. In some cases, it may be many metres away; in others, the contact is much closer; but rarely do the two properly unite in one centred single and coherent unified field. More often than not, the physical and the soul are in discord. The soul linked directly to the Divine Creative Field under the law of self-similarity should be the overarching governor of all thought, words and actions, as this follows the fundamental law of higher vibratory realms directing and influencing the lower. Through our gift of free will, we may have chosen not to be guided by the divine inherent in our being. We may have instead chosen to follow the lower vibratory energy of the manifested physical planes. Because of this disastrous choice, our being in all its fields is a war zone. This complete reversal of the natural order has a grave effect on us and everything in the multiverse and it can have only one end result which is involution. It is impossible to stress this too strongly. Some situations disconnect us more from our souls; other situations draw us closer and give greater coherence. However, if we are to be mentally – thus physically well and happy we must accept and adopt the fundamental law in which the higher vibratory order governs the lower. While we stay immersed in the physical, taking instruction from the physical and with all our focused attention on these lower vibratory planes, we cannot and will not evolve to a higher state of wellness, happiness, love and joy.

The object and entire focus of this book is to show the way to ever-greater alignment, coherence and subsequently higher levels of evolutionary progress, spiritual power and assured immortality with all the love, peace and joy this brings with it. The vision we each must hold for ourselves is of paramount importance here, as we are only ever able to experience, create and affect that in which we believe. Therefore, if we were to see ourselves as Divine Immortal Souls on an empowering evolutionary journey, much that is out of balance and negative in our world would cease. For us to see ourselves in this way we would need to believe that we are possessed of an energy field (our soul) that is the essential part of us and that this soul field, which has a higher rate of spin than our physical body, is permanent under all but the direst of circumstances. This field of our soul has as its igniting spark the Divine Creative Field, and even though our soul field is often no more than a minuscule spark, as it is in its entirety the Divine Creative Field, it is always coherent, harmonious and unified and therefore always calm, peaceful, perfectly loving and imbued with a wise intelligence. As such, it can be a constant source of strength, wisdom, love, joy and power. Our soul is the fundamental seat of the only real power available to us in the multi-verse, as the power of the Divine Creative Field flows primarily to us through the agency and mechanism of our soul. The conscious acknowledgement and possession of our own soul is the key here as the soul is the *only* ultimate access or portal to the Divine. Access to and interaction with the Divine Creative Field is only to be accomplished through the agency of our own Divine Immortal Soul. This is the most important and profound knowledge because only from this understanding and acceptance can further evolutionary work proceed. We must learn to be guided and directed by our Divine Soul so that once again the higher order is directing the lower.

Here it might be helpful to gain a greater understanding of the soul's various qualities. As we have seen, it is believed to be immortal. We cannot see it or touch it but we can become fully conscious of its presence and interact with it and work through it. In all spiritual texts, the soul is described as being the highest conceived expression of God and the fundamental qualities of the soul are described as being wisdom, spiritual power and love. These qualities are also the qualities ascribed to the Divine Creative Field, with wisdom and power being the natural products of the resonance of love. Again we have the trinity, the three in one. To the degree that we have inherent in our fields and manifest these three qualities is the degree of our evolutionary progress. Our progress from the dark chaos of the unformed to the spiral light-emitting high vibration of individual yet not separate formed perfection can be easily measured by our ability to hold within our fields the resonance of these three qualities. In this physical world of manifested forms, we should only ever revere and emulate those with these three qualities in abundance, and we should acknowledge that those lacking in these three fundamental and primary qualities could not be inspirations for us. If we wish not only to survive as souls but also to continue our evolutionary journey, these three qualities must be our only signposts – there are no others.

As physical beings emanating from our metaphysical Divine Soul, we need to be aware of other important aspects. Our soul, which no matter how enfolded and misaligned it may be at this time, is itself a spark of the Divine. This spark of the Divine Field is ever-present, all-powerful, has all knowledge and, most important, is independent of our will. It may be a frightening thought that our soul is independent of our will. What exactly do we mean by this?

Here we enter again the realm of paradox. Paradoxes appear to litter profusely our evolutionary journey. If our soul, our small portion of the Divine, is independent of our will and if we become aligned and coherent, i.e. run by our soul, does this not mean we lose all independence, power and free will? Will this mean that someone or something else is running us, and we are not in charge? Well, the answer is, "Yes and No." Both are correct. This is the paradox: when our soul is paramount then and only then are we truly operating from as much free will as is possible within the system. The fundamental reason for our gift of free will is that we are free to make this choice.

Until we do make this life-giving choice, we are primarily controlled and run by our puny, limited physical wills, egos and all outside influences. We are like so much flotsam and jetsam washed this way and that, each passing storm causing us grief. More importantly, we are easily led astray and may become imprisoned in the dark realms of low vibration, immersed and lost in the manifested physical world of low vibratory forms. Being lost in the physical will engender a subsequent attachment to all things physical as in the darkness this is all we can see and know, and we will cling to these illusory forms in the belief that they represent our entire world because that is truly how it seems. The result of being lost in this way is often hopelessness, addictions, anger, depression, violence and worse. In this lost, obsessive and materialistic state of being, we will often find a little mantra is playing in our heads: "Is this all there is?" The answer, of course, is, "No, this is not all there is, not at all, it just seems that way when immersed in darkness." Our true essence is our eternal divine aspect, our soul; we can choose whether to be guided by our soul or guided by our egoic personal will and/or external forces. Our personal will, while initially promising personal freedom, actually leads us into prison. Our soul guidance, which initially seems to be a giving up of our free will, our freedom to choose, actually leads us not to complete unfettered personal freedom – how could this be possible in a system where all is connected? – but to a greater unfolding and evolution of the soul and thus increasing free will and power. A more highly evolved soul has a greater energy field of higher vibration, therefore greater wisdom, love and power. This is the paradox – by giving up personal will and seeming personal power by submitting to the higher authority of the soul and hence the Divine Creative Field, one gains greater freedom and power. By submitting to higher dimension causes rather than controlling lower dimension effects, one quite naturally gains power, as the higher dimension cause is the source of all true power. Therefore, in order to gain greater freedom and power one must give up all previous notions of freedom and power – this is the inbuilt safeguard against misuse and one of the great natural laws. To be guided solely by our soul is the whole point of our existence: until we learn how to do this, we cannot evolve. If our soul is paramount, the entire landscape changes in ways beyond our imaginings while we inhabit those dark regions of soulless materiality. Until we are able to see, hear and know for ourselves, faith is required at this point, because when immersed in the physical most are blind and deaf.

Dr Andrew Powell– Royal College of Psychiatrists, U.K., has this to say on the subject:

> "The impact of the Newtonian world view has been immense. Our scientific model of the psyche has no place for the soul; there is nothing before birth and nothing after death. Everything has to be understood as arising from within this temporary, physical existence, with the human self the only source of consciousness. We are all separate beings, bounded by the envelopes of our skin and moving around in a fixed, impersonal, three-dimensional universe, which is utterly indifferent to our comings and goings. Little wonder that depression is the ailment of the modern world. In the first five years of Prozac's coming onto the market, over ten million prescriptions were handed out".
>
> — Dr Andrew Powell, *Quantum Psychiatry – Where Science meets Spirit*

It is important to remember that our Divine Soul is, above all else, intensely personal and unconditionally loving. When we are consciously connected with our Divine Soul it is impossible that we may feel depressed, unloved, unhappy. Impossible that we should seek often eternally and hopelessly for love out there, as we will know that under all circumstances, the vibration/resonance of Divine love is to be found within through the mechanism of our own soul which emanates the Divine coherent, unified field of unconditional love. Remember also that sound is a key throughout the multiverse, when our soul has been encouraged to unfold, if only in a small way, (and by merely thinking about it, will cause a shift) not only will we begin to be guided by it, but also, we will become aware of our individual and unique sound. As we develop our soul, as it is enabled to unfold ever further, as we align more and more with it, we will begin to hear the glorious individual and unique sound we each make. When conscious and focused, all our being intent on the core, the celestial high spin sound of our Divine Soul is heard. The sound will bring tears to the eyes – once heard it is impossible to forget – and it will change the image one has of oneself forever. It is by this unique sound that each of us is recognised throughout the multiverse. Of course, if our soul is greatly enfolded, then we will be almost silent and it will be more difficult for us to be heard, more difficult for us to communicate with the multiverse at large. If however, our soul field is large and powerful then communication is enhanced accordingly.

> "Quantum physicists discovered that physical atoms are made up of vortices of energy that are constantly spinning and vibrating; each atom is like a wobbly spinning top that radiates energy. Because each atom has its own specific energy signature (wobble), assemblies of atoms (molecules) collectively radiate their own identifying energy patterns. So every material structure in the universe, including you and me, radiates a unique energy signature".
>
> — Bruce H. Lipton, Ph.D, *The Biology of Belief*

All in the multiverse, whether material – energy held temporarily in physical form – or immaterial, emit a unique energy signature. We urgently need to revise our belief systems and our view of ourselves and the multiverse, because many of us think we do not have a soul, or if we do think we have one it gets little or no attention. Certainly, we have little or no interrelation, or interaction, with our souls. Our soul for the most part languishes unrecognised, disputed and ignored, far from the centre of things. For most of us it lies dormant, a potentiality for evolution, but yet undiscovered. We remain half-man, half-spiritual being, more physical than spiritual, vibrating almost wholly at the level of our lowest common denominator, our physical mortal body.

Some may believe they do not have a soul, as their analytical left-brain has worked out for them, and wish to hold onto the old software. Now in our rapidly fragmenting world they are faced with the consequences of that uncomfortable, limiting even dangerous belief system. If in scientific terms this belief system is equally as unprovable as the one put forward here, why not opt for a more comfortable, more meaningfull belief system? One could, I suppose, give life some meaning by placing all the importance and focus on family and friends, on material possessions and all the fun we have with them, on worldly importance, but essentially what does this give us? The end game is nothingness: we cannot take our loved ones with us when we die, nor our material possessions, worldly power or anything else we have collected along the way. The whole game rests on our individual shoulders and there is no real help forthcoming for the desperate times, as with a soulless belief system it is all down to us alone, as we are alone with nothingness at the end. We may with this belief system act in any way we wish as there is no ultimate retribution or karma. (Although Newton's third law of motion – that every action has its reaction which is equal and opposite, applies as much to the world of morals and principals as to the laws of physics). This playing field is the only one, and as long as we are bigger, stronger, better or cleverer than the next person, we may think we are fine and can pat ourselves on the back for succeeding.

Some may be afraid they will look foolish adopting a possibly illogical belief system, one they cannot concretely prove is correct, but then try concretely proving the soul does *not* exist. Anyway, does it really matter what others may think about our belief systems? Those who believe in a Divine Soul as part of their being think that those who do not are foolish and blind. They find it hard to understand how anyone may choose to live in such a cold isolated place as a soulless world, missing all the benefits that come from this vital, life-giving and positive belief system.

Should we choose to believe that we possess a Divine Soul, then immediately the dead end opens out into a wide prospect. The entire multiverse shifts from a stagnant, blocked dead end, an accident without meaningful life, into a meaning-full landscape, packed with infinite possibilities. We may now take something with us when we die; life has infinite meaning and purpose as greater wisdom, love and power emanating from an increasingly unfolded soul goes with us when we die. We must also consider the inherent danger in choosing not to believe that we are possessed of a Divine Soul, in choosing mortality and death over immortality and life. If it is possible for our soul to be destroyed, if we have the free will to destroy the tiny unevolved spark that is our soul, we should be extremely fearful of doing this. We should be fearful of suffering involution rather than evolution, with our chance of evolving towards divinity lost. If we choose not to go so far as to destroy our soul but to do nothing one way or another, we may never evolve any further than we are now: we may remain stuck, endlessly going round in the natural cycle of birth, death and decay.

In a rational sensible society, one would expect us to be fearful of neglecting the health, welfare and growth of our soul, as this should be of primary importance to us all. We should be putting the state of our soul at the forefront of all we do, all the thoughts we have, all the decisions we make, all actions we take. Instead, in our egoic rational, mechanistic, left-brain separated material world, our souls are of no consequence – we are so immersed in the physical we have lost all sight of what is real. We are truly blind and have mistaken the real for the unreal, and the unreal for the real. In any other area of life, if we had things upside down or in the reverse order, we would expect confusion, negative consequences, bad energy, chaos and violence. So why do we not now look at our world and understand that all that is incorrect, out of balance, fractured and negative about our physical plane of existence would be immediately corrected if we just did this one small thing. If we all recognised, interacted, paid attention to and worked under the guidance of the Divine Spark, our Soul; then all that is sane, coherent, truly rational, aligned, wise, healthy, happy, loving and Divine, would naturally flow.

They say the eyes are the windows of the soul, and in truth, our eyes reveal much about the state of our soul. They clearly reveal the general state of our entire being. It is possible to recognise an individual merely by looking at a photograph of the iris of their eyes. The very depths of our being are clearly depicted in the eyes for everyone to see, should they choose. If we wish to know the state of our own soul, we can gaze deeply into our own eyes and much will be revealed. Whatever is seen there, it is always helpful in moving forward as it clearly tells us where we are right now.

In this space-time continuum, we inhabit a sea of energy which is in a perpetual state of flux – all is fluid, nothing is fixed and concrete – so the choice of our belief system is entirely up to us. We may think and believe whatever we choose. As our belief system creates and forms our reality, it makes sense to choose one that is drawn from a higher order than our own, a belief that is living, vital, positive and helpful to us in all things. Our belief system describes our level of consciousness and evolution.

> Be in truth eternal, beyond earthly opposites. Beyond gains and possessions, possess thine own soul.
>
> — *Bhagavad Gita 2:45*

Each individual and unique soul is the key, the vehicle and pathway to all. To be under our souls' direction is the reason for life on the physical plane, as it is only when our soul is paramount, that it may develop and grow from a tiny spark, a minuscule single-faceted diamond into the glorious multi-faceted brilliant gem of power it is desired that it become. The Divine pattern is that we acknowledge and accept the natural order whereby higher vibratory realms direct and organise the lower. It is only in accepting this that we may evolve. As the *Tao Te Ching* says, "What really matters most, your image or your soul? What do you care about your money, or your life?" Our soul is the ultimate portal to expanded life, but all evolutionary progress involves the entire being and this of necessity involves all our fields as they expand outward from the soul. Because of this, we must come to fully know and understand the entire vehicle we are working with and through. This is why "Know thyself" has for aeons been the first great command prefacing all spiritual evolutionary journeys.

Chapter 4
Know Thyself

> My heart do not take pride in every thought, do not
>   flutter like a moth around every light.
> Until you know yourself you will be distant from God.
>
> — *Rumi*

There has been one great injunction echoing down through the ages, "Gnothi seauton" – "Know thyself". This is because we cannot journey further on our evolutionary path to a higher vibratory state with its subsequent unfolding of our soul unless we take this essential first step.

Socrates said, "I must first know myself, as the Delphi Oracle inscription says, for to be curious about that which is not my concern while I am still in ignorance of my own self would be ridiculous." Socrates would today judge many of us ridiculous. The Greek sages' injunction "Gnothi seauton" has always been paramount because the key to Wisdom, Interaction, Divine Love, Joy and Peace, does not lie outside of us. It is not to be found from a point of contact beyond. One can only ever make progress towards greater spiritual power with the knowledge, ability and practice of going within. The vehicle we need is ourselves and the access point/doorway is only to be found within, nowhere else.

If we refer to the wonderful *Tao Te Ching* again, Lao Tzu wrote that "those who know others are wise, those who know themselves are enlightened". The *Vedas* teach: "All men should seek to know one thing (thyself) knowing which, all else is known." The Sufis say: "He who knows himself, knows his Lord".

In the *Gospel of Thomas*, discovered at Nag Hammadi in Egypt in 1945, there is much written regarding "knowing thyself":

> For he who has not known himself has known nothing, but he who has known himself has at the same time already achieved knowledge about the depth of All.
>
> When you know yourselves, then you will be known and you will understand that you are children of the living Father. But if you do not know yourselves, then you live in poverty, and you are the poverty.
>
> — *Gospel of Thomas 3*

Those are all strong and clear messages. To put them another way, we are in our essence a spark of the Divine Creative Field that is held in manifested existence, and if we were with conscious awareness, knowledge and power to direct our focus within this soul field, we would immediately come into contact with and have direct knowledge of the Divine Creative Field or God. The Divine Implicate Order is not to be fully contacted and understood by looking in the explicate realm, the realm of low vibration. The only portal we have for this access is within ourselves, through a very specific point, in a very specific way. The left-brain, for instance, will not afford access. This clearly defined process and path is particular, and access is denied through any channel other than the correct one. The correct path may be instinctively followed by many who possess an inner wisdom, an inner knowing – to them this path seems as natural and as simple as breathing – but for others the way must be learnt. Here again we have another underlying immutable law: to "know thyself" is to know all. It is all quite simple, really. Without going within, without knowing thyself, no real progress can ever be made, as this instruction is a fundamental prerequisite for union with the Divine which will subsequently bring greater love, joy and peace, together with greater knowledge of and union with the Divine.

Now, before a great wail goes up, "I don't want to become just another navel-gazer," wait a moment. Navel-gazing is not what is being advocated here. A journey through yourself and beyond is the project and it will be the most fascinating, exciting, interesting and, yes, sometimes frightening journey you will ever take. It will leave all other journeys you may take in the explicate, material realms in the shade. Many of us are dissatisfied with our often extremely privileged lives. Our work does not satisfy, our personal relationships often do not give us all we are looking for and all our material possessions leave us wanting something more. The problem is, we do not know what it is exactly we are missing, what it is exactly we want. All we know for sure is that there is a feeling of dissatisfaction, a hollow in our centre, sometimes a large black hole that we are often quite consciously aware of but seem unable to do anything about. The more we look "out there" for help or assistance, the greater the sense of emptiness and loss increases within.

There are possibly various mantras running through the brain – "I don't want to be doing what I am doing", "I don't want to live like this", "Why do some people have a magically blessed existence while my life is difficult and troubled?", "There must be more than this" and so on. Well, of course there is more than our daily manifested physical existence. There is much more than emptiness, trouble, pain and difficulty. The only real problem is that we are looking for relief with incorrect belief systems and in incorrect places, so nothing changes. Even if one has a seemingly blessed life, there may still often be a feeling of lack; as a life lived without a spiritual dimension, without conscious connection to the source of all life, is out of balance – it is a half-life and instead of being fed from the source, it feeds primarily upon itself. This source of power is finite and a life lived this way can only end in tears.

> Nature is the source of all material things: the maker, the means of making and the thing made. Spirit is the source of all consciousness which feels pleasure and pain.
>
> The spirit of man when in nature feels the ever-changing conditions of nature. When he binds himself to things ever-changing, a good or evil fate whirls him round through life-in-death.
>
> But the Spirit Supreme in man is beyond fate. He watches, gives blessing, bears all, feels all. He is called the Lord Supreme and the Supreme Soul. He who knows in truth this spirit and knows nature with its changing conditions, wherever this man may be he is no more whirled round by fate.
>
> — *Bhagavad Gita 13:20–23*

How do we make changes, how do we start to look in the right place in the right way? How do we go about changing our lives so that we are not only certain of continuing our evolutionary journey, but are assured of greater peace, love and joy while journeying? We must first believe that it is possible to become strong, positive, fulfilled, at ease with ourselves and filled with a reason for living, as this belief will naturally bring with it a measure of that in which we believe. However, a truly joyous life filled with wisdom, love and spiritual power, may come about only if the Divine is consciously woven throughout the warp and weft of our lives. We are usually unable to do this until we have direct knowledge, personal familiarity with, or a gnosis concerning the Divine. It is true that often in order to learn how to "know thyself" we must start by reading a book or listening to someone for direction. However, after we have received the direction, after we are given a few tools, a few simple exercises, then the path is only to be found within. If we wish to change direction, to let go of negativity and take control of our own mind, emotions and desires, if we wish to make our lives meaning-full, if we wish to know the reason we are here and to live an expanded life on all levels, then the journey to accomplish all these things starts from within.

Is it not possible that a spark of the Divine, a coherent unified field/soul, a small universe which is itself a reflection of the vast universe outside itself, resides somewhere about each physical manifested energy field/body, and it is to this that the spiritual teachers are referring when they say "the Kingdom of God is within"? The doorway to all the spiritual mysteries, the *only* entranceway to all the mysteries of the Divine, is within. You will not find anything at all without: if you look there, you will be left without.

For our journey to succeed we need to understand the whole vehicle we will be working with and through. We need to understand all our inherent blocks to full unfolded spiritual gnosis, we need to know the pathways and to be able clearly to see any work that is required to be done in order to proceed. This is as essential as all other preparatory work we undertake before any journey in the explicate realms.

The Buddhist monk Hui Neng spoke to a student in this way: "When your mind is enlightened, you will know the Essence of Mind, and then you may tread the Path the right way. Now you are under delusion, and do not know your Essence of Mind. Yet you dare to ask whether I know my Essence of Mind or not. If I do, I realise it myself, but the fact that I know it, cannot help you from being under delusion. Similarly, if you know your Essence of Mind, your knowing would be of no use to me." Instead of asking others, why not see for yourself, and know it for yourself?

If we go back to the image of the two different fields of energy, the lower vibratory physical and the higher vibratory Divine Soul energy, this is our equipment (together with other fields we will get to later). This is what we must work with and through. If we hold that image for a moment, focusing in the centre, and then imagine moving the focus to the outside of the two fields, out into the world around, energy drains away does it not? Any feeling of concentrated power we had while focusing in the centre drains away the moment attention is directed outwards. This is a simple exercise to show how energy fields start to dissipate and lose power once our aligned, centred and focused attention wanders from the source. We lose power and much more besides. Our ability to perceive, to understand, to know, in fact to do anything of real importance of wisdom and power has been depleted, negated by the simple act of directing our attention outwards away from our centre.

Now go back to that image again, focusing inwards upon the centre of the two energy fields, the fields that are "you", see how much stronger the energy is while (even if only in a partial way) your fields are centred. This therefore is the place to start.

Another thing you might do that you may find interesting is to close your eyes and find where you think your final boundary is. You will find that you don't seem to stop anywhere – you appear to go on into infinity. Of course, we know the boundary of our physical body, but if we were to look with our mind's eye at our energy fields, sensing them, where do you suppose you actually end? Interesting, isn't it?

The Bible makes many references to looking within for the Spirit of God:

> Do you not know that your body is the temple (the very sanctuary) of the Holy Spirit Who lives within you, Whom you have received as a gift from God? You are not your own.
>
> *— 1 Corinthians 6:19*

Therefore the place to look for God is within you, nowhere else. There are also warnings:

> If any man defile the temple of God, him shall God destroy; for the temple of God is holy, which temple ye are.
>
> — *1 Corinthians 3:17*

Here, religious scripture is quite clearly saying that under certain conditions God may destroy us, should we choose to defile our being, "the temple". As we saw in Chapter Three, we may also choose to irrevocably destroy ourselves by our own negative/low vibratory thoughts, words or deeds. When we engage in these actions, we put our feet on a downward, lower vibratory path into yet denser material planes where the very real risk is that our soul may be diminished or fragmented to such a degree that it can no longer be termed a unified, coherent field. Electrical output is nil, and we are destroyed. Elsewhere the Bible makes reference to the Kingdom of God being within:

> And when he was demanded of the Pharisees, when the kingdom of God should come, he answered them and said, The kingdom of God cometh not with observation: Neither shall they say Lo it is here, or, Lo it is there! For behold, the kingdom of God is within you.
>
> — *Luke 17: 20–21*

We find wherever we look the same information, whether ancient or modern. The texts consistently say that the place to look for contact with the Divine, and therefore Wisdom, Love, Joy and Peace is within. All the great mystical traditions of the East teach that the Kingdom of God is within. They also say, as Jesus did, "Knock and the door will open to you. Seek and you shall find." In other words, all the qualities of the Divine are there for all. All that is required is that we wish to know, that we seek, that we ask; but the answers are within, not without. All the religions clearly speak the same and simple truth, but the only way you will really know is to seek for yourself.

So how do we begin? There are many, many ways. This book offers step-by-step instructions. The *Bhagavad Gita* offers another, perfect in its simplicity:

> A single oneness of pure love, of never-straying love for me; retiring to solitary places and avoiding the noisy multitudes; A constant yearning to know the inner Spirit, and a vision of Truth which gives liberation: this is true wisdom leading to vision. All against this is ignorance.
>
> — *Bhagavad Gita 13:10–11*

It will be helpful here if we look briefly again at the quantum view of the multiverse and all in it. We now know we are a great deal more than just the physical body we are programmed to experience; we are in fact a replica of the universe/multiverse but of course on an infinitely smaller scale. Each of us is a small universe, although more accurately we are an infinite mass of universes as each cell in our body is a universe, rather like those carved Chinese balls one inside the other that keep getting smaller but with intricate detail on each that is the same. Each atom in each cell is a still smaller universe. This gives us the view of ourselves as a vast system of universes, even millions of universes held together in a seemingly separate unit by something scientists would call quantum coherence. This single unit "you" could be viewed as but a single electron in the great macrocosm of the multiverse, and as we are a pure image of the vast system outside ourselves and the smaller system within ourselves then it logically follows that "he who knows himself, knows all". This quantum view confirms many spiritual texts, the Bible for instance:

> So God created man in his own image, in the image and likeness of God he created him.
>
> — *Genesis 1:27*

The Sufis say, "The macrocosm is the microcosm" or "As above, so below". The Egyptian prophet Hermes Trismegistus said, "One of the great secrets is, the without is like the within of things; the small is like the large." The Greek philosopher Empedocles wrote, "God is a circle whose centre is everywhere, and its circumference is nowhere." And Edgar Cayce, the American healer and prophet, said, "Each cell of man is as a representative of a universe in itself."

We are a microcosm of the macrocosm, "as above, so below". For example, if we look at the nucleus of each atom surrounded by its electrons; the relative distances between those electrons when compared with their sizes are quite as great as those distances between the Sun and its planets. Further, if each single "unit" is an entire universe in itself in a universe of self-similarity, then it becomes very easy to understand how we may contact other units/quantum coherent energy fields/electrons in the multiverse, sidestepping time and space as we saw electrons doing in Chapter One. It is important to understand that we have been so constructed that we may be in conscious communication with and move to/through all in the multiverse at any time we consciously choose ("consciously" is the key word here). As individual electrons are able to communicate non-locally with each other and to move great distances in zero time, so may we consciously function in this way when we know how. (I am not saying that our physical bodies at this time are able to do this – first we must learn to consciously do this with our metaphysical bodies.)

Instead of seeing ourselves as tiny, meaningless, separated fragments alone in this vast multiverse, we need to understand we are fractals, connected to all that is by our self-similarity. Because of this we are able to move to and through all realms and communicate with everything else that is. We are not alone and we may contact and interact with all in the multiverse as we choose, when we know how. The *Gita* speaks clearly about consciousness and communicating with the Divine Creative Field:

This body, Arjuna, is called the field. He who knows this is called the knower of the field.

Know that I am the knower in all the fields of my creation; and that the wisdom which sees the field and the knower of the field is true wisdom.

Those who with the eye of inner vision see the distinction between the field and the knower of the field and see the liberation of spirit from matter, they go into the Supreme.

— *Bhagavad Gita 13:1–2, 34*

Now do you think you might like to do a bit of navel-gazing, or to be more accurate third-eye gazing? The third eye, located in the middle of the forehead, is the eye for inner vision or internal sight (clear vision without the use of your two physical eyes). It is the initial focal point when embarking on all spiritual work. When our energy fields have stabilised and aligned with our soul into one centred, unified coherent field of high spin, then we may fuse with the Divine Creative Field under the law of self-similarity. We are able to do this as our field's vibratory rate has become (if only for a second, as that is the most that is possible at the beginning) the same as the Divine Creative Field's. In other words, you and God have, if only momentarily at first, become one. In this sublime state of being, we see all, we know all, we become one with all that is and we are infused with and melt into the Divine Creative Field, the field of pure unconditional Love. There is nothing like it – once achieved, all other states of bliss, happiness and joy pale in comparison. With this priceless wisdom and knowledge of spiritual union, joy and love, then and only then do we begin to understand the true nature of all. The wonder is that we can accomplish this while in the physical body. It is not required that we have to die, or even leave home. The following passages from the *Bhagavad Gita* are a wonderfully clear description of what happens when, on the inward path in our quest of "knowing thyself", understanding our true identity and place in the multiverse, we merge with God:

Now I shall tell thee of the end of wisdom. When a man knows this, he goes beyond death. Beyond what is and beyond what is not.

His hands and feet are everywhere, he has heads and mouths everywhere: he sees all, he hears all. He is in all, and he is.

The Light of consciousness comes to him through infinite powers of perception, and yet he is above all these powers.

He is beyond all, and yet he supports all. He is beyond the world of matter, and yet he has joy in this world. He is invisible: he cannot be seen. He is far and he is near and he moves and he moves not, he is within all and he is outside all.

He is ONE in all, but it seems as if he were many. He supports all beings: from him comes destruction, and from him comes creation.

He is the Light of all lights which shines beyond all darkness. It is vision, the end of vision, to be reached by vision, dwelling in the heart of all.

I have told you briefly what is in the field, what is wisdom, and what is the End of man's vision. When a man knows this, he enters into my Being.

He who sees that the Lord of all is ever the same in all that is, immortal in the field of mortality – he sees the truth.

And when a man sees that the God in himself is the same God in all that is, he hurts not himself by hurting others: then he goes indeed to the Highest Path.

— *Bhagavad Gita 13:12–18, 27–28*

Not everyone has a desire to find and merge with God. Not everyone is on a conscious spiritual path. However, if we wish to refine and perfect ourselves, or if we just wish to be happy and peaceful, if we wish to evolve to ever-higher states of being, we must start somewhere. Some may wish only to start at the surface and tinker about there resolving issues around relationships, anger, childhood, sex, money, fear (the biggest of them all) and so on. Understanding such issues, getting to really know yourself, bringing resolution and dropping off redundant stuff, trauma and pain is a good and necessary idea. However, it is worth noting that it is easy to get lost in our stuff. It is quite possible to spend the rest of one's life bogged down in this way, lost in the negativity and the physical morass of our own personal version of the explicate world.

Admittedly, a great deal of this work will probably have to be done in order to get to where we wish to be, as it is impossible to become at one with God when we have negative/low vibrations in our own fields. There are, however, simple effective ways to bring our being to some semblance of coherence and to then align our energy fields. To gain a holistic view it will be most helpful if we are able to rise above all the many and various personal issues and looking down upon the whole see the totality of the being in all its glory. Keeping this view always front and centre of our vision will ensure we will not lose our way, will not become engrossed in our stuff as if we are to spend the rest of our lives walking around telling "my story" in an endless round of relationships, therapies, workshops and so on, we will remain stuck. Quite apart from the enormous amount of money we may spend in this way, it can become a diversion and worst of all it can be addictive. As with so many of the other diversions on this plane of existence we can easily become lost in our own negative pain and so lose our way.

At this point you may wish for further information, more names, dates and localised information: where exactly is the mind located, what is the name of the location, how exactly does all this function, how many other realms are there, what are they called, how many energy centres are there in the being, what are they called, what are the other aspects of the soul, what are they called? You may think, "If we do not have names, dates, locations, how are we to find our way and depend on anything?" Exhausting, isn't it? Not to mention pointless and confusing, for there are as many names for things as things, there are as many theories as there are things, there are as many ideas as to where things are located as there are things and so on. We need to ask ourselves, does any of that really matter? Is any of that going to help? It is also by the way a pure left-brain mouse on the wheel process.

When we are immersed in the darkness of the manifested physical world, all appears complicated because everything is so close to our face. We do not have a long view; we are unable to stand back and see more of the whole. We tend to seek complicated answers and will not accept simple ones. If we are immersed in matter, we will have difficulty seeing, we will have difficulty in experiencing gnosis, for the further from the light of God we are, the greater the apparent complication. There are thousands of books, documents and scriptures out there that may be examined, but take care not to spend the rest of this life reading and never getting to the doing and the knowing of the point of existence. Once we are able to "know thyself" and contact the soul in a meaningful way, the darkness, blindness, deafness and complication together with a great deal else that troubles us now will just fall away.

All wisdom, all knowledge of the multiverse is available to us through the agency of the Divine Soul; therefore, the relationship with our soul is of paramount importance. Too truly "know thyself", we must be able to contact, interact and become intimate with and thereby know all there is to know of our Divine Soul and beyond. It may be helpful if we have a picture of what we will really look and sound like once we have reached a particular stage of our journey, even though once there we will be able to see and hear for ourselves. Anyone who has ever had a Kirlian photograph (electro photography) taken of the energy fields already has some idea of their true beauty and luminosity. Many scientists are now studying the human electrical field as part of new and ongoing medical research. The results of which will be the new healing paradigms of the future. We are a grid of energy channels, fed from seven primary vortices, or chakras (spinning wheels of energy) and several thousand other vortices of varying degrees of size and importance. In the energy soup in which we live and breathe and have our being, we draw in and are electrically charged/vivified by the highly charged energy within the surrounding fields. The vortices act as circuit-breakers: they lower the voltage to the amount our bodies can absorb without annihilation. We are electrical energy beings, cleverly held within a water bag (water being a brilliant energy conductor). While we are at our present level of evolution our fields are unstable – the slightest thought, the slightest emotion that ripples through our fields changes them, and the colours wax and wane. One could have a Kirlian photograph taken every five minutes and, depending upon the change in our mood or thoughts, the picture will change as the colours emitted by the various fields vary in intensity and sometimes greatly differ in their placement. However, once we are in any way aligned and coherent and our intrinsic soul energy is primary, our thoughts and our emotions are ever more aligned with the qualities of our soul field and so have little or no effect upon our fields, as all is becoming one. If we arrive at the point where we dwell for the most part in the numinous light of God via the mechanism of our Divine Soul, then no matter what events may arise from the explicate fields, because we also dwell consciously and powerfully in the implicate realms, we have complete mastery not only over our own thoughts and emotions/fields, but over all in the explicate realms. The higher orders are now directing the lower, as they should. This is our evolutionary journey towards greater spiritual health, well-being and power.

If our physical body has not been irreparably damaged, and the soul is awakened to a degree and some alignment has already taken place, then this is how we would look and sound. Yes, sound. As we saw in Chapter One and Three, sound is integral to the system and the multiverse is one great symphony. We are part of this symphony and so it is not possible that we are silent.

The energy field at the base of our being is showing as the largest and most vital at this stage. It would be coloured brilliant red and would be moving in such a way as to suggest tongues of flame licking upwards. The feeling of this energy field is one of power, but physical power. Eastern religions often show this flame effect as the petals of the lotus flower. The sound of this field would be as the bass in an orchestra, except that until you have heard the music of these fields this is a very poor comparison as divine music is indescribable in our limited languages.

The second field is a luminous orange, gently pulsating with a slight humming background noise, but a humming of exquisite beauty.

The third field is an incandescent yellow, with a mellow sound that flows as though it were molten gold.

The fourth field is a shimmering apple green, gossamer light, glowing and gently pulsating. The sound is higher than the last, more delicate, more complex, many-stringed.

The fifth field is intense sky blue. Moving with force the sound is crystalline.

The sixth field is a powerful pulsating indigo. The power is not physical but spiritual power, therefore far greater with force behind it from the source. The sound is as of horns blowing in a clear triumphal manner.

The seventh field is a glowing violet; in a strange way it seems to hold in its light all the qualities of the other fields. The sound is of indescribable delicacy, much as one would imagine fairy music. This is the crown of the being and the vortices in this field are together with the heart the primary centres for the inflow and outflow of the Divine Creative Field's energy. The heart Chakra is also the primary exit point for the soul upon physical death.

While each field has its own particular sound, they all fuse to become a whole Divine and indescribably beautiful sounding. Each individual being is a glorious celestial symphony, itself a reflection of the whole. However, there is one important thing that sets each of us apart from the other: our signature sound is unique. This is how we may communicate with all that is, and yet be recognised as simply as we can be recognised by our fingerprints. The unified field that is God is deeply personal, our relationship with it is deeply personal and unique, and therefore we can communicate with and are recognised by all that is by our own particular sound. The more conscious and aligned we are, the greater is our ease to communicate in this way, for the higher our spin, the greater and more glorious is our sound. Just as a baby has difficulty communicating at first, so do we at our current evolutionary level.

All the fields fuse as they move upwards, but with the heart of each field keeping its own colour and having the brilliancy of a glaze. As one moves higher in the vision, the fields narrow towards the summit so that we are viewing a triangular shape of three equal sides in three-dimensional form (a tetrahedron, one of the Platonic Solids). The triangular field of energy starting at the feet finishes at a point above the crown of the head in a spiral column of pure silver light. This column moves to a point about a third of a metre above the physical head, then spirals out into a beautiful silver chalice, wide at the top, narrowing down to the spiral cord, then to the crown of the head. The base of this chalice later moves to a point midway of the energy being, the heart chakra between the breasts. This beautiful spiraling energy chalice of cascading silver light is our individual sending and receiving station, rather like a satellite dish. This chalice is known by another name, the Holy Grail. The word comes to us from the Latin "gradale", meaning taking place by degrees – the energy field graduates out spiral by spiral until it forms a grail or cup.

Much has been written of late about this fabled object and all of it is nonsense, as the Holy Grail is not and never has been a physical object. The legends passed down to us have lost their real and original meaning over the millennia. As we sank further into the darkness of the explicate world, spiritual knowledge and wisdom was lost and this led to us interpreting the ancient stories from a limited physical-plane bias. Immersed in materiality, we could only give material meaning to ancient myths. The Holy Grail of ancient legend changed to become a jewel-encrusted cup. The ancients who valued spiritual knowledge and power above all else were now, according to us, not on a spiritual quest but on a quest for material wealth. Even if, as some claim, great spiritual knowledge was somehow encoded in this fabulous object of gold or silver and precious stones, it still does not make sense, as anyone with true spiritual knowledge and power would have no use for such a device. It is neither sensible nor logical and it shows how sunk in materialism we have become that such an idea could have taken hold in the first place. If on a spiritual quest, one does not go chasing after, so-called, priceless material objects found only in the explicate realms. In ancient times, spiritual knowledge and power was regarded as the only thing worth seeking. Sadly, this is no longer the case. Today, we go chasing after metal cups.

The real meaning of the Grail quests is this. When we are sufficiently aligned and when we know how, we can develop our own Holy Grail. Once we have developed this very efficient and reliable sending and receiving station in our energy field, we are well along the way to achieving wisdom, love and spiritual power. Spiritual communication, both sending and receiving, and union (if only briefly) becomes a matter of fact in our daily life. Should we choose, we will never need to read another book to learn anything we want or need to know. All spiritual knowledge is ours for the asking – depending upon our degree of alignment. With the Holy Grail as part of our being, we are on the path towards Divine union and power. All true Grail quests start with the injunction "know thyself", and from that starting point we may move towards becoming a fully unfolded, highly evolved, coherent and unified Divine Being of light, Joy and power. There are simple exercises that will assist to bring all to this point; all that is required is a desire for a higher evolutionary state, dedication, love for the Divine and practice.

> For this reason I say, if one is whole, one will be filled with light, but if one is divided, one will be filled with darkness.
>
> — *Gospel of Thomas 61*

In other words, if we are aligned with our unfolded soul, if our fields are coherent and unified, then we will be filled with the light of the Divine Creative Field under the law of self-similarity. However, if we are misaligned, fractured, incoherent and therefore divided, we will be filled with darkness (fractured, incoherent = low vibration = less light). There are, of course, many degrees between the two ends of the spectrum.

This vision of how we may look and be when once further along our evolutionary path is a glorious one, is it not? It is a far more wonderful vision than most of us have previously held of ourselves. This vision, while glorious and beautiful beyond words, when once experienced and seen is extremely liberating and powerful. From the moment we recognise and adopt this vision of ourselves, we raise our energy field's vibratory rate. It is as simple as that. Our individual energy field will respond as it does to all our thoughts and emotions in a profound and positive manner. Our vibratory rate will take a sudden upward shift and a degree of alignment and coherence will immediately occur from this one powerful thought and belief system alone. From that one, seemingly small change in our consciousness, the resulting change in our fields will be tremendous.

> There are two spirits in this universe, the perishable and the imperishable. The perishable is all things in creation. The imperishable is that which moves not.
>
> But the highest spirit is another: it is called the Spirit Supreme. He is the God of Eternity who pervading all sustains all.
>
> Because I am beyond the perishable, and even beyond the imperishable, in this world and in the Vedas I am known as the Spirit Supreme.
>
> He who with a clear vision sees me as the Spirit Supreme he knows all there is to be known, and he adores me with all his soul.

Know Thyself

I have revealed to thee the most secret doctrine, Arjuna. He who sees it has seen light, and his task in this world is done.

— Bhagavad Gita 15:16–20

The journey within ourselves and thence to other realms is the most challenging, exhilarating and rewarding journey we can ever take. This is a journey that will be far, far better than any we may take with our physical body. What is more, it will not cost anything, not in terms of money anyway, and it offers the richest of all rewards – Wisdom, Unconditional Love, Joy, and Spiritual Union with all that that brings.

This journey within is part of the greater journey, that of our spiritual evolution. and it should be paramount that this journey be consciously undertaken as soon as possible, which brings us to the concept of evolution.

Chapter 5
Evolution

You do not see me for I am hidden inside the soul.
Others want you for themselves, but I call you back to
    yourself.
You give me many names, but I am beyond all names.
While you remain blind and deaf, I will be invisible.
Come to me and I will take you to the depths of spirit.

— Rumi

If we take on the belief that we are all evolving through this space-time continuum and beyond, in an interconnected musical dance with all that exists, then where are we right now? Are we fully evolved and at the end of the line, have we nearly reached our full potential or are we a long way from it? In other words, are there further evolutionary adventures awaiting us while journeying through the multiverse? We need to know where we are, as then we may consciously choose to speed our evolutionary journey towards greater unfolded spiritual union. Without this knowledge, we are like shipwrecked mariners knowing not where we are nor where we should aim.

There is currently great debate raging over whether we were created by God in exactly the same place evolutionarily speaking as we are today, i.e. instant creation with no evolution from then until now; or whether we evolved over time quite by accident and with no guiding intelligence involved whatsoever as set forth in Darwin's theory of evolution. Does it have to be one or the other? I would have thought the more logical framework was they are both right in part. Yes, there without a doubt appears to be a Divine creative intelligence at work in all; and yes, we together with all else in the multiverse appear to be adapting and evolving over time due to various external factors together with the more ephemeral, all-encompassing, intelligent and creative evolutionary force that we as yet do not fully understand. If we presume that we and everything else are evolving – because to presume we are not is to presume the multiverse is a static place without progressive change, and it patently is not that – then we must presume we are at a particular place in our evolutionary journey. We must presume there was a beginning and there will be an end. With this idea in mind, it is quite clear from our actions that we are not highly evolved. We so obviously still have some way to go. What the final goal may be is a matter for speculation, but it seems because we are essentially energy beings that any evolution is not ultimately about our physical bodies but about our energy core, our soul. The ancient spiritual texts, together with current scientific thought, appear to have reached some sort of consensus, which is that the multiverse is evolving and this includes our planet and everything on it. All energy appears to be moving in an infinite spiral action towards ever-increasing realms of higher vibratory refinement. This is the constant elemental thrust of the multiverse, driven by the Divine Fire inherent in all. The quantum coherent fields of our souls are called to evolve to ever-greater degrees of unfolded alignment, coherence, refinement and subsequent loving relationship with the Divine.

We have three choices when it comes to evolution. As we have been given the gift of free will, we may choose one of three paths. As we saw in Chapter Three, we may not have an automatic right to immortality, to successful evolvement, but we may choose to destroy our immortal soul by our actions and thus cease to be part of the evolutionary thrust to greater spiritual refinement, power and immortality. Should we not do this, there remain two other choices – and as the multiverse is not a static place, we must take one of them. To exercise choice is to be conscious and should we not exercise choice, the dynamic evolutionary thrust of the multiverse will move on regardless within which we may evolve successfully over time, or we may not. Should we choose the third option, which is that of conscious involvement in our evolutionary progression, we will thereby ensure our speedy and successful evolution. The choice as always is ours.

We need now to understand the influences and energies that are in place to assist us in our evolutionary journey. However, we must hold in our minds that all entities that are assisting us are themselves part of an evolutionary process. If everything in the multiverse is made of the same stuff and if everything is interconnected, then all must be able to affect all else to greater or lesser degrees. Among the entities that have the most profound effects upon us all are the heavenly bodies. We all accept that the moon has a direct and powerful affect on the Earth and all life upon it. We accept that the action of the moon creates the push and pull of the tides and that menstrual cycles are affected by the waxing and waning of the moon. We know seeds grow better when planted in some cycles of the moon than in others; indeed, the mathematician Lawrence Edwards demonstrated using data collected over twenty-seven years that "as different constellations come up over the horizon, then the buds of a variety of trees and plants fluctuate in size in response to the rising constellation". We know magnetic field fluctuations have a profound effect on all living systems and that institutions for the mentally ill; not to mention the police are often kept very busy at full moon. Many people experience difficulty sleeping at full moon and some sea life is influenced to reproduce by the particular cycles of the moon. However, many of us exclude all the other heavenly bodies from having an equal or greater effect upon us. This is not logical; it does not make sense. If we are to look only at our physical makeup, which is predominantly water, we should realise that the enormous energy fields of all the celestial beings must affect us to greater or lesser degrees depending upon their position to each other and the earth:

> The seven major glands in order of their distance from the heart obey the same laws as the planets in the order of their distance from the Sun, and each gland is revealed to be a sensitive instrument, which not only transforms human energy to the tension (resonance) required for its function, but is tuned to a similar instrument on a cosmic scale and obeys it guidance.
>
> — Rodney Collin, *The Theory of Celestial Influence*

All works upon the same principle, all follows the same underlying pattern and laws, "as above so below". Our own spiral evolutionary progression is the same spiral evolutionary progression that all else is engaged in. An interdependent musical dance engages us all; knowing this, we also need to know the cycles and attributes of the heavenly bodies as then we will begin to understand our path and ourselves a little more. More importantly, we can begin to engage in a conscious relationship with these great beings whereby we may hear, feel and understand the clear urgings and pressures that the heavenly bodies exert upon us all in their intelligently designed and programmed efforts to guide us along our evolutionary pathway.

There is another important aspect we need to understand, that of the great heavenly cycles. To do this we need first to look at something known as planetary precession or equinoctial precession, as this plays a fundamental role in every aspect of our lives. If we will look at the diagram, we will see that as our day is ordered by the hours on the clock face, so the universe runs on a larger clock. The great cosmic clock, if it were drawn, would also have twelve segments to its face. This is because there are twelve grand constellations, represented by the twelve well-known astrological signs. Astrology does not attribute effects to the constellations themselves but rather it defines the signs as thirty-degree segments of longitude, and it is the correlation of signs with seasons which is of central importance.

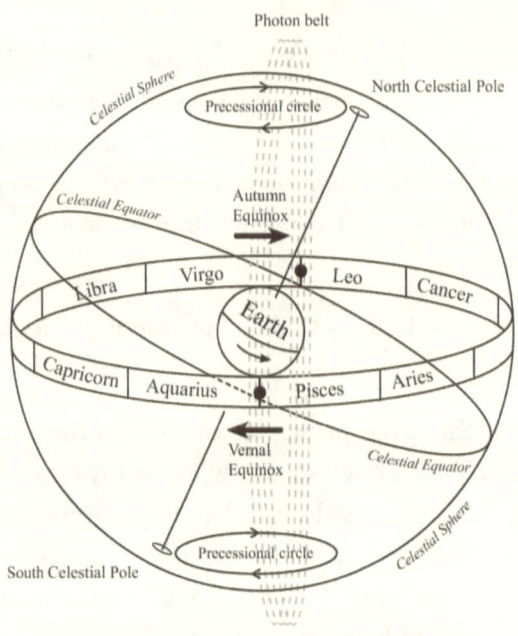

Earth's precession through the zodiac

The sun currently rises on the spring equinox against a background of the midway point between the constellation Pisces and the constellation Aquarius. The constantly shifting cosmic scene is because the Earth's axis wanders and wobbles (just like the atom Bruce Lipton referred to in Chapter Three) – it can be likened to a giant gyroscope – and this wandering produces a slow clockwise motion of the equinoctial points. In other words, the movement of the Earth creates an apparent orbit for the Sun called an ecliptic. Looking at the great circle of the celestial equator we can see two points at opposite sides where the path of the ecliptic crosses the path of the celestial equator. These are known as the equinoxes, the other two key points in a year being the winter and summer solstices. If the sun rises in Pisces at the spring equinox, it will rise in Virgo in the autumn equinox, Gemini in the summer solstice and Sagittarius in the winter solstice. As the great clock moves from one segment to another, all moves with it, so that soon we will have Aquarius, Leo, Taurus and Scorpio, instead of Pisces, Virgo, Gemini and Sagittarius taking the influential positions. The great celestial clock is now in the middle of moving from a background of the constellation of Pisces to a background of Aquarius, hence the song from the 1967 musical *Hair*, "This is the dawning of the Age of Aquarius".

The cycle of precession is the time it takes the Earth to complete the full circle, approximately 26,000 years, and the great circle described in the sky is known as the Great Year or Platonic Year (as Plato was aware of this action). It takes approximately 2160 years to move through each constellation, so the change from one age to another does not happen overnight. The full force of the new age will not be felt until a reasonable degree of progression has been made into it. To be fully into the new age, so that one could truly say we are now in the age of Aquarius, will take approximately another eighty years. We are seemingly at a critical and important time in the great cycle, as we are at the end of one great revolution of the clock i.e. at the end of a 26,000-year cycle. So, we are not only nearing the end of the age of Pisces, but the clock as a whole is about to change gears as it shifts into the beginning of another great cycle of 26,000 years. The precise date given for the end of this great cycle is December 21st, 2012. Precisely on this date, the sun rises directly in alignment with the rift at the centre of our galaxy – the Galactic Core. This alignment both Terrestrial and Celestial only happens once every 13,000 years. To move through the entire evolutionary cycle of the great clock would take 312,000 years. It is believed that with each small cycle shift, one age to another, the energies that play upon the Earth are subtly altered; to shift from one great age, the full 26,000 year turn of the clock, the energies that play upon the Earth are changed in even greater measure. The entire system is about to pass through a spiral evolutionary leap into ever-increasing degrees of refinement, so we can expect to be subjected to the play of these different energies in an ever-greater degree over the next coming years.

If we go back and look at the historical records of ancient civilisations, together with the myths and legends passed down among indigenous people, it becomes clear that this knowledge of planetary precession is not new. If we look back to the time it is thought the pyramids of Giza in Egypt were built, and if we were to recreate the sky as it would have been at 11,000 BC, we find some interesting things. The Great Sphinx, which points due east, was at the time of the spring equinox gazing directly at the constellation of Leo. It is thought to have originally had the head of a lion to match the rest of its body; it was only much later that the lion's head was re-carved with that of a pharaoh – so the Great Sphinx, carved as a lion, was facing towards its own image, the constellation of Leo, at the time of its construction, pointing the way to the halfway point of the great cycle.

There is a great deal more information available regarding the entire Giza necropolis delineating how it replicates the Great Belt stars' layout in the constellation of Orion. In other words, the pyramids of Giza are a replica on Earth of the heavens above, or as they were at the time of construction. The ancient Egyptians believed it was essential that man should be familiar with the heavens and the heavenly bodies since man's ultimate goal – according to the most ancient texts known to man, the Pyramid texts, together with hermetic and other Egyptian texts – was to achieve immortality of the human soul. They believed they could not take immortality for granted, but rather had to earn it. They believed they had to gain wisdom, develop spiritually, and evolve if they were to achieve an immortal soul. The Pyramid texts are written in precise astronomical scientific language: they give specific directions and co-ordinations for navigating the cosmos.

If we move forward in time to the great civilisation of Crete, the most revered animal was the bull, which is representative of Taurus. Traces of bull's images are to be found decorating engraved tablets and remains of temples. The racial memory of this reverence for bulls at this time has been handed down in myth and story to today. If this representation of bulls during this particular time period was an isolated incident, we could perhaps say it is just coincidence, but curiously enough once the age of Taurus passed away and the background constellation was then Aries, we find many of the bull's heads were re-carved to represent a ram's head. This practice of rams decorating many buildings and artefacts continued until the time of Jesus, which was exactly at the dawning of the age of Pisces. The symbol of Pisces is the fish, which is also the symbol often used to represent Jesus. Another coincidence?

Each constellation of the zodiac is represented as predominantly displaying a particular energy, with all twelve being broken down into the two aspects of positive/masculine and negative/feminine energy. The constellation Pisces is considered masculine and the constellation Aquarius feminine. Therefore, we are not only moving into a generally different influence, but we are moving from having a powerful predominantly masculine energy at play, to having a predominantly feminine energy paramount. This will have profound effects upon our evolutionary progress. We are moving from an age where the underlying support system was one of a positive energy field to one that is now negative. The masculine active, out-thrusting, dominant and resistant, is changing to the feminine, passive, reflective, fluid with markedly less resistance. This energy shift will continue to affect everything and everyone on the planet. Any power structures of fundamentally masculine energy will subconsciously, if not consciously, recognise that their support system is draining away. This loss of power will cause a consequent clinging in ever more aggressive manner to the old power base, and as the fundamental cosmic energy support drains away, so threatened individuals will increase their inherently doomed activities in an effort to retain the familiar support. A massive last-ditch outpouring of energy in order to retain control will eventuate. We are already seeing clear signs of this with innumerable new laws being enacted worldwide, with seemingly greater and greater control being exerted as the old power bases flex their muscles in increasingly impotent ways. This frantic, desperate desire to hold on will become stronger before it collapses altogether, as with the loss of its cosmic power base it cannot be sustained. The new energies will flow in; they cannot be stopped. The changeover will take place as the great cosmic clock grinds on. The planet and all upon it will respond and adapt one way or another, as the New Age is a reality and ultimately all in the physical (the physical is the last, because it is the lowest vibration) will manifest this change in time. If we understand and, more importantly, accept the process instead of reacting to and possibly resisting it, then we may consciously choose to align with the new energies. Should we do so, we will empower ourselves as we may then safely consciously navigate through all the darkness and turmoil that these changes bring. Remember: in the physical, breakdown and chaos must, and always does, precede great change. The old order must die before the new can be born. This is another law of the multiverse: the new is born only out of the death of the old. Understanding the great evolutionary cycle, we can see we would be wise to practice the art of Wu Wei and follow the flow allowing no resistance.

We know from archaeological evidence that greatly advanced people lived on Earth before us. Possessing knowledge far superior to any we have today, they appeared, populated the Earth, and then vanished, sometimes overnight. Yet we do not know why. We have progressed from being cave dwellers who used predominantly what we now call the old brain, located at the base of the skull. We then moved to developing the right-brain, which is feminine, responsible for art, music, creativity of all kinds and, more importantly intuition, spirituality, and communication with realms other than this one. During the period our right-brains had ascendancy we created great art and glorious architecture; all the fabulous man-made beauty of our current world comes from this time. The great evolutionary spiral moved on and the focus shifted from the right to the left hemisphere, which is masculine. We went from beauty and the spiritual to the analytical, mechanistic, logical, scientific and the madness of separating all into its component parts. The left-brain is also the seat of the will or ego, and as a result, this period of evolution has wrought horrors of epic proportions that we are only now beginning to become aware of. The resulting trashing of the planet is the natural outcome of the separate, will-driven egocentric seat of the left-brain having dominance in almost all aspects of current life. Today the predominant focus in our education system is still the development of the left-brain.

Now, however, we are arriving at the time in our evolutionary spiral where both hemispheres of the brain are reasonably well developed and the use of both equally is now required that we may achieve balance and a greater wholeness. We need to arrive back at our understanding of the interconnectedness of all things, back at our understanding of the spiritual realms. We are being called to balance all aspects of our brain. Do not suppose this change from predominantly masculine energy to predominantly feminine means in any way feminine domination over all – we are being called to balance the two energies in all ways. All we have learnt and embedded in our beings up to now must be integrated and balanced in order to achieve a greater balanced unified wholeness. With our new understanding that co-operation and communication with all are key, we must weave into the whole the middle way of the Buddhist, the flow/non-resistance of the Taoist, the almost scientific spiritual understanding of the Hindu, the respect of the Jew, the love of the Christian, the deep submission of the Muslim and the rationality of science. These are our necessary markers along the way if we are to succeed in making this evolutionary leap towards greater spiritual union with its promise of immortality.

Humans have had knowledge of the heavenly bodies, their movements and their effect on the Earth and all living upon it from time immemorial. However, we in our mechanistic left-brain age of separation have forgotten, or do not wish to know. We feel these beliefs are merely silly superstitions that cannot have any place in reality; possibly we do not wish to acknowledge that there are more powerful beings/ aspects than ourselves. The ancients, however, possessed something that is sadly lacking today – wisdom. Wisdom's portal into our daily lives is through the right-brain and we need to urgently reclaim the importance of this aspect if we are to evolve successfully.

> The journey through the planetary houses/constellations boils down to becoming conscious of the good and the bad qualities in our character, and the apotheosis means no more than maximum consciousness, which amounts to maximum freedom.
>
> — Carl Jung, *Mysterium Coniunctionis*

The Divine Mathematics of the Spheres as they not only move across the heavens, but spin the creative music of the Divine whilst making relationships and communing with each other and all else, have been the subject of wisdom seekers through the ages, and for good reason. It must be rational to conclude that these great beings have similarly great energy fields and that these particular energies playing upon the Earth to greater and lesser degrees at different times will create particular effects. Certain characteristics have been assigned to each planet based upon the particular quality of its energy field. I am listing these only briefly here, as although the science of astrology is a vast subject and one well worth studying, it is not what we are about here.

Sun: represents pure concentrated spirit, vitality, wholeness, power.
Moon: represents the unconscious, feelings, emotions, fertility, reflection.
Mercury: represents mental, communication, mental agility, teaching, mediation.
Venus: represents love, harmony, feminine sexuality, beauty, art.
Mars: is the opposite of Venus, traditionally represents war, aggression, masculine sexuality, strength.
Jupiter: the giver of life represents the individual nature, which extends beyond the physical world, optimistic, generous, realization of the higher self.

Saturn: is the opposite of Jupiter, it is depressive, oppressive, limiting, can represent evil, melancholy, reserve, limitation, economy, authority.

Uranus: represents the unexpected, eccentricity, invention, independence, intuition, impulsiveness, integration, originality.

Neptune: represents physic activity, mediumship, dreams, illusion, extra sensitivity, drugs, and the immaterial world.

The nine major heavenly bodies (there are of course others all playing their part) as represented above cover all human conditions; they also influence physical health or sickness. The planets influence minds individually and collectively, their energetic influences constantly pulsing out into the multiverse to greater and lesser degrees as the great cosmic clock turns. Incarcerated in our bag of water, delicately, subtly and in the most minuscule of ways, we register each outflowing magnetic field that arrives here from these great beings. As these beautiful heavenly bodies move across the heavens, their energy vibration/resonance and subsequent sounds play upon our energy fields, moving us to do this, pressuring us to do that, guiding, teaching, inspiring, illuminating, always in a helpful manner. The guiding will never be detrimental in any way. They are our ultimate teachers and they rule our lives; nothing in our life escapes their attention. We respond to them, act upon their urgings and our moods reflect their presence, to all of which we are mostly unconscious. Should we choose to become more conscious, we may then actively and consciously listen to, work with, move and flow with their urgings. Then, instead of being as fish swimming against the tide, we move effortlessly with it, spiraling upwards towards greater consciousness, refinement and power. These astounding beings are our direct teachers. Those of you more aligned and sensitive will already know this. When we become more aware on all levels, in the fullest meaning of the word, we will find our life following a path directed by the planets. Once we consciously choose of our own free will to closely follow the direction of these celestial beings, then we are no longer will and ego driven, we cease to make incorrect choices and the wisdom of the multiverse opens to us. Once this happens and we notice consciously their guidance and help, then our relationship with them becomes one of student and teacher, with gratitude, awe and love being our gift to them in return.

The heavenly planetary bodies are of course living beings as is everything else. They are rainbow-hued, musical spheres, living, interacting, communicating and evolving as we are. In addition, each has its own signature note and when they as a group sound, it is the most extraordinary indescribable music ever heard. When the composer Felix Mendelssohn visited the mystically beautiful and remote Hebrides, he wrote *The Hebrides (Fingal's Cave),* a short piece that is a faint echo of the celestial, eye watering, soul-uplifting Music of the Spheres – once heard, never forgotten. Mendelssohn obviously heard it himself when in meditative mood and tried to recreate the sound. If you should be fortunate enough to sit in any of the great cathedrals in Europe during a Bach organ recital you will again hear echoes of the Music of the Spheres. Of course, you must first hear it to recognise it, and to hear it one must progress at least a small way along the spiritual evolutionary path. The Music of the Spheres alone is well worth the effort.

Now I am aware that the left-brain scientific view of the planets is entirely different from the above description. However, if all of "out there" is merely a virtual reality that we create on a moment-by-moment basis, then the virtual reality described above is merely the one that goes beyond the first level of reality created in order to explain and describe the physical world. In other words, there are many virtual realities, one for the physical realms and another for the metaphysical and so on. Some may still find these concepts hard to accept, but if we are to accept the theory that everything is composed of the same thing, energy, interconnected with all else in a creative field of infinite possibilities, then there is no reason why the planets should be left out of the picture. If the vision is to be whole, then we must include all in it. If sound is integral to all else, then there is no reason the planets should be silent and no reason they should not be possessed of intelligence and memory, as is all else. Remember: as above, so below. In addition, as the multiverses are purposeful realms then presumably all within are purposeful also. Why should the function of the planets and the constellations as represented by the twelve astrological signs not be that of instructor/teacher assisting us to evolve to a higher vibratory rate of being? They themselves will also be assisted by a higher order and so on, as the higher orders, organise and direct the lower. Many will not wish to think of themselves as a lower order, but the fact remains we are. Once we have managed to stabilise our energy fields into a sufficiently unified and coherent state then communication with all that is will be possible. In particular, we may converse with these great beings and start a conscious instead of unconscious relationship with them. We only need to contact them in this way once. From then on, no further proof will be required as the experience is profound. Once accomplished it is not possible to deny it and the memory never leaves.

When new and powerful evolutionary energies begin to flow in, we need to understand what to expect in order to respond appropriately. A good example of the changes we may expect can be found in the following. Almost all spiritual texts contain strong warnings against saying, "God and I are One", or as Jesus said, "I and my Father are one" (*John* 10:30). Dire things, we are told, will happen to us should we be so foolish as to say or think such a thing. If we wish to incur the wrath of any religious organisation, all we have to do is tell the religious teacher that this is what we are doing, and we will be accused of being presumptuous, arrogant, ignorant and blasphemous or worse. Unfortunately, they are correct, in part anyway, in their views on the matter. It *is* presumptuous and arrogant that we should contemplate saying "God and I are One", as we are for the most part in no fit state to make such a statement. It is not only arrogant, it is also dangerous. Where religions go wrong is in not explaining why we must not do such a thing, which is this: if we, as a discordant, misaligned, blocked, fractured and chaotic energy field were to express the intent to become one with a field that is coherent, harmonious, unified and unconditionally loving and therefore infinitely shareable, permeating throughout all that is, what would happen to us? It is true that should we choose to make that statement with pure intent, in full consciousness and with bravery, it would be a very fast evolutionary track. Our thoughts are extremely powerful and, suffice to say, the moment we make that statement, "God and I are One", the spoken words following the thoughts have set a most powerful thing in motion. We have expressed the desire to be the same as God, to be coherent, to have a unified energy field with the same resonance as God, which is pure Love. Now if we are possessed of a less than perfect field when we make this statement and have this intent, it doesn't take a brain surgeon to work out what is going to happen next. All our rigid blocked ways, all our negativity and incoherence, are going to have to change and quickly, and we will possibly become more incoherent and fractured with the inrush of the higher vibratory field, even if it is minuscule at first: we can't handle it, we are not in any way ready for it, and we may quite literally shatter. When a higher vibratory field comes into abrupt contact with a markedly lower, it is expressed thus, "we run the risk of being toast", burnt in the resultant friction. If we talk on a more physical plane, inviting in those energies, saying that we are ready for them when we so patently are not, will result in enormous upheavals in our physical life. Life cannot stay the same if we invite in a higher vibration: anything and everything that is keeping our vibration where it is will have to go and that may cause an enormous amount of physical grief.

In a similar way, when we experience the inrush of a higher vibration as the result of an involuntary evolutionary leap, i.e. one that is thrust upon us by the turning of the great cosmic clock of the multiverse, if we are not in fit shape, if we are not prepared, we may also find ourselves in serious trouble. The influx of the so-called "New Age energies of Aquarius" can be similar in effect to aligning one's self with God, and depending where precisely we are situated on the evolutionary scale the shift can be painful, dramatic and in some cases cataclysmic. We can take heart from the fact that the shift, though substantial, is relatively gradual and we have time to prepare. However, we may find ourselves in difficulty if we do not prepare – our lives will become ever more difficult as we will suffer trials and tribulation almost without end until we are able to assimilate and integrate the new energies.

The energies that are playing more and more powerfully upon the Earth are the age-old energies of evolution. The Earth itself is experiencing convulsions as it is called, as is all else, to assimilate these higher energies. All at this time is in a dramatic state of flux and upheaval as these new energies flow in, calling us to evolve to a higher vibratory rate, to more coherence and greater alignment with the Divine Creative Field. The pressures for us to do this will build and build as no one can escape the evolutionary thrust. If we cannot escape it, it makes good sense for us to learn how to raise voluntarily our vibratory rate easily and naturally as the multiverse dictates. Once we learn how to do this, our physical daily life will flow with ease and instead of grief, we will have joy, because a higher vibratory rate brings with it a natural effervescence, a natural lightness of being and a natural sense of well-being. Once we have accomplished a greater alignment with our own soul, a greater stability within all our individual fields, then and only then may we ride the evolutionary forces with some measure of ease. When we have reached this stage, we may learn to steer our soul with intent and power and finally we may consciously communicate with all that is. Once we have mastered this new state of being, we will also become aware of a greater sense of personal power, as the more consciously aligned and attuned we are the greater is our connection to the Divine Creative Field and the more those powers are ours to use for the greater good. This is our immediate evolutionary task and goal. This is the next step that is coming upon us. We will not achieve this in totality, that is too great a leap, but a small step in the correct direction is imperative for all right now. It is increasingly urgent not only that we understand this, but also that we embark on our task sooner rather than later.

The above is vital to understand as there is another aspect coming into view that makes this shift even more imperative. "Imperative" because we do not know if we have six years or one hundred to make this important alignment, but all the signs are pointing to less time rather than more. It is always better to be sure than sorry, so it makes sense to work consciously towards an effortless, painless growth during the potentially tumultuous times of energy changes ahead. None of this evolutionary work will be wasted as it brings with it so many other benefits that help on a minute-by-minute basis throughout the day and for that reason alone it makes sense to work consciously at raising our vibratory rate.

This other aspect we have to consider is the Photon Belt or Band. Much has been speculated and written regarding this phenomenon. Some even deny its existence, though recently there was an article in the *Daily Telegraph* stating that the Earth appeared to be entering a band of fine star dust and that what exactly it was and what effect it would have on Earth was not known. These intriguing articles often appear, tiny and tucked away, of no seeming consequence; the topic then disappears. (Perhaps it is not considered wise for the public to be too well informed.) However, if we decide to examine what is known or speculated regarding the Photon Belt, we will find some interesting ideas to ponder.

If we look again at the diagram, we will see a band or pathway wrapped around our solar system rather like a giant rubber band. This band crosses our path twice each 26,000 years. Where does it cross? During the ages of Aquarius and Leo! Therefore, it is more than 12,000 years since the Earth last travelled through this band. It is believed the Photon Belt is a large band of heightened and intense electromagnetic radiation, emitting radiation in extremely high frequencies beyond the visible spectrum. This band of heightened energy will have an enormous impact on the planet and us as we pass through it. It is not known how long it will take for the Earth to pass through – estimates vary from 2000 years to possibly only fifty, but if we were all to pass through a band of such heightened energy now, a great many of us, if not all, would perish as we are not prepared. It is possible that the effects of the field will be only gradually registered, the fringes less powerful than the centre, and of course if it takes hundreds of years to pass through, we have time to adapt. The problem, however, is that we do not know how long we have. As a great many of us today are seriously misaligned, together with having great dense masses of negative almost concretised areas in our fields caused by fixed points of view, a belief in separation and negative behaviour patterning, this together with a lack of spirituality or any higher vibration; then if we were to come into relatively fast contact with a higher vibratory field, the result would be conflagration. We would be toast. This could well be how other great civilisations vanished overnight from the face of the Earth. We just do not know. What we do know is that with greater spiritual awareness, with a higher vibratory rate in all our fields, we have a greater chance of surviving. The entire focus of the multiverse is that we should all succeed to a state of high spin refinement and therefore become truly immortal souls. The thrust of the multiverse is to this end. If we neglect this work, we run the risk of being destroyed, not just physically (that is not important anyway) but spiritually. If we are of too low a vibration, we will not be able to survive the new and heightened energies that inflow.

On a positive note, it is believed that the main function of the Photon Belt is to elevate consciousness. It is there for our evolution, it is there to assist us, to carry us to higher vibratory planes of consciousness. As with everything else, once we understand something then to work with it is easier. Therefore, the pre-eminent message for all of us now is we must do whatever we can to elevate our vibratory rate. Anything that is a negation of the Divine must go. It is imperative that we delete/let go of anything inherently heavy, of a low and dense vibration; it is imperative that we remove blockages and resistance. We must elevate our being and focus only upon the positive and higher vibratory aspects, and then when we encounter the energies of the photon belt we will not suffer or worse be destroyed from the resulting friction of a higher vibratory field coming into possibly abrupt contact with a lower vibratory field. We will be able to ride the higher energies and steer ourselves to ever-higher realms of vibratory existence.

The Earth in the past has gone through massive and often dramatically quick changes. From geological and scientific evidence, it appears that Ice Ages have rapidly come about in previously warm areas. Great, all-obliterating floods, massive changes from earthquakes, volcanic eruptions and subsequent tidal waves have demolished or sunk beneath the oceans what were great cities and civilisations. These things will continue to happen, and we are approaching a time of very great and rapid Earth changes. We are starting already to see rapid climate change of a sort unprecedented for many thousands of years. Indeed, only a few short years ago the climatologists and scientists were arguing that all climate change would be gradual. They have had to change their opinions. The massive Earth changes that are rapidly approaching us are part of a great cosmic cycle, and already the frequency of the Earth's pulse has increased. This, together with the Earth's geomagnetic field weakening (30% in the last one hundred years), should tell us we are in for significant earth changes. Speculation is increasing that a pole reversal is immanent; this is how the earth recharges its spin, much like a dynamo. We now know this has happened many times before. We are all now experiencing an overall increased rate of vibration. This in itself may go a long way to explaining the increasingly bizarre behaviour we see around us: if we do not or cannot raise our vibratory rate as required by the system in which we have our being, we will start to fracture ever more, and with greater fracturing comes increased incoherence. If this situation is allowed to continue unabated, madness will result.

It has been said that "those whom the gods wish to destroy, they first make mad". We all need to think upon this, as human behaviour the world over is increasingly becoming quite mad. Reason is deserting her throne; common sense is an almost unheard of attribute. Is this because we are beginning to fracture as we rigidly endeavour to hold ourselves in place, to hold ourselves in opposition to the inherent and natural action of the multiverse? Is this also because we are so cut off from our source, the Divine Creative Field/God? We need to understand that we can in no way avoid or stop these changes. Indeed, it is extreme arrogance on our part to presume, as popular belief has it, that we have caused these changes and that we may therefore stop them. Do we hold onto this belief because it gives us some semblance of power and control? We may have contributed to the acceleration of these changes, but in so small a way as to be negligible. All runs on the time of the great Divine Cosmic Clock, and we can neither change nor interfere with the process in any meaningful way. This does not mean we should not change our ways, quite the reverse. We have been raping and pillaging our beautiful planet for far too long. Our behaviour towards our physical home is an outward manifestation of our inward condition, of our deep unconsciousness, a manifestation of the inward incoherence, misalignment, and lack of spirituality that a great many of us suffer from. All we can do now is to find out how to adapt in order to survive what is coming, and there is only one direction in which we may face: the higher order of the Divine needs to be our guide. We must acknowledge that higher orders organise and direct the lower. There is no other way.

According to ancient scriptures, we are nearing the end of a great cycle. Hindus call it "the Kali Yuga – the age of vice and darkness". Many Mayans and Christians believe we are in the end times. If we look at our recent history (i.e. our known history, as that is recent in Earth time) we would be hard-pressed to dispute that this has indeed been an age of darkness. However, as with all else, this age has an end and we are currently moving rapidly into a time of great change, the result of which will be a higher vibration, therefore more light with the resulting greater consciousness, greater refinement and therefore less darkness and all else that this implies. The time band of rapid change, however, will be a period of chaos and danger, so it is imperative that we all understand what is going on. We all need to acquire the wisdom, understanding and soul/God contact in order that we may navigate successfully through this coming period of great change, as only then can we be assured of our successful evolutionary leap towards the promise of immortality and greater spiritual power. In doing this, union with the Divine, with all the gifts that come with it, we will have acted in accordance with the Divine Intelligent Will and will be practising the noble art of Wu Wei, flowing with the Divine Intent toward the penultimate meaning and object of our life which is the greater development and unfolding of our soul on its journey towards wholeness and union with the Divine Creative Field. The time is now, and in religious language, a successful evolutionary life is the degree to which we are attaining or reaching for eternal life, without which we will be mortal souls running the risk of perishing. If we are to align with the Divine Creative Field, then we need more perfectly to understand its nature – and to do this we need to understand the nature of love, as Perfect Unconditional Love is the fundamental vibration of the Divine Creative Field.

Chapter 6
Love

By Love he knows me in truth, who I am and what I am.
And when he knows me in truth he enters into my
   Being

— Bhagavad Gita 18:55

What exactly is love and what does it have to do with greater unfolded spiritual evolution? We talk about love a great deal, we sing songs and write poems about it and many of us spend our entire lives seeking it. We pity those seemingly without love and those seemingly with it in abundance are envied. How often does the cry go up "I just want someone to love me"? If no one loves us, we feel alone, afraid and/or incomplete. Often, we may find love but do not recognise it, or we may find love but find it too frightening and so reject it. We may feel we have never really found it at all, it is only something we have heard about, dreamt of, imagined, and yet we have an ever-driving inner urge to obtain it. The urge for love is as remorseless as the urge to evolve and this is because they are one and the same. "Fully unfolded spiritual evolution is the attainment of Perfect Unconditional Love".

So how do we define love? Is love another person being around us, doing things for us, taking care of us? Is it us doing things for, or taking care of, another? Is love taking care of a child, nurturing it? Is love being with another person and feeling whole and complete? Is love something to do with sex? Is love feeling happy or exultant when surrounded by nature on a beautiful day? Is love looking into the smiling old eyes of our dying mother, father, husband, or wife? Is love the love of God?

Love can be all of these things, but it is also much, much, more. It is in fact the very stuff of the multiverse, the essence of the Divine Creative Field, of God. In Chapter One, we saw that some scientists have found that love, or the resonance of the energy field we call love, corresponds to the Golden Mean Ratio. In addition, the energy field generated from the heart (which is one part of the physical apparatus the soul directly functions through while in the physical plane) when in the moment of loving has the same harmonic as that of the essential warp and weft of the multiverse, i.e. it is coherent, harmonious, unified and infinitely shareable. This means that all the particles which are us respond to this field and that under the law of self-similarity we have the ability to wholly respond to and become one with the essential fabric of the multiverse – God – while in the moment of loving. The reason we are not at one with this field all the time is because we have to a greater or lesser degree negativity, incoherence and much else of a low vibration held within our fields. Without this negativity we would permanently be of the field called love, which is also called God.

When the mystics speak about being in a state of oneness or pure enlightenment, what they mean is that our energy field corresponds with that of the Divine Creative Field and as this field has been found to correspond to the vibration of the thing we call love, they are saying that oneness equals pure love. We are at one with the Divine, bathed in a sea of perfect love. Further, when mystics, sages, Jesus and other spiritual teachers say "God is Love", they are speaking of a reality.

If love is the energy field of God, then if we love we are familiar with having the same resonance (if only for a short time) as God. If we know how to do this then we must have, at some time, made contact with God – and further, we will be able to consciously, at will, make contact again as and when we wish, when we know how. Conversely, if we do not love, we are not interacting, communicating, and becoming one with God (even momentarily) the unified shareable and coherent, loving field of energy, we are separated from God. If we have never loved, it will be more difficult to start as we will have no conscious memory to guide us. However, with intent, focus and knowledge, all is possible. The Bible confirms this:

> Beloved, let us love one another: for love is of God; and everyone that loveth is born of God, and knoweth God. He that loveth not, knoweth not God; for God is love.
>
> *— 1 John 4:7–8*

The *Bhagavad Gita* has this to say:

> Only by Love can men see me, and know me, and come unto me.
>
> He who works for me, who loves me, whose End Supreme I am, free from attachment to all things, and with love for all creation, he in truth comes unto me.
>
> *— Bhagavad Gita 11:54–55*

Jesus spoke a great deal about love. In fact, if you were to ask a Christian, "What is the main message that Jesus brought?" the reply will invariably be "Jesus was Love, or he taught about love." For us to become unified with the Divine in loving relationship, the integral, the most important activity we must accomplish is to consciously and at our deepest levels come to know, understand, interact with and love the Divine Creative Field, we call God. If we are to do this, then we must first have a real understanding of love itself. We must be able to recognise the resonance of the energy field of love; for to love what in the initial stages may be an abstract is difficult indeed. This does, however, have to be done, as it is in the act of love for the Divine that we open ourselves – unfold to the Divine energies – and to the degree that we are able to open is the degree that we can receive. We need to explore love in its many manifestations because to succeed we need a clear and accurate vision of this thing we all so desire. Some of our ideas of what real love actually is are grossly incorrect. We all need a clear understanding of it in all its power and glory, as this knowledge is an integral key to success on our evolutionary journey to full spiritual health, coherence, and joy. However, in order to reach the exalted state of ultimate unfolded loving spiritual union we need to first look at what love is *not*. A misconceived idea of what love is can lead us astray as an energy that we call love may well turn out to be merely yet another diversion, as these are so abundant in this explicate realm. Let us first look at what we experience and call love in the realm of physical manifestations in this particular space-time continuum. It will be instructive if we look at love as described by one of the world's greatest lovers. Sadly, this kind of love is the least enduring and often the most superficial. More often than not, it is not love at all but need, lust, fear and many other negative things beside. Nevertheless, it makes up a great part of the vast body of work around the subject of love and is probably the one we all are most diverted by.

We will start with the poetry of Lord Byron, one of the world's great lovers and an expert, you might say, on the subject of loving. If we think about the ideal of Romantic Love, we cannot help but think of that glamorous and handsome poet of the eighteenth century whom the opposite sex so adored. What did he have to say of love?

The First Kiss of Love

> Away with your fictions of flimsy romance;
> Those tissues of falsehood which folly has wove!

Love

Give me the mild beam of the soul-breathing glance,
Or the rapture which dwells on the first kiss of love.

Ye rhymers, whose bosoms with phantasy glow,
Whose pastoral passions are made for the grove;
From what blest inspiration your sonnets would flow,
Could you ever have tasted the first kiss of love!

If Apollo should e'er his assistance refuse,
Or the Nine be disposed from your service to rove,
Invoke them no more, bid adieu to the muse,
And try the effect of the first kiss of love!

I hate you, ye cold compositions of art!
Though prudes may condemn me, and bigots re-prove,
I court the effusions that spring from the heart,
Which throbs with delight to the first kiss of love.

Your shepherds, your flocks, those fantastical themes,
Perhaps may amuse, yet they never can move:
Arcadia displays but a region of dreams:
What are the visions like these to the first kiss of love?

Oh! Cease to affirm that man since his birth,
From Adam till now, has with wretchedness strove;
Some portion of paradise still is on earth,
And Eden revives in the first kiss of love.

When age chills the blood, when our pleasures are
    past –
For years fleet away with the wings of the dove –
The dearest remembrance will still be the last,
Our sweetest memorial the first kiss of love.

So there we have it, the whole thing on this physical plane of existence, a thing more than mere romance, inspirational in itself, with a power greater than poetry or art to move. It makes other amusements pale by comparison, it brings the Garden of Eden down on to this Earth plane and the lasting memories of it stay with us into old age and beyond while still giving pleasure. Powerful stuff! Is there anything else that is able to do all that? No wonder everyone wants it. However, love has another aspect, some might say its dark side. Byron waxes lyrical about all the positive aspects of love, all the wondrous gifts it brings and the powers it has. Kahlil Gibran (of whom it was said, "His power came from some great reservoir of spiritual life, else it could not have been so universal and potent") gives us another view of love:

On Love

> When love beckons to you, follow him,
> Though his ways are hard and steep.
> And when his wings enfold you yield to him,
> Though the sword hidden among his pinions may
>   wound you.
> And when he speaks to you believe in him,
> Though his voice may shatter your dreams as the north
>   wind lays waste the garden.
>
> For even as love crowns you so shall he crucify you.
>   Even as he is for your growth so is he for your
>   pruning.
> Even as he ascends to your height and caresses your
>   tenderest branches that quiver in the sun,
> So shall he descend to your roots and shake them in
>   their clinging to the earth.
>
> Like sheaves of corn he gathers you unto himself. He
>   threshes you to make you naked.

Love

He sifts you to free you from your husks. He grinds you to whiteness.
He kneads you until you are pliant;
And then he assigns you to his sacred fire, that you may become sacred bread for God's sacred feast.

All these things shall love do unto you that you may know the secrets of your heart, and in that knowledge become a fragment of Life's heart.

But if in your fear you would seek only love's peace and love's pleasure,
Then it is better for you that you cover your nakedness and pass out of love's threshing-floor,
Into the seasonless world where you shall laugh, but not all of your laughter, and weep, but not all of your tears.

Love gives naught but itself and takes naught but from itself.
Love possesses not nor would it be possessed;
For love is sufficient unto love.

When you love you should not say, "God is in my heart," but rather, "I am in the heart of God."
And think not you can direct the course of love, for love, if it finds you worthy, directs your course.

Love has no other desire but to fulfil itself.
But if you love and must needs have desires, let these be your desires:
To melt and be like a running brook that sings its melody to the night.
To know the pain of too much tenderness.

> To be wounded by your own understanding of love; And
>> to bleed willingly and joyfully.
> To wake at dawn with a winged heart and to give
>> thanks for another day of loving;
> To rest at the noon hour and meditate love's ecstasy;
> To return home at eventide with gratitude;
> And then to sleep with a prayer for the beloved in your
>> heart and a song of praise upon your lips.

Some of that doesn't sound like too much fun, does it? We are told that the ways of love are hard and steep, with mention of swords and dreams being shattered. Gibran talks about love crucifying, and if that is not bad enough we are also going to be pruned, threshed, ground, kneaded and then consigned to a fire. You may think "He got that right" as your experience of so-called love was all that and more. Or you may think you will go with Byron's version and forget this depressing Lebanese character. In all fairness, we need to consider the entire poem as it actually gives us an extremely clear picture of how and why love most often manifests, acts and interacts in the explicate realm. More importantly, it tells us why it is so important that we engage in love, why love in our life is a necessary part of our evolution. If we wish to evolve, we must have this aspect or energy in our life. The poem continues and says in effect that it is better to love than, in our fear of possible pain, to avoid love, for then we will never plumb the full depths of our emotions, of joy and laughter as well as pain and sorrow. We will stay on a more even keel emotionally, but in so doing we will miss all the great highs and lows of a full emotional life. In order to gain full possession and control of all our emotions, we must first experience them, as to experience them is to understand them – eventually. If we seek only for pleasure in love then it is better that we should abandon the idea of love, as in this realm love and pain are closely entwined. It also makes clear that when loving we are as though naked, and therefore vulnerable. The poem tells us we cannot possess love nor can we direct its course, meaning we cannot control it. It is sufficient unto itself – desiring nothing other than to be complete in itself. The poem marvellously relates that should we have any desires at all to do with love then these should only be that we allow it totally, even if this should end up causing us pain. Then, should it cause us pain, we are told to be joyful about this and, what is more, grateful.

Love as we for the most part experience in these realms will have elements of all the above within it because when we allow the perfect field of love to have contact with our imperfect fields, something within us has to move. Old wounds, buried anger, resentment etc., will rise to the surface and cause us trauma as the action of love attempts to heal our fields. Any fracturing, negativity, and rigid blocks we own will all be under assault, as love is the most powerful and solvent force within the multiverse. When we in all our imperfections encounter the harmonious, powerful and perfect field of love, even if for a split second, then an effect is registered in all our fields which can be, and often is, quite dramatic and painful.

Even if the Love we are receiving is imperfect because it is flowing through another imperfect field and is not completely of the Divine but is a lesser thing, it can still cause enormous upheaval in all our fields, depending on our inherent negativity, resistance to change and fixed points of view. Therefore, our experience in loving is always first and foremost a reflection of ourselves and the only way to lessen pain and trauma is to let go, practise the art of Wu Wei and allow the field of love to heal as it is designed to do. If we cling on to our positions, if we fight that we are right in all our pain, the wheel will keep turning and we will experience again and again the same pain until we understand and let go. Some might add "let go and let God" which is love. Let love have its way and heal us all.

Kahlil Gibran was a deeply spiritual and wise man, so is there something else he is wishing to impart here in this poem on love? Apart from the above, is there a yet deeper message here? If we look again at the poem, we will see a key passage is, "All these things shall love do unto you that you may know the secrets of your heart, and in that knowledge become a fragment of Life's heart." The process of being pruned, ground and fired by loving is one of the many ways the universe encourages us to "know thyself", to contact our soul and discover our true reality. It is one of the ways it urges us to clear our negativity, the low vibrations that overlay, obscure and disconnect the soul, because once the soul is revealed, is more accessible, even visible, we may then consciously interact with it and thereby initiate its alignment, development and unfolding. The vibrational frequency of pain has a very efficient scouring action on our other fields. In the midst of great pain (mental, emotional or physical) we are ground, scoured and depleted until we are able to contact our innermost being. In the midst of great pain all else falls away; in the depths of our pain we are less conscious of the normal things of explicate life, we retreat within and are thus able to reach and touch our soul and hence the Divine Creative Field. In our pain, we let down the barriers, let go of control, we go within, and so we gain an understanding of ourselves that we did not have before. Hence, we may know the secrets of our hearts and once we know this, we begin to know all. The fire of love may leave us with an emptiness, a vacuum that was not there before into which a new and different energy may move. This is an invitation and a great opportunity to allow the right energy to replace what was there before.

But what is the right energy? It is the unfolding and expansion of the loving field of our soul. Our soul is now able, has been allowed (the choice is always ours) to unfold a little, and as our soul is itself a fragment of Life's Heart – fragment of the Divine Creative Field, which is pure unconditional and perfect love, we have not only expanded the field of our soul, but we have expanded our experience and field of love. This love is of the highest and most complete vibration, unconditional love that has within it only the pure light of the Divine Creative Field and therefore no lesser vibration of negativity or pain. An important pathway to experiencing and possessing in ever-greater capacity within each of our individual but not separated fields the pure unconditional love of God is through the experience of love in the explicate realms, which will be by definition imperfect.

Out of the experience of loving, even if it causes great pain, comes the capacity to unfold, and so the capacity to love in a more whole and unconditional manner than before. With the further unfolding of our soul we become ever closer to the Divine Creative Field under the law of self-similarity – we move ever closer to becoming coherent, unified and infinitely shareable, therefore towards a more complete and conscious "fragment of life's heart". With this experience we have been given a great gift: this is why we should bleed willingly and joyfully and why we should give thanks and praise. There are other ways to accomplish this unfolding of our soul without the pain and trauma of love in the explicate realms, but for most of us, at this stage of our journey, this is the method we so often seem to employ.

In order to understand and become familiar with the vibration of the energy called love, and if we are to acquire the ability to be a channel for it at will, a Buddhist meditation called the Metta Bhavana will greatly assist. The process is, as for all meditations, to be as comfortable as possible. Sit cross-legged if possible as this will help to focus your energy fields. Focus your mind, relax and still all, as much as possible. Now think of someone you love very much: observe how you feel while you are feeling loving; observe the quality of the energy and its flow from the heart centre. Move more and more into this stream, giving it greater space and power while thinking of all the ways you love. Hold this focus and intent for as long as possible. Once in a powerful field of love, the guided meditation then moves through its various stages listed below. The object of the meditation is that the flow of love's energy does not cease even while contemplating someone you do not love. It is quite difficult in the early stages, but with practice it becomes easy and is a very useful, enlightening and powerful exercise on the path to full spiritual love and power.

Focus on and generate the energy field of love to:

1. Someone you love.
2. Someone you don't know very well, maybe just pass in the morning.
3. Then a friend.
4. Someone you actively dislike.
5. Neighbours.
6. Your town.
7. Your country.
8. The world and the multi-verse beyond.

This meditation is an extremely useful tool as it enables us to recognise the quality and generate the field of the energy called love. With practice, we gain the ability to run it at will to whomever, whatever, wherever we choose. By doing this, we are able to change energies and therefore situations and places; elevating all to a higher spin, without fear of doing harm. Sending out a field of love is highly effective in areas of conflict and it is possible with practice to change powerfully the energy in a room, which also affects all within in a positive manner. We need never again say, "I want someone to love me", we need never again feel we are not loved. We all live within a Divine unconditionally loving field of energy; we are just for the most part so unconscious and disconnected that we are unaware of it. We can choose to change this.

When we are immersed in a field of perfect love, we are immersed in a coherent, harmonised, unified and infinitely shareable energy field, which is the coherent, unified and infinitely shareable field of the Divine Creator. All our acts of love in large ways and small are our unconscious efforts at striving to contact and become one with this field. All our sexual unions, not withstanding the primeval urge to procreate, arise out of our desperate, urgent, and omnipresent need to merge ourselves and become more at one with God, as when we merge with this field we unfold a little further, we become greater in our fields – we evolve. At the sublime peak of orgasm, we merge for a moment in time and become one with all that is, but often in our confusion we may think it is our partner that is the Divine. The better the sex, the more we elevate our partner in our mind. In the darkness of the material, explicate realms we are easily confused: great and loving sex is union with our partner but, more importantly, it is union with the Divine Creative Field, or God, and hence an experience, for a second in time, of pure unconditional and perfect love. The sexual act is primarily a spiritual act or should be regarded as such. The more it is degraded, by the many and varied means we often employ, the more it becomes only a limited physical act of low vibration, with the true meaning and positive effects lost in the mire of dense physicality, resulting logically in deeper unconsciousness with progressively lower vibration. Instead of generating an elevated, more conscious and coherent loving energy of higher spin, the opposite is created, which if continued risks damage or destruction to the soul. This is involution, not evolution, and is highly dangerous.

Love of the greatest quality, in fact the only thing we can truly call love, is unconditional love, loving without requiring any return for our gift of loving. Loving and allowing the energy to flow in a healing, nurturing, expansive and generous gift, in prefect alignment with the Divine Creative Field – this is what love truly is or can be. Love expressed in this way is a most powerful solvent and the most potent and powerful energy there is in the multiverse, as this kind of Love is the Divine Creative Field expressing itself, it is God in action. Unconditional love raises the vibration of all, from the smallest cell to the Earth itself and out to the wider cosmos. Unconditional love is energy in a fast-track evolutionary spiral. In an act of unconditional love, we invite the flow of the Divine Creative Field more perfectly into our lives. This is the ideal; this is where we should all aim. Unfortunately, in this explicate realm if we talk about unconditional love, we are liable to hear, "If you wish for unconditional love, get a dog." We recognise, it seems, that human beings are as a rule not very good at generating unconditional love, and unfortunately to a great degree this is true. All our various ways of loving do often tend to come with strings attached. It is common to hear, whether it be parental love or other kinds of love, the words "If you really loved me, you would...".

We use love as a bargaining chip, we manipulate with it and we even sometimes use it as a weapon.

Let us look more closely at unconditional love and try to see why we think dogs are better at it than we are. To do this, we will return to Byron for a moment. He adored the opposite sex and had a reputation as a great lover, yet who does it appear offered him the greatest love?

Inscription on the Monument of a Newfoundland Dog

> When some proud son of man returns to earth,
>   Unknown to glory, but upheld by birth,
> The sculptor's art exhausts the pomp of woe, And
>   storied urns record who rests below; When all is
>   done, upon the tomb is seen,
> Not what he was, but what he should have been; But
>   the poor dog, in life the firmest friend, The first to
>   welcome, foremost to defend, Whose honest heart
>   is still his master's own,
> Who labours, fights, lives, breathes for him alone,
>   Unhonour'd falls, unnoticed all his worth, Denied in
>   heaven the soul he held on earth: While man, vain
>   insect! Hopes to be forgiven, And claims himself a
>   sole exclusive heaven.
> Oh man! Thou feeble tenant of an hour, Debased by
>   slavery, or corrupt by power,
> Who knows thee well must quit thee with disgust,
>   Degraded mass of animated dust!
> Thy love is lust, thy friendship all a cheat, Thy smiles
>   hypocrisy, thy words deceit! By nature vile,
>   ennobled but by name,
> Each kindred brute might bid thee blush for shame. Ye!
>   Who perchance behold this simple urn,
> Pass on – it honours none you wish to mourn: To mark

a friend's remains these stones arise; I never knew
but one, – and here he lies.

— *Newstead Abbey, November 30, 1808*

The inscription which precedes this reads: "Near this spot are deposited the remains of one who possessed beauty without vanity, strength without insolence, courage without ferocity and all the virtues of man without his vices. This praise, which would be unmeaning flattery if inscribed over human ashes, is but a just tribute to the memory of Boatswain, a dog, who was born at Newfoundland, May 1803, and died at Newstead Abbey, Nov. 18, 1808."

In his 1861 will, Byron directed that his body should be buried in a vault in the garden, near the faithful dog he knew for only five years. Poor Byron, his bitter words concerning the human race in general are, of course, a reflection of himself. It was *his* love that was lust, *his* friendship that was a cheat, for he sought for love outside himself and looked only for love to be given to him instead of realising it is only in the giving that we are able to receive. He devoted, some would say, his entire life to love's pursuit and it forever eluded him. He remained only able to receive that which he put out, an endless reflection of himself. He wrote about love, endlessly waxed lyrical about it, but in the end love eluded him. He died feeling that the only true and unconditional love he had experienced came from his few years' acquaintance with his dog. Without this experience, one supposes he would have died utterly disillusioned in his search for love. If the unconditional love of a dog is the only love we are able to manifest in our lives, it is certainly better than no love at all. It is a wonderful gift indeed and if it assists us to recognise what love feels like, if it helps us to allow the energy of love to flow, there is nothing wrong with that. Anything that assists in this regard is better than nothing at all.

So, love in the explicate realms is often a mere shadow of what it should and can be. We are not very good at loving, as a general rule. In fact, we appear to be naturally better at hating, at conflict. This makes sense because this is the field we are evolving from. We are evolving from darkness towards light, from low vibration towards high spin and right now we have greater darkness in our fields than light. Darkness, low vibration, is what we must leave behind on our journey towards the complete unfolding of our soul and spiritual power. If we remember that our primary journey is from darkness towards light we need never take a wrong turning, as anything that is of lesser light, of lesser vibration, of lesser love, is the wrong direction.

For the next stage of our journey forward, we need to know three all-important instructions. These come in a particular order.

The first thing we must resolve to do on our journey from darkness to light is to love God and, as we saw in Chapter Two, Jesus said, "Thou shalt love the Lord thy God with all thy heart and with all thy soul, and with all thy mind. This is the first and great commandment." It is all very well to say, "love God", but how are we to do this? How do we love something our left-brain is perhaps not exactly sure even exists? How do we love something with all our heart, soul and mind if it is for us an abstract? We can't see God, can't touch God, can't with any of our physical senses make God a reality. Further, how are we to love God, the Divine Creative Field, whose very essence is Love itself, if we have never felt or had any real understanding of love ourselves? It is impossible, is it not? Nevertheless, however impossible, it absolutely has to be done, because for us to become fully unfolded, of a light-filled high vibration, and complete our evolutionary journey, this is key. In addition, this huge leap is – surprisingly, maybe – the first step, not the last. It is the first as all else will flow from this one point of resolve, this one point of faith, this one point of contact.

> Those who set their hearts on me and ever in love worship me, and who have unshakeable faith, these I hold as the best Yogis. Those who worship the Imperishable, the Infinite, the Transcendent un-manifested; the Omnipresent, the Beyond all thought, the Immutable, the Never-changing, the Ever One;

> Who have all the powers of their soul in harmony, and the same loving mind for all; who find joy in the good of all beings – they reach in truth my very self.
>
> They for whom I am the End Supreme, who surrender all their works to me, and who with pure love meditate on me and adore me – these I very soon deliver from the ocean of death and life-in-death, because they have set their heart on me.
>
> *— Bhagavad Gita 12:2–4,6–7*

For us to move at all, we have to, at our deepest level and consciously, come to know and love the Divine. It is in the act of love for the Divine that we open ourselves to the Divine energies; and the degree to which we open is the degree to which we are able to receive. It is all up to us – the system is there waiting to be accessed:

> Ask and it shall be given you; seek, and ye shall find; knock, and it shall be opened unto you: For everyone that asketh receiveth; and he that seeketh findeth; and to him that knocketh it shall be opened.
>
> *— Matthew 7:7–8*

These are clear directions, clear promises. However, here we venture more clearly into understanding the primary importance of "belief". A fundamental key to all is belief or faith: the degree that we believe we will receive and find will be the degree of our success. If we approach this in the spirit of testing or enquiry, with a mind to prove or disprove, we will only prove our lack of faith and love. If we approach with faith and with the powerful energy field of love, we possess a primary key to the system. The measure of our success will be the degree to which we have faith and love. So, there it is: we must first have love in our field in order to receive it; if we do not have love in our field, we cannot receive it. Fun, isn't it? In addition, we must first believe that God exists, as we would find it impossible to love something we do not believe is a reality and it would be equally impossible to receive anything from that which we do not believe exists. Therefore, in order to love God, we must first believe in God's existence: we must have faith. Once we have faith and are able to love, then the proof of the reality of God is given. Another of those wonderful paradoxes – who says God does not have a sense of humour?

The second instruction is to love ourselves, as without this it will be impossible for us ever to become a unified and coherent field. A lack of self-love will render all our attempts to further unfold and evolve impossible, also, if we are to be a perfect channel, if we are to manifest the energy of love, then for this to flow into us and out into the world we need to be as aligned, unified and coherent as possible. If we do not love ourselves, our fields will be fractured by degrees of darkness, low vibration and negativity and this will render null and void all our attempts to manifest the Divine Creative energies.

> And the second is like unto it, Thou shalt love thy neighbour as thyself.
>
> — *Matthew 22:39*

Jesus seemingly accepts as a given that we do love ourselves as he instructs us to "love thy neighbour as thyself" and so refers to only two important commandments. In truth, for a great many of us, loving ourselves is enormously difficult if not seemingly impossible. However, if we follow the injunction "Know thyself" – for how may we love ourselves when we have no real knowledge and understanding of ourselves? – then we are on the path. Further, if with a clear understanding that without self-love it is impossible to love anything else, as we cannot give that which we do not have and it is impossible to receive and out-flow the perfect divine energies through a disordered channel, then we will see that love of ourselves is a key. Indeed, how may perfect unconditional love flow through a disordered vessel and not become contaminated by it, thus rendering it imperfect love? It is not possible. Without love of ourselves, our inner darkness will overwhelm any tiny amount of perfect love we should allow into our fields, always supposing it were possible for us to allow any in at all, because if immersed in darkness, the pure white light of love can only initially cause us pain. It is a conundrum, but it can be done and that is by first choosing to believe that it is possible.

So, we see that there are three all-important instructions to consider rather than two. Jesus crucially goes on further to say:

> On these two commandments hang all the law and the prophets.
>
> *— Matthew 22:40*

It appears that for Jesus everything hangs on these two simple instructions – all the law, everything. Love God and love others. One could say, therefore, there is nothing left for anyone else to say – just understand and live these two simple instructions, or three, if you do not yet love yourself. Unfortunately, it has not been that simple. If we wish to create some semblance of balance, of correct priorities in our lives, then in all our relationships, in all our thoughts, words and deeds, in our holistic view of the multiverse, the image we would be wise to hold in our mind is as follows:

First place, in pre-eminent position, before all else; we must learn to love God, the Divine Creative source of all things. We must learn to live in a state of loving gratitude for our "whole" relationship, together with all that has naturally emanated from it. In other words, love and gratitude are the frequencies we are consciously and with intent manifesting in all our fields.

Second place, we must hold our vision of ourselves in a field of love and deep respect, while keeping a conscious connection (as much as possible) at all times in all ways to the above.

Third place, we outflow all the positive fundamental energies derived from our direct contact with God the Divine Creative Source, which flows through us, to significant others, all others, all beings and everything in the multiverse as we consciously choose.

Should we get our order of priority in any other way, we are heading for trouble. Should we, for instance, put another being between the Divine and ourselves so that we no longer have direct contact with the Divine, or should we have no Divine at all, with ourselves or another being taking its place, we are in trouble as we have cut ourselves off from our source of all. If we put material goods or money in place of the Divine, the same thing happens, and we cut off our access to the infinite abundance of God. If we do not always place ourselves second, receiving all that is our birthright directly from the Divine, if we so devalue ourselves as to place ourselves in any other position, we will not and cannot have anything of real value to give to anyone else. What we do give will come from an imperfect source and as such will be imperfect and finite. It will not and cannot be infinite, shareable and perfect unconditional love. It may masquerade as love, it may sound like love, but it will not be love. We must be clear that unless we have a conscious connection with the Divine and are to a degree centred and unified, it is impossible for us to give perfect unconditional love, as any gift we make will reflect only our own fields and their lack of connection to the Divine and thus lack of perfection. The quality of our loving is a clear manifestation of our primary relationships and the subsequent state of our own energy fields and level of our evolution. From an imperfect field, disconnected from the primary source, only limited and imperfect love can be generated. The way forward now is clear: all we need to do is follow the very clear simple directions. It makes no sense to do otherwise if we remember that without the frequency of love nothing can be accomplished, as without love we will continue to be closed – enfolded and therefore unable to receive love, unable to evolve further and thus will remain primarily misaligned, unconscious and incoherent. If we look around us now at this time, 2024, what do we see?

Many years ago, I attended a six-week workshop whose focus was deleting the negative software programs/belief systems inherent in every cell of our bodies. These programs stop us becoming whole, they keep us fractured and keep us from being free, as they trigger us to react to almost everything instead of acting out of our conscious free will. One hundred and sixty people of all races and creeds, from the four corners of the globe, came to attend this workshop. One day during some of the early intensive psychological processes most were going through, I was struck by an almost universal and desolate cry I heard echoing round the great room regarding love, which was, "No one loves me" or "I just want someone to love me", or "I want love in my life" and so on. I did not once hear, "I just want someone to love". I found this curious, as the cry was wishing only to be given this thing called love; the desire was only to receive, never to give.

The key to love resides within each one of us. The fount of all love is the Divine, the point of flow comes from within each of us, through the facility of first our Divine Soul and thence in the physical explicate realms through the portal of the heart chakra. If we do not have the wisdom, understanding and focus to unlock this flow from its Divine source, through its natural channels, how may we get love from another source, from an imperfect source in the explicate realms? This desire does not make sense, as how may another incoherent being give us perfect love? We are doomed to failure if we look outside ourselves for love. More importantly, if we do not have love within us, even should we get it from another, we would not recognise it as love, because how could we recognise something we had no real knowledge of? In addition, if we do not have love within us, we are incapable of receiving it.

In order to give anything, we must first have it, as how may we give something we do not have? Everything comes from the Divine Source, and we know that in order to give, we must first receive, but here is the paradox: in order to receive, we must first give. So how does that work?

I will explain. The Divine Source of all is giving all the time. That is what it does: the energy field is active always. The Divine is always there for us to receive it, but if we are closed, or we don't believe, shut down, fractured and/or incoherent, we will be unable to receive as we should. As the extent that we are able to give is the extent to which we are able to receive, we are in trouble because this means we are limited in our loving. Once we have perfected ourselves as channels for the Divine energy, then the love we may give will be infinite. There is a very simple, yet extremely difficult way to receive all that the Divine has to offer, as we will see later, but for now the statement "Not my will but Thine" is a clue. We must give of ourselves in gratitude and love, we must open our minds, open our hearts and offer our entire being in trust and faith as a child does with a good parent, and as we give of ourselves so then shall we receive. It is impossible that we will not, as once we open ourselves in the act of faith, in the act of giving our gratitude, in the act of loving, the Divine Creative Source will inflow and God's existence will be no more in doubt. To the degree that we are able to do this is the degree that we are able to receive, which will then be the degree to which we are able to give love. It is as simple and as difficult as that. Know that as we give of ourselves, and to the extent that we do this, so then shall we receive, and as the Divine coherent, harmonious, light, love, wisdom and spiritual power flows in, then we may consciously direct its flow outwards as we choose. What is more, to become masters of this process is why we are here.

In the explicate realm at this time, we may have reached the stage whereby we can pour out wonderful unconditional love, but this does not necessarily mean we will receive the same amount and quality of love back. In fact, it is quite possible we may not receive any at all, because we may be giving our love to someone who is not able to recognise or receive it. However, if our love is unconditional as it should be, then it will not matter. Should our love be received and returned, it is only possible to receive back that which already resides within, unless we choose to evolve. Great love may be given, but we may only receive it in a mean and miserly manner. If we are capable of only giving in a mean miserly manner, the very best that we may hope for is to receive a mean and miserly amount back. We are only ever able to receive that which we may give. All is in balance always; it is not possible that it be otherwise for "As ye sow so shall ye reap". This not only means that what we put out, is what we will receive, but also that unfortunately, unless we choose to evolve, which is often painful, we are only able to receive, that which we are able to give. What we are able to receive is always a reflection of what we give, which is a reflection of ourselves. Some may ask why, if love is the greatest solvent, does it not, no matter the source, assist us to unfold and thus evolve? Because our soul may only unfold and evolve when in direct conscious relationship with God. Loving exchanges in the explicate realms, while cut off from the source, result only in another turn of the wheel. It is only through a holistic experience – that is, relationship with the Divine and loving explicate exchanges – that we may unfold and the soul may grow. We cannot evolve if we choose to cut ourselves off from the Divine source of all. It is important that we understand these simple laws, as how else may we progress along our individual path? How may we respond to having possibly given great love when it is not understood, received, or returned? We may often in such circumstances get upset, feel we are not appreciated or have not been properly treated, and all sorts of trouble may follow. However, if we understand the system, understand the laws, all becomes clear and with understanding we can keep our connection with the Divine Source, and give, just give without regard for any return. If we allow the pure beautiful flow and let all who are able to mop it up to whatever degree they are able without expectation of any particular result, then all will be well. As we unfold and open ever more to the energies of the Divine, we are able to give more and more and so we are able to receive more and more. It is a wonderful and beautiful divine dance of exchanging energies in perfect balance, symmetry and harmony. The infinitely shareable Divine frequency of love unfolds, heals, harmonizes and unifies and thus we evolve with the exchange.

Once we understand the power and the ways of love, once we have integrated this understanding in some measure in all our fields, then we begin to become a pure beautiful coherent and light-filled, unified field, which is moving ever closer to the point of perfect self-similarity in partnership and union with God. Once we have arrived at this point, then the Divine reveals itself to us in all its glory. As always though, we must work to attain this privilege:

> He that hath my commandments, and keepeth them, he it is that loveth me: and he that loveth me shall be loved of my Father, and I will love him, and will manifest myself to him.
>
> *—John 14:21*

This is our reason for being, our soul's evolutionary pathway and goal; this is also the emergence of Divine Spiritual Power. In order to be a successful human being, to evolve and become power-full, we must be able to recognise, access, receive and generate the coherent, infinitely shareable Divine Field that is love. Without love in our life, and more particularly without the ability to generate pure, powerful unconditional love at will, we are incomplete, incoherent, finite and powerless. Our ability to master this process of generating pure unconditional love at will, should be the only yardstick we employ when measuring the success or otherwise of another fellow human – when one understands the entire system, money and fame are laughable measures of success. They are finite, have no enduring life and add nothing to the unfolding of our soul. Often they do the opposite and thus the result is involution rather than evolution.

Unfortunately, there is a major obstacle that keeps us from union with the Divine and from realising pure unconditional love. This obstacle keeps us enfolded, fractured, incoherent and powerless and if it is not to be found immediately on the surface of our fields, it will appear lurking in our depths as we peel away layer after layer. This one great obstacle we call "fear". Before we can move forward from here, we must understand how to slay this ancient and powerful enemy. To slay fear, we must first understand it, as once we understand and know a thing, once we are able to look it wholly in the face, it loses its power over us and we then begin to have power over it.

Chapter 7
Fear

> My God do not give me back to myself.
> Do not let me settle for anything but You.
> In You I hide escaping from my ruin
> Please, do not give me back to myself.
>
> — *Rumi*

Fear is the only thing to fear, as it will make it impossible for us to become coherent and aligned with our soul, thereby aligning with God and thus becoming spiritually empowered. As we examine fear we see ever more clearly the importance of love:

> There is no fear in love; but perfect love casteth out fear: because fear hath torment. He that feareth is not made perfect in love.
>
> — *1 John 4:18*

Love and fear are at the opposite ends of the spectrum. There is no fear in love, as how can there be an incoherent and fractured field within a coherent and unified field? How can there be disunity within unity, disharmony within harmony? Perfect love casteth out fear, because a coherent, unified, harmonious energy field cannot have the opposite residing within it and the frequency of love is greater, more powerful than the frequency of fear. Therefore, this statement of John's is an accurate statement in fact regarding the characteristics and behaviour of particular fields and their frequencies.

According to the dictionary, fear is a painful emotion caused by impending danger or evil. The dictionary gives the impression that fear only ever comes into play when danger or evil are present and if this were the case then fear would be a very useful and necessary thing. Fear manifesting as the result of real impending danger propels us to take some action that will protect us or remove us from the source of danger. Therefore, some might say we need this fearful alarm system to keep us safe. In the right place, at the right time and at this stage of our evolutionary journey, fear performs a necessary function. (When one is fully coherent and aligned fear will never arise no matter the situation, indeed it is not possible that it can, and it is neither required nor useful.)

The real problem with fear is that it is not just present during dangerous or evil times, it is pretty much rampant to one degree or another in our lives all of the time and it spares no one. The consequences of this all-pervading chaotic energy are many; we see it manifesting in our lives in large ways and small, of consequence and seemingly inconsequential, as it directs and controls us. Fear may keep us from heights, depths, water and contact with some members of the animal, insect or human kingdom, from various kinds of work or various kinds of pleasure. Fear may keep us from many things we desire. We may fear the future, being penniless, alone, sick or debilitated and very often fear may keep us from getting a good night's sleep. We have only to look at how recently so many of us plunged into an unthinking, unhinged state of overwhelming fear regarding the Covid so-called pandemic.

Fear blights our lives because it stops us from realising our full potential. We may do foolish things because fear – like anger, its offspring – clouds our judgement and our minds. Fear keeps us disconnected from each other, from the physical world and from all else that is. Most destructively, fear keeps us from alignment and union with our souls and therefore fear keeps us separated from God the divine source of our being. You may ask, "If fear is not from the Divine, what is its source? Why is it in our lives in the first place"? If we go back for a moment to the idea that everything is energy, fear is the primeval, inchoate (just begun, undeveloped, the origin) energy field of darkness out of which all is fashioned. Fear, the opposite of light, is where all darkness is to be found; fear is the opposite of unity and wholeness. Out of the inchoate energy fields of darkness, light is spun into creation by the resonance or focused intent of the Divine and all else in creation is thence spun from the light. So fear is the beginning of things – the myriad strands or strings are discordant, without Divine intent and therefore without intelligence, unity, coherence, purpose or pattern. Fear is all the musical notes jumbled together in an inharmonious, discordant and chaotic, jangled energy field. Fear is the raw material out of which the multiverse is fashioned. That is why we need it: the multiverse needs it; we cannot do without it. It is the stuff from which all things evolve, which is why it is so frightening, as fear is a slipping back into the darkness, the soulless, incoherent, mindless and without hope or purpose primeval energy field of the origin of all things. Fear is the negation, the end of us, back into the void of all beginnings. Fear is the death of our Divine Soul, the negation of life.

This is why fear is ever-present, as it is what we are moving away from – but as in the Buddhist wheel of life, until we are well along the spiral path, we may fall back into the field of fear at any time. At this stage of our journey, we are all still very much on the slippery slope where fear is often more familiar to us than love; where fear is ever-present but love is not; where what we are moving from exerts greater control over us than what we are moving towards; and where the possibility of losing our tiny spark of potential immortality is greater than our possibility of attaining it.

As fear is ever-present, so also is the urge to control. In our fear, which is inherently inchoate, we attempt to bring order and pattern by our finite control and this is why, where fear is present, one will always find the need to control. The amount of control we manifest in our lives is in direct proportion to the amount of fear that is present in all our fields. The two go hand in hand. We will never find one without the other. In our fear of fear, in our desire to create order, coherence, harmony and a sense of purpose where there is none, we endeavour to navigate the senselessness of the field of fear in our beings, and so construct false boundaries, points of reference, controls, dictates, rules, laws, methods, regularities, systems, routines, rituals, fixed points of view and judgements. Weaving all these false constructs around us in a moment by moment, self assuring, comforting and seemingly stabilising web of self-deception we do not defeat fear but actually feed it. The deeper we are immersed in fear and subsequently control, with all its structures, the more unconscious we become, the more blinded and the more removed from contact with our Divine Soul and hence God. If we are expert at weaving this web of self-deception, we may become almost powerless to change, because fear is voracious: the more we feed it, the greater it grows. It recognises no boundaries and no controls; it will take us over until we become almost only and purely fear, with the tiny spark that is our Divine Soul seed of unity, coherence, purpose and light almost extinguished by the all-encompassing, overwhelming field of inchoate incoherence that is fear.

If we look to the ever-wise *Bhagavad Gita* for guidance we will see there is a simple way out of the morass of fear:

> If thy soul finds rest in me, thou shalt overcome all dangers by my grace; but if thy thoughts are on thyself, and thou wilt not listen, thou shalt perish.
>
> — *Bhagavad Gita 18:58*

Grace is Divine regeneration, an inspiring and strengthening influence; in other words, the only way out of the inchoate field of fear is to turn in the direction of, focus upon (through the agency of our divine soul) the Divine Creative Field – God. If our focus is primarily anywhere else, such as on ourselves and or our material needs, materialism in general, or outwards in any way, then we will be unable to evolve and we run the risk of destroying our divine immortal soul, or at best we remain stuck in the field of fear without end. This should bring all to the realisation of the truth of the statement, "The only thing to fear is fear itself."

In order to make greater sense of all this, let us look at the whole or holistic view. Everything is evolving out of the field of fear towards the field of love. Fear is as complex, yet in essence simple and essential in the whole scheme of things, as love. Fear is the evolutionary process thrusting out of itself towards the light. This is a dynamic and natural process and not one to be feared. It is a process to be understood, then with understanding we can move with facility from the field of fear towards the field of love as it is desired we do. Falling back into fear is an act of involution, therefore not something we really want to be doing. Destructively, fear keeps us from alignment and union with our souls; it obstructs us from unfolding and evolving as we are meant to; and ultimately it hinders our alignment and union with God. And without completion of this process, immortality is only a potentiality.

It is extremely difficult for most of us to confront and slay this ancient enemy in all its myriad guises. I will not here go into all the many and varied fears we all suffer from suffice to say, it is a good idea to acknowledge our fears and look them in the face, because the odd thing about fear, for all its seeming power, is that it is actually quite powerless. As we confront a particular fear, it will dissolve away. This is because the incoherent nature of a field of fear means that as soon as it comes into contact with a field that is more inclined to coherence, if only to a small degree, it has no option but to become more coherent. It will appear to move back and away, thereby automatically allowing the field of greater coherence more space to unfold. This is because the natural movement, the thrust, of the multiverse is towards greater coherence, hence there is greater power when moving in this direction. Once again the art of Wu Wei comes into play, because when flowing with the intent of the multiverse our actions are automatically possessed of greater power. Therefore, even though fear is irrational and one can't reason with it, and even though fear's origin is from the beginning times and its field is part of ours and our memory of it is buried deep within our psyche, all that is required to rid ourselves of it is that we replace this field of fear with another of greater coherence and refinement. Once we understand the essential nature of the bogeyman, once we have accomplished "Know thyself", once we understand our pathway and the power of love, once we rest secure in our contact with God, then a great deal of the power fear has over us will fall away quite naturally and easily without any conscious effort on our part to address it.

Many of the people we so mistakenly call "successful" are those most run and controlled by fear. It is in the fear of being out of control that they become politicians, heads of the world controlling us all, or so they think. Their need to control is often out of control and grows ever-greater with each passing moment so there is no respite for them. Often the wealthiest among us arrived at that position through their immense fear of poverty, of being no one of importance and without power. Their temporal power and control give them the illusion of having beaten their fear. However, fear is not easily slain in this manner, it is only fed, and so the fear grows until death or dis-ease causes change. There are numberless people living with fields composed primarily of fear. In an interview with the *Daily Telegraph*, the rock singer Ozzy Osbourne describes his ever-present, all-pervading irrational fear:

> I have always been in fear, always blamed myself for situations that have got nothing to do with me. You wake up every day and think, "Why am I feeling like this?" I'd be afraid because I didn't feel afraid.

Alcohol made it temporarily go away, but, as time went on, the fear was breaking through the alcohol.

There are possibly many who wish to hold on to their fear, as within their field of fear and seeming control they have a very nice little kingdom indeed. They are the king or queen directing and controlling all within their sphere. They are running the universe, everything is down to them; they are in supreme control of all. Of course, this is not so, because about all any of us manages to control is our own massive delusion – and isn't it exhausting? How often, although we would never admit it to anyone, we wish that it would all just stop and we could let go and have someone else take over for a while as it really is just too much to ask of any one person, and above all else it is just not fair! Although we feel quite virtuous, as how would everyone around us manage without our stupendous effort at keeping everything under control? Everything would be a shambles, wouldn't it. So, we can't stop, because if we did, we would just disappear, as it is only our enormous control that is keeping everything held together in existence, isn't it. That is the scariest thing of all, the possibility that we would cease to exist if we did not keep exerting all this controlling energy. We feel the world would stop turning on its axis, the stars would darken, the sun would disappear, and all would disappear into a Black Hole never to be seen again. In our darkness and ignorance, in our field of fear, we think this is about as good as it is possible to get and anyway, we don't have a choice, do we? Also, we are so used to the darkness and the seeming smallness of our world that it is comforting in a funny sort of way. Everything has become so blocked, almost like concrete, that we have a semblance of stability which helps to make us feel safe, so it is probably better to keep everything as it is, isn't it?

If all or part of the above is going on, we need to bear in mind that our position is one of complete powerlessness despite apparent appearances. Our seeming grip and control on all aspects of our lives is an illusion; we have no power source but our finite, fearful will. More importantly, we are stuck, we have ceased to evolve. Depending upon how deep in the mire we have allowed ourselves to become, we may find that great effort will be required if we are to extricate ourselves and move forward. We will probably decide to do this only when we have finally had enough. When we can't take any more of our field of fear, or when because of outside agencies we are no longer able to hold the control in place, then we will move. It is so much better if we choose to move, as if we do not, the multiverse will force us. We will be thrust into change, even if we are the greatest controller of all time, as exhaustion, dis-ease, death and the evolutionary thrust will get all of us sooner or later. As we are driven towards ever-greater refinement, if we should cling to fear and its offspring as the only familiar things we know, then we will suffer endless pain and distress as we are striving against the powerful intent of the Divine Creative Field. It is always better and less painful if we of our own free will consciously choose to evolve, releasing all fear, as we then can to a degree direct and control our pace along the evolutionary path. If we must be coerced/forced by the ever-present natural forces of the evolutionary thrust, we will undoubtedly suffer pain, confusion and maybe greater fear, together with the ever-present risk of falling back altogether into the field of fear and being lost within it. On this subject, the *Bhagavad Gita* says eloquently:

> If thou wilt not fight thy battle of life because in selfishness thou art afraid of the battle, thy resolution is in vain: nature will compel thee. Because thou art in the bondage of Karma, of the forces of thine own past life; and that which thou, in thy delusion, with a good will dost not want to do, unwillingly thou shalt have to do.
>
> — *Bhagavad Gita 18:59–60*

The greatest fear for most of us lurking beneath everything else is the fear of death. Many people would say that fear of death is their greatest overall fear. Death is the one thing none can escape, although we can, when we know how, direct and control the process of dying and beyond. If we must be controllers, at least let us use that ability intelligently where the control is real; use it to direct and control what is possible to be directed and controlled, where there is real benefit. Let us use the ability to control only with real knowledge, understanding and power. Let us use it to direct and control our flow towards the field of the Divine Creative Field of Love. Let us not use our ability to control to hold ourselves frozen in the field of fear.

What is this thing we call death? Why do we fear it? I do not believe it is possible to live without fear, unfolding/evolving as we should with power, unless we fully understand death and its processes and thus lose all fear of it. Unless we are comfortable with and knowledgeable of all aspects of death and dying before, during and after the point we call death, we will always retain an element of fear in our fields. Most people's belief systems on living and dying will fall into one of two categories. In the one, we have all those who believe we are born out of nothingness or perhaps something, but they are not sure what. Most likely, it was all some big accident without any rhyme or reason. We then live for a short while, enjoy ourselves, or suffer pain, loss, drama and then die, which means we are extinguished, cease to exist. What we were, somehow magically vanishes forever. That all sounds very sensible, rational and logical, doesn't it? It makes nonsense of so many things we experience and see on a daily basis, but many people cling tenaciously to this belief system.

The second category is composed of all the people who hold a variety of beliefs that encompass innate morality, conscience, an immortal soul and some form of life after death in heaven, hell or various other space-time continuums. Some belief systems hold that we are born repeatedly, shedding the physical body when it is time, to return at another time in another physical body; this process is called reincarnation.

If we look at the first category, famous left-brain thinkers such as Richard Dawkins espouse this view, declaring that there is no God, there is no soul etc. If the left-brain can't comprehend the implicate realms – which it can't – then the implicate realms do not exist.

Simple, isn't it? These brilliant left-brains say, "We live and die and that is the end of it." However, as we have seen, the path to the soul and thence to God can only be travelled utilising the entire being: employing just the left-brain will be of little assistance. To look at the idea of death through the left-brain alone is so limiting as to be impossible. Again, we must employ the entire being.

Words are inadequate to explain profound things. Words are great for cat, cow, dog, telegraph pole and so on, to identify things in the physical world, but when we try to describe metaphysical processes, we run into trouble. This is why the religions of the world use allegory and symbols in their often vain attempt to describe the metaphysical and associated processes. Their message as a result is often lost and the religion is then ridiculed as being so much myth and nonsense purely because we fail to understand or cannot discern the truth hidden in the allegory, myths and symbols.

To come to grips with death and what it is exactly, let's look at some passages from the *Gita:*

> Interwoven in his creation, the Spirit is beyond destruction. No one can bring to an end the Spirit which is everlasting.
>
> For beyond time he dwells in these bodies, though these bodies have an end in their time; but he remains immeasurable, immortal.
>
> Therefore, great warrior, carry on thy fight. If any man thinks he slays, and if another thinks he is slain, neither knows the ways of truth. The Eternal in man cannot kill: the Eternal in man cannot die.
>
> He is never born, and he never dies. He is in Eternity: he is for evermore. Never born and eternal, beyond times gone or to come, he does not die when the body dies.
>
> When a man knows him as never born, everlasting, never-changing, beyond all destruction, how can that man kill a man, or cause another to kill?

As a man leaves an old garment and puts on one that is new, the Spirit leaves his mortal body and then puts on one that is new.

Weapons cannot hurt the Spirit and fire can never burn him. Untouched is he by drenching waters, untouched is he by parching winds.

Beyond the power of sword and fire, beyond the power of waters and winds, the Spirit is everlasting, omnipresent, never-changing, never-moving, ever One.

Invisible is he to mortal eyes, beyond thought and beyond change. Know that he is, and cease from sorrow.

But if he were born again and again; and again, and again he were to die, even then, victorious man, cease thou from sorrow.

For all things born in truth must die, and out of death in truth comes life. Face to face with what must be, cease thou from sorrow.

Invisible before birth are all beings and after death invisible again. They are seen between two unseens. Why in this truth find sorrow?

The Spirit that is in all beings is immortal in them all: for the death of what cannot die, cease thou to sorrow.

— Bhagavad Gita 2:17–30

There is not much lost or obscured in that message, is there? According to the *Gita,* there is no such thing as death. What we call death is only the death of the bag of water that contains our primary energy field. The bag of water drops off and decays as we leave this particular space-time continuum. According to the Hindu and many other belief systems, our modern view of death is quite incorrect. Death, like so much else, they say, is an illusion and scientists are beginning to agree with them. Merely because we are unable to see the primal energy field leaving the bag of water is no reason to say the primal energy field no longer exists. Because most of us in the explicate realms (not all) are unable to see it is no reason for illogically presuming that it has magically vanished into nothingness, back presumably into the field from whence it came. (Of course, the left-brain thinkers believe there is no primal energy field to begin with, that we are merely and only a manifested physical bag of water.)

The Bible is more obscure on the subject, but one of its most often quoted passages on death is as follows:

> Jesus said, I am the resurrection, and the life: he that believeth in me, though he were dead, yet shall he live. And whosoever liveth and believeth in me shall never die. Believest thou this?
>
> —*John 11:25–26*

Here again we have the subject of belief entering. Belief appears to be an integral part of the process, as to believe in something is to imbue it with life. In the fluid energy field of constant creation that is our multiverse, for something to be, there must first be the sound or focused intent spiral of creation forming in the background field and a belief system must presage these processes. Accordingly, what we believe in becomes our resultant reality, if for example, we live a life believing in and imbued with fear, then that will be our experience of life, so we begin to understand that belief is a fundamental piece of the puzzle. If we believe we are a divine immortal soul, in loving interaction and relationship with a loving God, then that will be our reality. Conversely, if we believe in nothing, then *that* will be our reality. If we believe in trauma, chaos and pain, *that* will be our reality. If we believe in all things positive, then *that* will be our reality. Belief is everything; without belief in the possibility of something, it cannot be made manifest. Here Jesus is saying that he himself is an aspect of God (as we all are through the agency of our divine soul) and further that with a belief in God we are giving greater life to our soul as it is then directly and consciously connected to its source, the Divine. Through this direct relationship which can only come about through our belief in the Divine, we are assured of immortality. Our soul is allowed free expression, growth and continuance. That which we believe in, we create, feed and evolve.

With this belief system in place, even if our physical body is dead, yet we will live through the agency of our immortal soul in relationship with the Divine, which we have imbued with life by making it a reality. Jesus repeats the same message but in a slightly different way: "If you are alive, if you believe what I am teaching, you will never die." This does not mean our physical body will not die; it will, but the essential aspect of us, our soul, will continue. As we have said before, we need to be aware that we are behaving in a dangerous manner if we do not believe in our own divine aspect, our immortal soul, for if we do not believe in the possibility of divinity and immortality, we risk destroying our soul: how may something live that we are denying life?

In order to move towards the light of God, to clear our field of fear and negativity, we must first believe in the process. We must believe these things are possible otherwise they will not be. More importantly, we run the risk of destroying our soul; so it is only with belief in the process that we can be assured of immortal life. Immortal life is something we have to earn; it is not an automatic gift or right. If the idea of a quantum coherent field/soul being able to remain in existence with memory and consciousness continuing on after the collapse of the manifested bag of water is a distinct rational and logical possibility, then our view of death, not to mention of life, must change radically. When we fear death, is this perhaps fear of an illusion, as so many of our fears are?

In looking at how best to rid ourselves of our all-pervading fears we need again to look at the power of our mind and our belief systems, as this aspect is primary in our journey along the evolutionary path. As we are ourselves tiny fragments/sparks of the Divine Creative Field, we also are creators; very limited, but creators nevertheless. As creators, what we believe in, what we dwell upon with focused intent, is what we will manifest. Remember, we must first have it to get it. If we don't have it, we can't get it. Or, to put it another way, in order to receive something, we must first believe that the thing we are wanting exists. If we don't believe it exists, then it is not a possibility for us. This is logical. If we believe in the Divine and immortal souls, this will be our reality. It is impossible for us to make something a reality that we do not first believe in. If we believe in fear, it will exist for us – we will be fearful. If we do not believe in fear because we believe in something else more attractive instead, then fear will not exist for us – we will not be fearful. It is as simple and as difficult as that. To the degree that we believe in the Divine, which is perfect love, is the degree to which the fear in our life falls away.

It is not possible to live in full conscious awareness as a wholly integrated being unless we lose our fear of death. To do that we need to understand death in all its ramifications, processes, meaning and full glory. It is logical that if we are afraid of death we will be filled with fear during our life, as there is one great certainty in our life and that is that we will die sometime. There will always be a part of ourselves that is fearful unless we understand death and so lose our fear of it.

So how do we go about understanding this forbidden subject? The quickest way to clear a room, a dinner party perhaps, is to raise the subject. No one wishes to discuss it, or very few will. Death is an integral part of life because we are living on an ever-changing planet that is itself within a solar system forever on the move, with all coming into being, changing and evolving as an integral part of its energy system and essential law. Without change, there is no movement and our entire known universe and everything in it is always in a state of flux. Those seemingly safe places we create to protect ourselves cannot protect us from death and its processes. In order to live fully and truly safely, our lives must be without fear of any kind. The word "death" is somewhat of a misnomer, as we understand the word to mean the end of life. However, we know it is impossible to destroy energy; the only thing that can happen with energy is it merely changes its form. Therefore, if we are energy beings as we must be, because ultimately there is nothing else, how may we disappear? Surely, all that we may do under the laws of the multiverse is to change our form. To die is merely to change our form, as all the ancient, learned scriptures expound. Death is nothing to be afraid of, as quite simply all that happens is that we leave our lower vibratory explicate physical body at the same time as we also appear to leave this space-time continuum. The degree that we identify with the physical will be to a large degree the extent of our fear of death. If our whole world of meaning is constructed almost solely of physical things, things that one can see, feel, taste and touch, then of course death is terrifying – because it appears to be the end of all that. Death is then something to be denied at all costs, something to put our heads in the sand about: don't talk about it, then maybe it will not happen; it happens to others, but it will not happen to me, not for a very, very, long time yet anyway.

Sorry, it could happen in the next minute. We all need to know about it; we need to understand how to do it properly, with ease, mastery and glory. We need to know what lies beyond so-called death in order that we may navigate with direction and power through those, at first, foreign realms.

It is because of our great fear of death that we modern beings, particularly in western cultures, look upon death as a dreadful thing, something to be denied, to be avoided at all costs and for as long as possible. We carry this avoidance often to the point of maiming ourselves both physically and spiritually. We befuddle our souls with medical drugs and medical intervention causing ourselves needless pain and distress. Many times, this results in our being not only unable to die in a state of full conscious awareness, but we die having no real awareness of any kind. We are often so sedated that our condition after death can only be painful and confused. Instead of our soul's journey being the beautiful rite of illumined passage and spiritual power it should be, we die drugged, and our soul at the same level of evolution it was at our birth. We have neglected and impeded the normal natural processes, and thereby our journeying through death and on to the other realms of the multiverse, we die in a state of ignorance and confusion, distressed and agonised – a hell indeed. Far better to accept the inevitable natural processes in full conscious awareness, with knowledge, skill and dignity, and to consequently experience a gracious, beautiful and peaceful journey infused with and guided by the Divine. Dying should above all be a cause for celebration, for a life lived well and for a soul which is hopefully now more fully unfolded, journeying on, infused with greater wisdom, love and spiritual power in its successful transformation to another phase of its epic journey. Dying can only be like this if we have the wisdom and understanding of the true reality and purpose of life, death and beyond.

We, the ones left behind, weep and wail, but we are really weeping for ourselves as we feel bereft, cut off from the departed soul. That person can now, we feel, no longer love us or help us. The great mistake we are making here is in believing in mortality. Because in fact, a soul that is discarnate is able to be closer, more helpful and to pervade our entire being in ways that were never possible for them while in the physical form. This is a comfort, and a warning. Discarnate beings out of the realm of physicality may have more power to connect with us and overlay our souls, pervading our entire fields, than they were ever able to do while in manifested physical form. Depending upon the degree to which this is happening, this is as bad for us as it is for the discarnate being, and as the next stage from death this is not a positive outcome.

Knowing this quite ordinary fundamental wisdom, when we find ourselves in the presence of death – from the centre of our being, aligned with our soul, in our unified field of spiritual power directly informed by God through the agency of our divine immortal soul – we will know there has not been any separation. In our state of loving unconditionally, without desiring anything for ourselves from the person who is dying, we will see the full glory of death and realise all that is required from us is to help them onwards, guide their journey, celebrate and acknowledge their life and give thanks for the gift of having known them. If it is our own death, then when we are able to generate a field of Divine unconditional love at will, we will be dissolved within this field. Even in the midst of initially great pain, unconditional love, the great solvent, dissolves pain instantly. We will then rest serene and peaceful within the loving field of the Divine Creator, through the agency of our soul, knowing that all is well and there is absolutely nothing to fear, because the field of love cannot contain fear within it. In this field we will be guided every step along the way as the Divine Intelligence desires and we will be again practising the noble art of Wu Wei. The next adventure starts here. When we can encompass death in this way, we will have lost all fear of it. Of course, there are all the degrees in between, but any movement in the right direction is helpful and positive.

Many ancient cultures that had conscious and acknowledged acceptance of the Divine in all things interwove this knowledge into their daily lives and as a result had great wisdom regarding the processes of dying and what one can expect immediately after the experience, we call death. A good modern source of this valuable information is *The Tibetan Book of Living and Dying* by Sogyal Rinpoche. To know how to die well, with knowledge and skill, read Part Two, "Dying", and Part Three, "Death and Rebirth". Living and dying well go hand in hand. We cannot be ignorant about or ignore death without causing problems in life.

There is a commonly held misconception about the afterlife, that after we have changed our form we will somehow magically know things we did not know before, we will be an improved character; we will magically be elevated to a higher plane spiritually by the mere act of leaving our physical body behind. In other words, the belief is that merely by dying we will be changed into a better, wiser, more knowledgeable and spiritually evolved being. This just isn't logical or possible. How can we obtain this extra knowledge, how may we obtain this greater goodness, love and spirituality, merely by changing our form? In fact, we will die as we have lived and, once dead, we will know only that which we knew before death. Our spiritual wisdom, awareness, level of evolution, love and power will be exactly the same dead as alive. How can it be otherwise? Jesus had this to say on the subject:

> Look to the living one [God] as long as you live, otherwise you might die and then try to see the living one, and you will be unable to see.
>
> — *Gospel of Thomas 59*

Our opportunities for growth, for the gaining of wisdom, love and spiritual power are here in the explicate realms. Once we are again in the implicate, the opportunity has passed. We have lost that time and experience. The time and place to evolve is here while alive. This is why we are here. So today set out to learn about all we have spoken of here, so that we may set ourselves free from all impeding fear. Then the words of St John will have real meaning in our life: "Ye shall know the truth, and the truth shall make you free." The truth without a doubt does set us free. Understanding the wisdom and laws that underwrite the multiverse, understanding the Divine Creative Field, our soul and ourselves is fundamental for the next step along our path to ever-greater freedom. With this knowledge, we will begin to lose our fear not only of death but also of change, which of course contains death within it. After the fear of death, this is the most powerful fear that has us in its grip. Just as with love the most difficult leap – that of loving what is possibly an abstract, God – was the first step, so it is with fear. The greatest fear – death – is the first one we must overcome, and after this the other fears, of change, the unknown, difference and so on, naturally fall away.

In reality, there is nothing to fear in all the multiverse except possibly ourselves. Only we can do real harm to ourselves. The only things that may harm us will be the natural consequences of all our thoughts, words, actions and inactions. Therefore, our thought could be, "If I choose to fear at all, then the only thing I need fear at all is myself." Another cannot hurt us unless we choose to allow it. Everything rests upon our responses to a situation. This does not mean we will not be hurt physically, as this material plane of existence is full of all those possibilities for learning. However, our reaction to the perceived hurt is everything. Should we choose only to observe it, to watch it pass through us and beyond, "leaving no residue", then our soul has not been harmed in any way and in fact we will have grown and expanded from the lesson inherent in the experience. We can choose to set ourselves free, to fly with conscious ease along our soul journey, knowing that it is fear and its offspring resistance, anger and all those other dark thoughts, words and deeds that cripple, ensnare and enslave us.

There can be no room in our life for fear of any kind, great or small. Look all fears in the face and ask, "What is the very worst thing that can happen?" Then look again and walk on. Understand all fears for what they truly are – illusory. Hit the delete button and walk on fearless. Install a new software program based on a loving, unattached, wise acceptance of all and in this greater alignment and therefore greater coherence walk on the evolutionary path to ever-greater wisdom, love, and spiritual power. Know that dying is merely changing form, as the chrysalis does into the butterfly. Choose to do this as naturally and as elegantly as the chrysalis, then we may hang gently, like a beautiful butterfly calmly drying its wings in the sunshine, before we fly on.

Chapter 8
Free Will

> Trust in the Lord with all thine heart and mind; do not rely upon your own understanding. Seek His will in all you do, recognize, and acknowledge Him, and He will direct and make straight your path.
>
> — *Proverbs 3:5–6*

We have talked a great deal about evolving which will result in our fields achieving a higher spin rate, and therefore greater refinement wisdom, love and spiritual power. We have expounded these ideas as though they are achievable. Are they really? Contemporary evidence and many ancient philosophies agree they are, but there are a number of aspects blocking us from easily achieving this advancement, and in order to advance and overcome these obstacles to our growth, we need to know what they are. In addition, we need to understand fully another great and primary key if we are to succeed in our quest.

Before too long in any discussion of a theosophical nature, the question will arise, "Do we have free will?" Are we able to do, have or be anything we want, as and when and how we want it, as some self-improvement philosophies teach? My answer to this question is always a resounding "No." This is because we are bound and limited by the patterns and laws of the Divine Creative Field together with the level of our own evolution. The inherent blocks and fracturing within our fields can be overcome with focus, intent and wisdom, but all can only proceed as and when the patterns and laws of the Divine Creative Field allows. It is important that we understand our limitations within the system, as to believe that at this time we are capable of achieving, with enough focus and intent, anything our hearts desire will lead only to inevitable failure and then disillusionment. If disillusioned, we may then give up our entire spiritual evolutionary quest. Therefore, it is vitally important that we understand the many aspects that are stopping us from being totally free and having absolute free will, because it is only with this understanding that we will be able to move forward towards the most freedom of will we can achieve. Gaining a clear understanding of our will in context with the Divine Will is another of the great keys to the mystery without which it will be impossible to succeed. So let us look at some of the aspects that are blocking us from unfettered individual free will.

An ancient Arabian saying is: "A man's fate is bound on his brow at birth." What this means is that our destiny is planned prior to birth, and only limited movement from the blueprint is allowed. The life path is predetermined, no matter the apparent freedom of thought or action. Fundamentally, we are only able to follow the pre-arranged pattern, and any apparent free will is within the confines of that plan. The creator of the pattern, Allah/The Divine Creative Field through the agency of the Divine Immortal Soul, has overarching control over all the aspects of the pre-set energy pattern which is itself an integral part of the interconnected cosmic whole. Therefore, there is no free will as such.

Palmistry dictates a similar idea in the belief that delineated on our palms is the map or blueprint of the forthcoming life. The pattern, written for all to read who have the wisdom, is the destiny, the fate and path the life will follow. As we know, no two people have exactly the same palm print; the markings on each palm of all the billions of people populating the Earth are unique. This in itself is quite extraordinary. We are marked for all to read who know how and there is a school of thought that proposes, that should we make advances of a spiritual or self-improvement nature, then certain of the lines will change, and it is by the changing of these lines that we receive clear confirmation that we have indeed made progress. However, any change in the essential blueprint is small and limited in relation to the entire plan. Therefore, there is no free will as such.

Pre-cognition, the action or faculty of "knowing" and sometimes "seeing (with inner sight) and hearing (with inner hearing)" before an event takes place, has been studied seriously by many scientists, particularly in Russia. If we accept pre-cognition as a reality, then we must also accept that some things are predestined; otherwise, how is it possible to see or experience something before it has happened and often many years before it happens? Therefore, there is no free will as such.

Astrology describes the metaphysical structures and the essence of the personality, carefully plotting in detail using only the information of the subject's birth date, time and place. The idea behind this ancient science is that the particular placement of the heavenly bodies and subsequent energy patterning creates a corresponding resonance which becomes inherent in and integral to the birthing energy field. Each individual arrives with a particular patterning in their energy field that is as unique as their fingerprints and will influence all aspects of their life – motives, actions, reactions, abilities, desires, physical weaknesses, emotions, family interactions, likes and dislikes and so on – to a great degree. Therefore, there is no free will as such.

Inherited genetic programming means that when we are functioning as physical beings in the explicate realm, we arrive here with particular inbuilt software programming. Inherited from our ancestors, these are memory programs as opposed to genetic ones: memory initiated by and embedded in an ancestor from their life experience is passed down through the generations, adding and mingling with each new arrival. As the Bible puts it:

> The Lord is long-suffering and slow to anger, and abundant in mercy and loving kindness, forgiving iniquity and transgression, but He will by no means clear the guilty, visiting the iniquity of the fathers upon the children, unto the third and fourth generation.
>
> — *Numbers 14:18*

Other passages change this slightly to say:

> I, the Lord your God, am a jealous God, visiting the iniquity of the fathers upon the children unto the third and fourth generation of those who hate Me.
>
> — *Deuteronomy 5:9, also Exodus 20:5*

This idea of a parent's (presumably it is not confined to fathers only) iniquity being passed on to offspring is a common theme throughout many spiritual texts. This is particularly interesting as it implies that only negative memories are stored and passed on. Memories from events that were in opposition to the evolutionary thrust and the Divine Creative Field/God remain stuck in the field and are passed on to those closely linked energetically. My experience with those who bring to their surface consciousness while engaged in particular energy healing modalities, recover only negative events. It appears that positive events are not stored and passed on in this way: events that send a negative charge out into the interconnected field of the multiverse must somehow be negated or resolved, under the law of "as ye sow so shall ye reap". If the source of the charge does not "reap" or somehow else negate the charge, then the offspring inherit the debt for resolution as the source of the charge is the only possibility for resolution and under this law the offspring are considered the same as the source. In other words, it is not possible that the field just absorbs a negative charge and deletes it without the source suffering some effect from the creation of such a charge. Even though the end resolution may be the fourth generation from the source, the law has still applied. This should give an added pause for thought before creating such negative events.

What this means for those of us who inherit these memory programs is that we may be acting out, or responding to, something in this life because of the embedded memory of an event experienced by, say, a great-grandfather. With these programs in place, we are unable to act from conscious free will, but rather act or react in particular circumstances according to a memory implanted in our being of which in most cases we are completely consciously unaware. In order to have greater freedom and to redeem the actions of an ancestor we need to become aware of these programs and work towards deleting them. There is a very clear and simple indication that memory programs of one kind or another are running: you hear the words "I had to do so and so" or "I have no choice, I have to do so and so". People speaking in this manner are running memory programs and are speaking the literal truth, as they are prisoners of the inherited memory programs and are acting as obedient automatons. When we are clear of these programs, we will never think or speak in this way, as we will know we have the free will to behave as we choose, albeit with limited free will.

If we add to this multiplicity of inherited memory programs our programming from parents, school, family, friends and so on, free we are not. We are reactive, polarised prisoners of our unconscious and subjective worlds. Our many acts and reactions are for a great part a pre-programmed response to stimuli both external and internal. To think we are in charge of our lives, in control and running things, is to function under a deep delusion. The sooner we realise what is really going on and start to make changes, as these programs are simply deleted if we are working from our higher vibratory soul field, the sooner we can set ourselves on the path to greater coherence and freedom. We may then begin to function from a centre of light-filled coherent conscious awareness, which will naturally generate greater freedom, rather than from the unconscious and incoherent darkness of pre-programmed captivity. While we are reacting unconsciously to stimuli based upon internal memory programs, there is no free will as such.

If we consider all the many addictions we may indulge in that often stem from the above inherited programs, such as anger, love of chaos, love of control, self-pity, being a victim, centred in the ego, fear, dis-ease, the need for constant noise, constant attention, constant diversion, constant activity, constant work, overuse of alcohol, drugs – legal and illegal – gambling and more, we can see clearly that free we are not. Therefore there is no free will as such.

If all the above were not enough, we have the hundredth monkey to consider. Studies carried out in the 1950s on a group of monkeys living on a Japanese island revealed a startling result. The researchers fed sweet potatoes to the monkeys, one of which started to wash the potatoes as they were quite dirty. Soon another monkey copied this action and in a relatively short space of time a great many monkeys were all washing the potatoes. When the number performing this particular action reached approximately one hundred, or critical mass, all the monkeys, including others on other islands – that is, monkeys without contact of any physical kind with the first group – also performed the same action. This phenomenon has been termed "morphogenetic resonance", or the hundredth monkey aspect. What is worrying is not only monkeys are susceptible to this process, but that we of course are too. Therefore, if enough of us think a certain thing, suddenly most of us are thinking the same thing as well. How scary is that? This hundredth monkey phenomenon shows us once again that it is not possible to take a single separated thought or action, since it will always affect the whole if only to such a tiny degree that we are unable to register it at the time. There is another way to look at this phenomenon – we have a glimpse of just how powerful we can be should we choose. We have the possibility to move millions in a positive manner, and the more aligned, coherent, and whole we are, the more powerfully we can promote change for the better.

With the hundredth monkey in mind, it appears that others may make enormous life-changing decisions on our behalf without us even being aware of it. With no coherent centre, no semblance of conscious free will, we will find ourselves swept along with the tide of public opinion, subject to all the winds that blow no matter their source, their quality or their direction. Suddenly we may find ourselves thinking, doing and believing things we never thought of before. These changes in our thoughts and subsequent behaviour due to a thought-form reaching critical mass may be positive or negative. If positive, that is well and good – but it may be, and often is, negative and is therefore detrimental to our entire being, the multiverse and everything within it. We need therefore to practise great vigilance, discernment and a constant and conscious connection to the Divine Creative Field to ensure our full protection at all times. It may well be a matter of life and death: it is not possible to over-dramatise the danger here. It is always wise to ask throughout the day, during all our activities, "How conscious am I? Why am I saying this? Why am I doing this? Is my behaviour making sense? Where are these thoughts coming from?" and, most powerfully, "Who does this belong to?" If the thought's origin is indeed within yourself, it will become stronger; if it is not your own it will move back and possibly completely away. In this manner we may start to take control of our own thoughts and actions. This constant policing of our thoughts is a good habit to develop as it will start to increase conscious awareness and hence free will. With the aspect of morphogenetic resonance at play, unless we have a profound and conscious connection to the Divine through the agency of our soul, we may find ourselves powerfully dominated and controlled by the thought forms of others. Therefore, there is no free will as such.

As a species we are at a particular point in our evolution, so until we choose to direct our attention towards the Divine (we have the free will to do this) we are controlled and limited by our level of development. Therefore, there is no free will as such.

Even should we choose to reject most of the above, there is one aspect we cannot overlook when considering the subject of free will – we must take into account the structure of the system in which we live and breathe and have our being. As the multiverse is a single contiguous field and there is no such thing as separation, our free will must of necessity be bound by the pattern, laws, intent and actions of the whole. If we are part of an immense web, how can it be possible that we may run amok and gratify our every whim as and when we choose? There is individuality, yes, different facets of the whole, rather like a large diamond with each one of us a facet, but we are an intrinsic part of the unified whole. So how can it be possible that one facet of the diamond has total free will? This intrinsic unity is why "we are our brother's keeper": if we harm others, we harm the whole, and therefore we harm ourselves. Conversely, if we harm ourselves, we harm others. Everything within the unified field is in relationship with and has an effect upon the entire field.

We obviously have some limited free will in that we may, for instance, kill our brother should we choose. This action, however, will harm the perpetrator far more than the victim, as this is an act of involution in opposition to the evolutionary forces and intent of God. It will fracture the soul field and propel the perpetrator into greater incoherence and chaos, back towards the inchoate field of all beginnings. The one who has been killed conversely suffers no real harm, as their soul field will not have been damaged by this act visited upon the enveloping bag of water.

We are too insignificant and powerless to cause irreparable damage to the unified field. However, the act of murder will have sent a negative charge out into the field. A negation of an aspect of life has been created and that will undoubtedly cause an effect, under the law of "what ye sow, so shall ye reap". Without question, we have the free will to behave badly should we choose, but our free will is of the order of a small child. Within a family that child may be destructive, violent, have screaming temper tantrums and refuse to eat, learn, play properly, share and so on, but all those acts of bad behaviour are within boundaries set by the parents. The child's ability to be truly free, to be totally evil and destructive, or even totally good and creative, is all limited by the system within which he or she is bound. We are that child within the multiverse, with everything dependent upon everything else: we are caught in and are part of a vast web. Therefore, there is no free will as such.

> Does aught befall you? It is good. It is part of the destiny of the Universe ordained for you from the beginning. All that befalls you is part of the great web.
>
> — *Marcus Aurelius*

There are literally thousands of books, videos and courses available today that offer the illusion of free will. They teach that if only we knew how to be positive, how to visualise and focus, we could create for ourselves all the things and events we wish. Most of these processes are merely tinkering about on the surface: they do not and cannot get to the core of the problem. If these processes are able to make life easier, happier and better in some ways, then of course they are a positive activity. However, it is wise to understand the limits of these relatively isolated processes with their inevitable partial result and dead end. We need also to recognise the inherent danger with a great many of these processes as what we are in fact doing is installing another program into our being – which probably has quite enough already. With each new program, we lessen our conscious awareness, possibly further fracture our being and therefore lessen our free will. Before installing new memory programs, the sensible thing to do is to delete the programs already present. Once this is accomplished to a degree, there will be no need of such processes; indeed, the idea of them will be abhorrent. Once our fields are clear to a degree, our soul recognised and allowed to unfold, once a clear and conscious connection to the Divine is accomplished, there is no need for any new programs. The power and wisdom that inflows from being aligned and connected to our source enables us to accomplish all that is required in the material realms and beyond. When we have a clear understanding of ourselves and the system in which we live, then we realise that these programs are at best just another overlaying of charge in an already overburdened and fractured energy field. These processes do not set us free; they do not generate wisdom, love and spiritual power. At best, they may enable us to procure more temporal wealth or power, or they are a temporary palliative. At worst, they lead us down an illusionary material path whereby we may become disillusioned, as we will be unable to make these processes work properly and may then give up all ideas of personal change. Often, these processes are promoted and used for the acquiring of more material goodies such as how to be more efficient and better at work, how to make more money. Many of these processes negate life; it is the work of involution and imprisonment. If we are on an evolutionary path, working towards a more fully aligned, coherent and conscious awareness, we will reject these processes as memory implants of the same old dead end warfare game of "survival of the fittest" dressed up with New Age or personal development labels. If all our activities take place with knowledge of the larger picture, in loving conscious relationship with and under the laws of the Divine Creative Field/God, then we are functioning as an aligned, conscious and powerful aspect of the Divine web of the multiverse. As such, we are able to receive the creative assistance, wisdom, love, power and abundance that we need, limited only by our ability to receive, our evolutionary level and the will of the Divine Creative Field.

As we have seen, and as worldwide events currently make clear, we are in a time of great change, that may be rapid progress for us all if we are able to navigate the tumultuous energies. Because of current powerful cyclical planetary positioning, solar cycles and other factors, we will all experience great and rapid change over the coming years. Old, buried, half-forgotten wisdom and knowledge is being revealed on a daily basis. It is imperative that we all come to know and understand that which has been lost. The energy shift that has revealed this information has also made possible our own shift in consciousness so that, for a great many of us, this knowledge is something we now wish to seek. Our minds are opening and consequently we seek and can understand this new – for us – information. This process has been going on in an intense way for the last twenty years. Consequently, we are getting close to the hundredth monkey – critical mass. Once this point has been reached, an immense simultaneous shift in consciousness will move vast swathes of the world's population without them ever having to take the deliberate and conscious step themselves to make change. When change happens to us in this way, without our full conscious awareness and willing active participation, aspects of ourselves naturally lag behind. Often, we will resist a change we did not seek and as a result will suffer great difficulty, stress, physical body breakdown, mental body breakdown, emotional body breakdown, confusion, and all other related effects. It is always far better if we consciously choose, in a willing and co-operative state of spiritual alignment to navigate these times.

Is there one simple way we may do this? Surprisingly, there is. It sounds easy but in fact it is extremely difficult. It is the great key mentioned at the beginning of this chapter, one primary overarching factor that we must include in all we think and do. We must bring the Divine Will into our equation, as how may we leave it out? How are we to accomplish anything at all, how are we to exercise our puny free will, unless it is with the consent of the Divine Will? It is amazing how many of us think we have the power to bypass this essential aspect, and when at play this is a clear indicator of an ego out of control. Wise, unconditionally loving people with a deep connection to the Divine acknowledge the Divine Will in all they do; this is how they became as they are. A devout Muslim will always finish a sentence in which he is saying he will do something, even just meet for a meal, with "Inshalla" – that is, "If Allah wills it." A Jewish friend used to write me long letters and scattered throughout the letters almost as a form of punctuation were the letters PG and TG. If he was writing about anything he had done or received, or in describing a day out, for instance, he would end the sentence with TG ("Thanks God"). If he was talking about things he might do in the future, the sentence would end with PG ("May it please God"). These devices are a constant affirmation that nothing happens in the multiverse but that the Divine wills it so. A conscious acknowledgement of the overarching power of the Divine not only strengthens our connection but also serves to protect us from all aspects of a lower vibration and creates an attitude of humility rather than egocentrism.

Just because our thoughts, words and actions which may be inherently negative and of low vibration do not appear to create a negative result for ourselves, just because we appear to get away with all sorts of things, is no reason to suppose that we actually do. Appearances in the explicate realms are deceptive and every tremor on the web is registered, as an ancient and wise saying confirms: "The mills of God grind exceeding slow, but they grind exceeding small." We do not get away with anything that is in opposition to the Divine Will; neither time nor scale escapes the notice of the Divine. How can it be otherwise? With the Divine Will paramount and with our will so very limited, then it must be foolish in the extreme if we are to pit our will against the will of the Divine. Therefore, if great change is taking place in our multiverse, to resist it is foolish, and to remain ignorant of it is foolish. If we are wise, we will consciously align ourselves with the Divine Will, practise the art of Wu Wei and flow with ease, knowledge and spiritual power where it flows. We may use our free will to choose to do this.

There is in fact one and one only ultimate purpose for the gift of our very limited free will and this is that we should choose of our "own free will" to make the Divine Will paramount. We must come to the point of consciously acknowledging that our will is not supreme, that it is second always to the Will of the Divine. Our reality must be in all things "Not my will but Thine". Then and only then are we able to lose all resistance, all negativity, as with this one act we are giving ourselves to the Divine. This act of a conscious gifting of ourselves is the one supreme and all-important action sought by God. This is the sole reason for our limited gift of free will.

We have, however, three choices we can make with this gift of free will. One, we can consciously of our own free will choose greater unfolded evolutionary life with the promise of immortality, in which the will of the Divine of necessity is paramount. Two, we can choose a slow, difficult evolution because we are resisting and unconscious and therefore we are forced, with great pain and difficulty our constant companions. Three, we may choose involution and death. Not a hard choice, I would have thought.

To choose the Will of the Divine is the only path to the maximum amount of free will possible for us within the system, and it is the only path to wisdom, unconditional love, spiritual power and immortality. To be able to say and really mean on all levels, "Not my will, but Thine", to be able to say and really live, "Not my will but Thine" is the key to all. This also is another wonderful paradox, that in order to exercise our will in any real way at all, we must first give up our will. Once we do this, we will have far greater freedom of will aligned with the Divine than we ever can have while in opposition to the Divine Will. We will have far, far greater ability to create, far, far greater ability to bring into our lives all that we desire, all that is good. If we function aligned with the Divine Will, then all power of the Divine is ours depending upon the degree of our alignment, the degree of our coherence and the degree to which we have surrendered our will. Until we are able to acknowledge the Divine as paramount, acknowledge that the Divine Will should take precedence over our own, acknowledge that the Divine in fact knows better than we in all things, then nothing further may be accomplished along our evolutionary path. We will remain stuck in incoherent and fractured fields and unable to evolve any further, because how may we become coherent, fully aligned with the Divine and at one with the Divine Unified Field unless our will is the same as the Will of the Divine? It is not possible.

There is great simplicity, beauty, and intelligence inherent in the system. An example of this is the inbuilt safety mechanisms which guard against misuse of Divine Power. Many of us, if we are wise, fear great spiritual power as we are aware that we relatively unevolved beings may grossly misuse it. However, the divine system is perfect. Once we have chosen to move towards great spiritual power, by becoming ever more coherent and aligned with the Divine Field in all our aspects, power of the Divine Creative Field then naturally floods in. However, and this is the beauty of the system, the split second that we move from our place of greater alignment by a negative, lower vibratory thought, word or deed, we will fall back from our place of greater alignment and thus will lose coherence and power. In addition, should we rapidly lose coherence (i.e. if the thought, word or deed is profoundly negative) we may fracture and fall back further than we were before we began. These processes are powerful and dangerous for the participants if not approached in the correct frame of mind and heart. The spiritual evolutionary progress and subsequent power to be achieved is immense and great harm might be done in the wrong hands, but with this inbuilt device no real harm can be wrought other than to one's self. Move from alignment with the Divine and we lose power; stay aligned and we keep our power. With the keeping of our power, we are maintaining greater alignment and are therefore working under the Divine Will in all things and thus it is not possible for us to manifest harm. Therefore, for those who in their humility fear they may abuse this great spiritual power and possibly hurt others fear not, it is not possible. We may only harm ourselves and this quite severely. It is for this reason that the instruction not to say, "God and I are one" or similar is to be found in all ancient scriptures. Until we are ready, until we understand what we are doing, until we have full knowledge of the dangers and power of these words, we should avoid them and all others of similar intent. Even "Not my will but Thine" comes under this heading, as with this intent we are moving ourselves powerfully out of our current energy field towards another of greater coherence and higher spin. We need to be sure this is absolutely what we want. We have the free will to decide.

Should we decide that we wish to move forward, then our paramount task is to make "Not my will but Thine" a reality. This is the hardest task for us on this journey forward. The more we live in our heads and egos, the more we are attached to the physical, the more we are in the habit of controlling, the more impossible it will seem. However, if we are able to comprehend the benefits this move will give us, we will find it easier. Once we begin to truly understand the limited perspective we all have because of our infinitesimally small place in the multiverse, we begin to see how distorted our general worldview is. The moment we open ourselves to the Divine Creative Field because of our greater understanding and the giving up of our will, we will be able to see and hear, where before we were blind and deaf. The multiverse in all its beauty, intelligence, glory and power will flood into our fields and we will know there is no other way to be but this. We then have no need to ask the question, "How can my will possibly be more helpful to me than the Divine Will?" We will know that beings as small as we are in relation to the whole cannot possibly have a clear, wise and holistic view unless we are consciously in relationship and aligned with the whole – the Divine Creative Field. We will know that we are not so clever after all and that relying on our own will makes no sense at all.

We call ourselves Homo Sapiens, "Man the wise". However, we should rename ourselves Infans Humilis, "humble children" as until we are able to assume this position in the multiverse, we are not going anywhere other than possibly to extinction. We are like small badly behaved children, racketing around the nursery out of control. We are arrogant, we refuse to learn, we shout and scream so that the cacophony we make almost drowns out all else. We are spoilt children believing the multiverse revolves around us, and it is only to this end that we have until now used our divine gift of free will. Until we come to the point of being humble enough to realise our tiny stature in the whole scheme of things, humble enough to say "I don't really know what is best" in any and every situation and to realise that we cannot possibly see the whole picture from where we are standing, misaligned, unconscious and disconnected as we are; until we choose to accept with equanimity the Divine Will in all things, we will never evolve our soul field to one of great wisdom, love and spiritual power.

> Verily, I say unto you, unless you change, turn about and become like little children, trusting, lowly, loving, forgiving, ye shall not enter into

the kingdom of heaven. Whosoever therefore shall humble himself as this little child, the same is greatest in the kingdom of heaven.

— *Matthew 18:3–4*

Should we choose to give up our will and become humble children within the multiverse, this does not mean we give up altogether and do not accomplish anything. Quite the contrary. Living under the guidance of the Divine Will we are actually far more effective and more powerful. We are consciously choosing to listen, choosing to learn, choosing to see and choosing to grow and evolve. We may still have desires, still have focus, still be ambitious; indeed, it is required that we do so, as there is an individual purpose to each life. The Buddhists have many teachings on the particular position one must hold oneself in while trying to live "Not my will but Thine". It is as though we are on a high wire, balancing and walking down the middle way of the Buddhists. Neither falling to the left nor the right, the focus is straight ahead on the thing we may desire and because we are centred and calm aligned with the Divine Will, our focus is intense. However, all is without attachment to the outcome as we are aware of our position in the multiverse, aware of the primacy of Divine Will. Therefore, whatever happens, i.e. we get what we want or we do not. We can truly say and mean "Inshalla". We rest in the field of the Divine, asking only that our request be granted should the Divine wish it so. How are we to know whether what seems to us to be a small and insignificant request might negatively affect the whole?

Until we are privy to the entire blueprint, we cannot possibly know if what we want should happen right now, later, or not happen at all. What we desire may not be in harmony with the entire web at that particular point in time; it may not be part of our blueprint. If everything we do affects the web, just as a butterfly flapping its wings may cause a tornado on the other side of the world, how may we expect that all our desires should be granted as and when we wish? If they are not, it is foolish to use our will to try to make it so. So often when we are denied our wishes, like spoilt children we cry, "There is no God. If there was a God, he would do this, or he would that." However, should we develop a conscious connection with the Divine and choose that in all things we are willing to follow Divine guidance, not only are we assured we will cause no harm, nor will we come to any harm, but also we will live a stress-free life and we will accomplish only that which is in accord with the Divine Will. The trick is in discerning the will of the Divine, finding the thread and then following it, doing always our best, giving it our all and then in the final analysis releasing it without attachment or resistance. We may choose to live our life in a different way, with different belief systems, believing that all that happens to us in the explicate realm is for our learning and growth. Under the Divine Will, we do not resist so-called negative experiences but choose to see that they are opportunities for learning, for our growth and therefore a closer alignment with the Divine. In this way, we choose to exercise our free will as a path to greater evolutionary refinement.

The Divine Field in which we all live and breathe and have our being is intelligent and interactive. It is omnific (all-creating), omnigenous (of all kinds), omniscient (of infinite knowledge), omnipresent and omnipotent. God speaks to the prophets and to all of us, should we choose to hear. To hear we must clear a space; delete rather than add; we must empty ourselves. It is only with emptiness, stillness, and a desire for unity that we will be able to hear, see and know. We are able to influence this field with our thoughts, feelings, actions, emotions and words; therefore, we can become conscious active participants in the processes of the Divine Creative Field working always under the acknowledged paramount Divine Will. We have the free will to choose to do this.

The underlying blueprint of the multiverse holds within it all aspects of the Divine Intent. The process of evolution with its continual process of refinement must follow certain primary divine laws, as does all else within the multiverse.

We have the free will to consciously choose to obey or disobey these laws. Intelligence and memory is stored throughout the physical body, including memories from our ancestors: we have the free will to work with and delete these patterns or not, as we choose. The multiverse and everything in it is one great and glorious symphony, we have the free will to choose to hear, listen and be guided by this music or not. We have the free will to choose to be aligned with our Divine Soul and, in full conscious awareness, engage in a cognitive relationship with all aspects of our mental, emotional, physical and soul fields or not. Should we choose to exercise our free will for the primary purpose it was given; that we may give ourselves in loving relationship to God and say, "Not my will but Thine", that is all we need do: as from this one great act all else will naturally flow. This last great task for us all at this critical point on our evolutionary path is to submit to the all-knowing, all-seeing, all wise, all-pervading loving Divine Will of the Creator. Let our every thought, every desire, every action be tempered with "If it is your will", "Inshalla" or a simple "PG".

> What is going to be diminished must first be allowed to inflate.
> Whatever you want to weaken must first be convinced of its strength.
> What you want to overcome you must first of all submit to...
> What you want to take over you must first of all give to
>   – This is called discerning.
> You see, what is yielding and weak overcomes what is hard and strong:
> (And just as a fish can't be seen when he stays down in the deep don't show your power to anyone).
>
> — *Lao Tzu, Tao Te Ching 36*

We have the free will to choose to interact and participate consciously in our and the multiverse's evolution. We have the free will to offer our love, our will – ourselves in an act of conscious co-operative relationship with the Divine Creative Field. However, it may well be that we find this conscious submission, interaction and participation difficult or impossible because of a lack of trust – which brings us to the next chapter.

Chapter 9
Trust and Faith

> Faith is to believe what you do not yet see;
> The reward for this faith is to see what you believe.
>
> *—Saint Augustine*

My mail was upon my desk and sitting there on the top was a paper from the RNZFB Guide Dog Services for the Blind – the motto under the logo is, appropriately, "Before guidance comes trust." If we wish to be guided, we must first trust the guide. The analogy of a guide dog leading a blind person is particularly apt when we consider the initial stages of progress along the evolutionary spiritual path to the Divine. For most of us, at the beginning of our journey we are blind and cannot see at all. We are in the absolute darkness of the lower-vibratory explicate realms. We can see neither around us nor where we are going, so trust is the fundamental quality we must employ. We must trust ourselves, trust our belief, trust the process and primarily of course, trust God. We are the blind and the light of the Divine is our guide dog. Without trust, we will not allow ourselves to be guided. Without trust, we will not take the first step and we will not continue. Without trust we will not pick ourselves up when we stumble and fall, we may allow our ego or will to direct our ways and so we fall back to our starting point or beyond. Finally, without absolute trust that what we are attempting is achievable, it is not possible for anything to be achieved. Trust, according to my dictionary, is "firm belief in the honesty, veracity, justice, strength etc., of a person – confident expectation". When it comes to the Divine, for the most part we do not have that. Quite the opposite – we do not feel we can rely on the Divine much or at all. We feel that if we do not look out for ourselves, we are going to be in a pickle. Often, we are anyway, but we think things would be a whole lot worse if we gave everything over to an abstract we are not sure even exists. Trust and faith are closely linked: for our quest to succeed, we must employ both qualities absolutely. This is another fundamental and extremely difficult task. Our left-brain and our will leap in to obstruct and divert us the moment we try to employ this way of being. Our left-brain does not like abstracts but to accomplish this fundamental task we must learn to believe in and rely upon what, in the beginning stages, is an abstract. We must set about forming a relationship with something that does not have substance, form or physical reality. The Divine, our guide dog, is an unknown, and certainly unknown to the left-brain which, for the most part, is not equipped to navigate the implicate realms. This is as it should be, as its function is primarily navigating the explicate realms. In order to succeed in our task of trusting our guide dog, we must develop some discipline and control over various fields of our being, and the field of the left-brain is one of them. To make this task even harder, we must love our guide dog, as without this essential act we will accomplish little.

Let's for a moment imagine we are physically blind and have just acquired a guide dog, but we do not know anything about dogs at all and do not really want to know. What is more, we certainly do not trust them, and the last thing we are prepared to do is to form a relationship with the dog. The dog's task will be so much more difficult if not impossible, as we will not allow ourselves to follow its lead. We will not allow ourselves to be guided. In the same way, if we are to be guided through the dark realms we currently inhabit, if we are to navigate our way along our evolutionary path, then we must love and trust God. We must love and trust something that is not manifest in the explicate realms in the ways we are used to.

Not only must we initiate the process, we must also develop the enthusiasm and the focus to keep it going. Together with trust and faith we are going to have to cultivate fidelity (in other words, faithfulness or loyalty). We must cultivate a certain resolve in order to win through to our place of spiritual wisdom, love and joy. We need to resolve to stick with it and it is best to do this at the outset. If we wish to succeed, we must have a confident expectation that our trust and faith will be rewarded. Unless we cultivate these three primary attitudes of trust, faith and fidelity, we will not succeed. Should we choose to further evolve and seek the Divine, the only sensible course of action, we can trust absolutely that we may rely utterly upon the following:

> Ask, and it shall be given you; seek, and ye shall find; knock, and it shall be opened unto you: For every one that asketh receiveth; and he that seeketh findeth; and to him that knocketh it shall be opened.
>
> — *Matthew 7:7–8*

The Amplified Bible stresses that we should keep on asking, seeking and knocking, then the door will open. In other words, we must be focused and determined and always the onus is on the seeker to make the effort. This is an absolute condition of the path to wisdom, joy, and unconditional love. The Divine is not out there proselytising, no one will chivvy us along, no one will actively try to keep us on the path, it may sometimes appear to be quite the opposite. However, we may take comfort from the fact, that although the system requires that we be pro-active, that we "keep on", if we will look again at the above passage from Matthew, we will see it is promised that should we ask, should we knock on the door, we can be assured we will receive. We will be answered and we will be assisted in our journey. This is an absolute and an essential aspect of the process, and we may trust in this absolutely.

There is a very good reason why we must take the first step, why we must initiate all action. The reason is this: if we choose to seek this jewel beyond price of unity with the Divine Creative Field, it will be hard-won and therefore valued. We will also have acquired profound memories, knowledge and wisdom from each step along the way. It is neither possible nor logical that such a jewel should merely be given to us without any effort on our part as nothing in the multiverse works in this way. For us to evolve, to develop a relationship with the Divine with all that this implies, if we are to achieve immortality, we must work for it. The Bible is quite clear:

> Give not that which is holy unto the dogs, neither cast ye your pearls before swine, lest they trample them under their feet, and turn again and rend you.
>
> *— Matthew 7:6*

This passage, which sounds quite harsh, comes from a time when profound spiritual knowledge was held in secret because of its potency and power. If we were to be just given powerful spiritual knowledge, we would not truly understand it or know its appropriate use, and in our ignorance, we would quite possibly spurn it. This pearl beyond price then is not given as a gift; without effort on our part. We are not even helped onto this particular path. However, once on it, we are assisted in our activities in large ways and small. As long as we keep earnestly seeking, help is always there – the right book, the right person – exactly when we need them. All we ever need to do is to ask. This is a promise that is always kept and we may trust that this is so.

We will also find once upon the path that together with having to be pro-active, we are often sorely tested. All aspects of our life, most fundamentally our trust, appear repeatedly to be put to the test. One could sometimes be excused for thinking the Divine is malign. Here we are giving our all, trying our hardest, trying to love this abstract that we barely know, and what happens? Our physical life turns upside down, difficulties and obstacles arise. The more we profess our love of and trust in the Divine, the more we are tested, and the further along the spiritual path we progress, the more severe the tests become. I liken it to being in school: the higher up one goes in the classes, the harder the exams become. The spiritual path is a similar process, but the apparent difficulties are merely natural phenomena arising out of our own inchoate fields as we move into ever-greater alignment with God. The apparent chaos, pain and trauma we engender should be a cause for celebration as these are all clear indications that progress is being made. When we are blocked in all our fields and do not seek change, our lives do not change much, but when we make conscious attempts to raise our vibratory rate, all that is not of the Divine will arise to be nullified – and thus healing and evolution take place. With understanding, we can see that unless we are aligned and coherent to begin with, the only way forward is to clear our fields of any negativity – fear and its offspring and the resulting chaos and fracturing they engender. The reason the tests appear to become ever more severe is that as we move into ever-greater alignment, we move into clearing the more deeply embedded, ever-lower vibratory aspects remaining in our fields. We move ever more into the darkest recesses of our being, into the places that up until now without true knowledge of ourselves, without love for and connection with the Divine, without trust and imbued with fear, we have been too afraid to go. At the beginning we are just skimming off the surface dross. The closer to God we become, the greater our contact with our own deeply embedded inchoate fields. It is for this reason that this is not a journey to be undertaken lightly. However, we may pause for a break any time we choose: the pace is ours alone to keep.

Throughout, it is paramount that we keep our trust and faith, because with the loss of these, fear and doubt rush in, the energy field loses the hard-won greater coherence and alignment and we fall back. With the lessening of alignment, we start to fracture, with the fracturing even greater fear develops and so on. It can be a rapidly spiraling downward escalation of negativity so it is important to understand that if great success has been achieved in a relatively short space of time, then the danger of a rapid downward spiral to low vibration is great, as the fields will not have had time to stabilise. In the early stages, this is something to be guarded against. It is better that the work proceeds slowly in balance with the whole being and the inner and outer world. Take time; proceed with care and caution; make sure each step has been firmly embedded before moving on to the next. Think of the process as being somewhat like a body-builder who has quickly developed his muscles and then neglects or stops altogether all exercise. We know that should this happen; the muscles will quickly degrade to a lesser condition than before he started. Fear and doubt are our greatest enemies in our quest for the Divine; trust, faith and love are our greatest allies.

Our belief systems are the foundation for all this work. If we were to look for something in the normal way in the explicate realms that we did not believe actually existed, we would be guaranteed not to find it. To embark on the search for spiritual wisdom, love and power, to attempt alignment with God, we must first believe that what we are setting out to do is a possibility. If we embark on this journey with the idea of proving along the way whether or not the Divine is a reality, we are guaranteeing our failure. As we have seen, the system within which we must work is a fluid energy field in constant process of change, of coming into particular form in the explicate realm through focused intent or resonance and then changing form, in a continual spiraling infinite dance towards ever-greater refinement. The key here is the creation of form through focused intent. Our beliefs are focused intent and create patterns in the fluidity of the field. However, the stability and power inherent within the patterns, i.e. the success of the patterns as originators of manifested form are inextricably linked with the quality of coherence and alignment behind the belief system or focused intent. If the belief system is aligned with the Divine Intent, then it will have power. If the belief system is a negation of the Divine, the power will only be the limited finite power of an individual will and ego. Because of this, the fluid field of infinite possibilities has a great many dangers inherent within it, as with incorrect belief systems we flood it with negative energy and, under the law of "As ye sow, so shall ye reap", we cause profound negative effects. Any belief system in opposition to the Divine Creative Field/God, even if for a moment through lack of trust, will engender an effect that we will later have to deal with.

If we are able to create with focused intent, some left-brain thinkers will ask, is it not possible that we have created the entire fiction of God by trusting in our own God belief system? This is true, as it is of any belief system. However, if the Divine is a reality, then our belief in it will have infinite creative power and life. If our belief and subsequent creation is only as living and powerful as our finite will and ego are able to infuse into it, then it will be possessed only of that degree of power and life, which will be lesser and finite. The proof of the integrity of a belief is always determined by the results. It is impossible for us to generate pure, powerful and unconditional love working only from within our own fields and our finite will and ego:

> Ye shall know them by their fruits. Do men gather grapes of thorns, or figs of thistles? Even so every good tree bringeth forth good fruit; but a corrupt tree bringeth forth evil fruit. Wherefore by their fruits ye shall know them.
>
> — *Matthew 7:16, 17, 20*

We are able, when we know how, to create our reality to the smallest detail (always under the caveat of "Not my will but Thine"). We are doing this all the time anyway, but as we are not consciously aware of the process and as it is mostly our programs that are doing the creating and not us from a fully conscious free will, we do not believe that we have this power. We believe stuff is just happening, and we are victims or at best only partially powerful (as some of us have powerful wills and egos that appear to produce what we want). In order to be creators, to evolve, to do all the things we have so far spoken about, we must trust and believe they are a possibility, trust and believe without any residual doubt or fear being present. The extent that we can do this will be the extent of our success. In order to align ourselves with the Divine we must first believe the Divine is a reality. How could we align ourselves with something we do not trust and believe exists? It is not possible. In order to proceed, we must first believe in God, must trust God absolutely and must trust ourselves. Then and only then may we start our journey. This is a very difficult thing to do, as in the beginning we are not only blind and deaf but are fighting our left-brain and will every step along the way. It will be helpful if we hold clear before us that belief, trust, faith, fidelity and courage are our necessary allies and that scepticism, mistrust, laziness and fear are our enemies.

There is some good news, however. Even though we must be pro-active there are two primary agencies assisting us throughout and both work under the umbrella of Divine Intention so we need never fear they will lead us astray. The first is the spiral force of the evolutionary thrust that is driving all in the process of refinement: we intuitively have knowledge of and respond to this force and we instinctively wish to move as this force is urging and directing. The second is our divine soul's inner urgings for greater unfolding and therefore greater multi-faceted life and spiritual power. Our soul's innate longing for coherence, union and interaction with God underpins all its activity. Note the word "interactive", because the moment we choose to step upon the spiritual path we are consciously choosing to interact with the Divine. Interaction implies a two-way flow of energy: once accomplished, we are no longer alone in our endeavours because helpful energy streams of wisdom, joy and love flow back to us in all we do, their power directly in relation to the degree of our alignment. We must trust that this will be so. We may rely on the fact that the moment we pause to be quiet, even just think about taking such an active step, our being in all its facets will awaken and will start to assist us as this activity is our primary task. This is the reason we are here: there is no other. Again, we must trust that this is so. We can consciously choose to assist the two aspects that are driving us forward. If we do so, we can fast-track our growth. Our tiny divine soul seed spark starts to unfold: the infinitesimally small, single-faceted diamond spark can be consciously developed until we are a glorious, multi-faceted, large and brilliant Divine source of light, wisdom, joy and unconditional love. It is part of the Divine plan that we accomplish this. We are working in union with Divine Intention when we choose to work towards this great goal. To accomplish it, as in all things, we must first believe and trust that it is possible.

> Because there is nothing like wisdom which can make us pure on this earth. The man who lives in self-harmony finds this truth in his soul.
>
> He who has faith has wisdom, who lives in self-harmony, whose faith is his life; and he who finds wisdom, soon finds the peace supreme.
>
> But he who has no faith and no wisdom, and whose soul is in doubt, is lost. For neither this world, nor the world to come, nor joy is ever for the man who doubts.
>
> — *Bhagavad Gita 4: 38–40*

There is another aspect on this journey that we must learn to trust absolutely. We must have trust in our abilities and ourselves. If we say, "This is too hard, I can't do it", or "I am not clever enough", or "I will never get there" or whatever words we may use to continually defeat ourselves, this will become our reality and we will accomplish little or nothing. In our relationship with ourselves, based upon the knowledge gained from "Know thyself", we must love ourselves, believe in ourselves and have trust in our ability to accomplish this task. Is this not so in any endeavour, in any relationship on this manifested plane of existence? All relationships on this plane will only work in their fullest sense if there is trust on both sides. Trust, apart from anything else, implies respect, for without both trust and respect most relationships will founder. Often in the explicate world in our varied physical relationships we may perceive that our trust has been betrayed. Whether this is factually so or not, we may still end relationships and primary ones at that, if we feel our trust has not been honoured. How much more important on this our soul journey to greater life, love and the Divine is the trust we have in ourselves and in the Divine. We must choose never to let ourselves down with a lack of trust, courage also is key here. We must choose always to say, "I can do this, it is possible, I trust myself to accomplish this." Then, in deciding to trust the Divine and ourselves, we must understand that our view of events is always going to be limited, we are often in our darkness going to spring to incorrect conclusions. We may in our initial tenuous interaction think the Divine has betrayed our trust, but we must absolutely trust that the Divine will never do this. We must trust that what has in fact happened is that we in our blindness have not seen, not understood correctly. The Bible is quite clear:

> For now we see through a glass, darkly; now we know in part; but then face to face: then shall we know, even as also we are known.

> —*1 Corinthians 13:12*

Once fully aligned, in union with the Divine Creative Field, with our negative energy, our low vibratory incoherence behind us, we will be able to see all and know all. Then also will we be known in our fullness, for what we have allowed ourselves to become, "a brilliant, clear, beautiful and Divine being of light, love and spiritual power". We can prepare for these times of misunderstanding by holding this vision always before us; we can prepare by vowing always to trust even if it appears our trust is misplaced. Then, when these times occur, as they surely will do, we will be pre-armed and danger of mistrust will not arise. Armed with this wisdom, we can say, "I must have it wrong somewhere. I can't see everything and know everything I need to know at the present time, but I trust that sometime all will be clear to me." We must behave as a humble, ignorant child and not only that, but as a blind little child, trusting that our guide dog will show us the way and that all will be well. We can know that some time in the future, we will look back and laugh at how wrong our vision was. Laugh at how distorted our point of view was, how we so misinterpreted something that with hindsight now appears so obvious, wonderful and wise, and with a far more brilliant, clever and ingenious outcome that we alone with our limited abilities and our tiny view could ever have created. Then we will stand in an attitude of awe, gratitude and love and will move forward with a deeper trust in the process, ourselves and God the Divine Intelligent, Creative, loving and Interactive Field. As we move into greater conscious coherence, love and union, our trust becomes an integral and automatic part of the process until it is inconceivable to us that we should mistrust God ever again. Potential mistrust of ourselves appears to linger on for longer because of our newly acquired humility which brings with it the clear knowledge that we so often do not see clearly, but through a glass darkly.

Remember that paradoxes will be encountered at every turn – the Divine has a wonderful sense of humour – and this is one of the most delightful and wonderful aspects of the journey. We can choose to laugh our way through the journey, and it is preferable that we choose to be light-hearted, looking upon the experience as an adventure, trusting and confident in our abilities to succeed because:

> The world exists only as an appearance: from beginning to end it is a playful game.
>
> — *Mahmud Shabistar*

If we are going to start to play this game, is there a particular way to begin? We must first choose between two paths, the path of action and the path of inaction. The Bible describes this initial point of our journey:

> Enter ye in at the strait gate: for wide is the gate, and broad is the way, that leadeth to destruction, and many there be which go in thereat.
>
> — *Matthew 7:13*

Now what does this mean? The wide gate, the broad way is the easy path, easy to find and easy to walk. This is the path most walked, the path we are nearly all on right now. Few leave this path, remaining instead on it for an entire lifetime. However, you can see the wide path can lead to destruction, presumably destruction of the soul and consequently loss of potential immortality. The very least that may happen upon the broad way is that we endlessly walk it without evolving. The second path, the strait gate that we are exhorted to enter is, by definition, a very narrow way. Therefore, the spiritual path is a very narrow path, meaning that there is a particular and singular way of entering and walking upon it. It is a fine line, a balancing on a high wire, falling neither to the left nor to the right. So where *is* the strait gate? How do we find it and how may we enter it? The strait gate is not a physical gate in the explicate realms, so it is not to be found there. Nor will one find it through the agencies of another. The entranceway is not through the right-brain, nor through the left-brain. The one and only narrow entranceway – the strait gate – is the point between the two brain hemispheres, the point between our two eyes in the middle of our forehead. This is commonly called the third eye. This is the strait gate and is the only entranceway. Walking, or we should say focusing, down the middle at all times, with our whole being centred in this one spot, there are certain paramount positions one must take, and we do not have a great variety of choices as to how we will walk it. However, even though the system is one, and all is interconnected, there is individuation within it, so the path once we are upon it, will be as individual to each of us as are our fingerprints.

We may educate ourselves with certain religious tracts, we may perform certain rituals and meditations, but our path in all of its tiniest details will be an individual one. It will not take exactly the same momentum as another's; it will have a different content at different times, a different rhythm and resonance. We are each unique, and our spiritual paths are tailor-made for us once we choose to walk them. The primary laws and levels are the same for all, but the flavour or, if you like, the music will be as different as your fingerprints are from mine. Therefore, any particular weaknesses we suffer from, any particular difficulties, will each attract particular and personal attention and assistance. You may trust that this is so.

> There are as many ways to Allah as there are human beings.
>
> — *Islamic saying*

St Matthew further relates warnings regarding false teachings, and that just calling upon the name of the Divine is not enough: one must follow a certain path and perform certain functions. It is not enough to bewail God in times of trouble, or to toss off casually a prayer at night as insurance. In doing this, we are giving nothing so we will get nothing. To the degree that we believe, we trust, we love and honour, that is the degree to which we receive. We must first seek in order to find, we must first give in order to receive, we must first love in order to recognise love and be loved. The extent that we move into relationship with the Divine is the extent that the Divine will reveal itself and move into relationship with us. Remember John 14:21 He that hath my commandments and keepeth them, he it is that loveth me: and he that loveth me shall be loved of my Father, and I will love him, and will manifest myself to him.

Many people find this concept difficult to accept. They have the idea that God should just appear, should just do everything we want, when we want it. God is God, so why not? If something bad happens, we weep and wail, saying, "How could God let this happen to me?" We try to work it all out from our necessarily distorted tiny point of view. We do not trust the Divine; we are if anything suspicious of our creator. Our thoughts are often fear-filled and even hatred can dominate us.

We are unhappy and our lives are not as we think they should be, therefore God is to blame. God is to blame for all that is wrong in the world, all the bad things happening. When we cannot make sense of all the negativity, we feel God is malignant or worse; God does not exist at all and we are all alone in this hostile hell. We do not trust anything or anyone and so we turn to diversions or mind-numbing activities or substances to help us forget the aching, empty black hole within us.

Here we are in the middle of this Divine, harmonious beautiful creation, with miracles small and large around us every day, but in our negativity, our fear and lack of trust, in our inner darkness and our blindness, we deny the existence of light. Because the whole of creation does not work the way we think it should, we then say God does not exist, or the creation is all wrong, unfair and without reason. Our point of view is understandable, as we are just ignorant and badly behaved children who hold the points of view, of ignorant and badly behaved children. Shall we choose to grow up and gain wisdom? Shall we choose to trust before we have proof? Many primarily left-brains will find this completely unacceptable, many egos too; however, it is the only way for "strait is the gate and narrow is the way" and the workings and paths of the left-brain and the ego are hardly that. The only way we can really know is to walk the path ourselves.

> Because strait is the gate, and narrow is the way, which leadeth unto life, and few there be that find it.
>
> — *Matthew 7:14*

At the beginning of the journey what is real, what is illusory and what is desired often become all tangled together and confusion reigns supreme. Many times, what appears as a truth takes us by surprise. Our conscious mind, we feel, would not have created what was seen or heard as we have no conscious memory of knowing such things. Often what we see and hear we mistake and misinterpret. Therefore, together with trust, faith and fidelity we must encourage an open, accepting and non-judgmental attitude. Our position in all our fields throughout the journey needs to be one of an open, conscious and aware pupil observer.

We need to assume the attitude of a small child with an open questioning mind, curious about the world around us but without so many of the judgements we collect during our journey in the explicate realm. Often the messages given to us are symbolic, or in pictures with the embedded knowledge obscure. We need at those times to rest easy, to allow time for all to unfold. If in our eagerness, we try to force concrete meaning we will misinterpret messages based upon our beliefs, points of view and our desires. If we do this, then as events unfold and show in the unfolding that our interpretation was incorrect, we may lose trust in the entire process, then question our beliefs and our abilities and thus lose coherence and spin. We fall back into the field of fear. We must become humble children waiting for enlightenment to come, as it surely will. Know that without trust, respect, and humility it is not possible to walk successfully upon a spiritual path. If we are always critically questioning the ways of the Divine, we show our arrogance, ignorance and disrespect. (As a note; know also, with incoming information, the brain looks for a match in relation to the beliefs, programs and points of view held within the brain as memory, should the brain not be able to find a match, it simply deletes the incoming information.)

Should we accomplish anything in the material world during our brief sojourn in it, our accomplishments are illusory and therefore finite unless they have coherent, harmonious and divine content. Without divine content, our accomplishments are as a brief ripple on the surface of a lake, here for a second, vanished in the next. Know that any creation without divine content is a negation and, apart from anything else, it is a waste of valuable time. Should we wish to accomplish/create anything lasting, anything that will outlive our memory, anything that will add immeasurably to the whole in a positive way, then our accomplishments must be creations of harmony that add to and align with the Divine Creative Intent. This is why great music, architecture, literature or great and beautiful art lives on longer than other creations. These soul-uplifting creations are the result of the ability to align with God and to infuse or embed the harmonious high spin refined field of beauty in concrete form in the explicate realms, whether it be on canvas, paper, wood or other materials, or simply in sound. Great art is the ability to place the soul on the canvas; even greater art is the ability to infuse the work with the Divine Creative Field in all its glory. A rare ability indeed, but one possible for all of us should we choose to believe it is a possibility. In the process of such creation, we ourselves further unfold and evolve and thus this modus operandi of life is one we should aim for. In small ways and large the principle is the same. We cannot all be great artists, but we can all work towards bringing the Divine into our daily lives, infusing all we do with Divine intent and in so doing, becoming great creative loving and powerful spiritual beings. Actively, consciously and powerfully, Divinely aligned and coherent, we may co-create under the will of God. We must trust that this is what is required of us and that it is possible to accomplish.

We have talked about being blind at present, but the spiritual journey will cure our blindness: we will be able to see all as it really is. We will no longer be in darkness; we will no longer be afraid. Fear and all its offspring – anger, hate, lust, addictions, stress and so on – will no longer be our constant companions. Joy, peace, absolute trust and the knowledge that we are looked after and unconditionally loved will be our lot every minute of every day. Is not that a better way to live? Trust that this is possible and take courage from the fact that the times are changing – we are entering a highly charged evolutionary threshold and the multiverse is pressuring us to knock and to seek. The evolutionary time is now for a leap in consciousness and an increased vibratory rate for us all, should we choose. All are being encouraged to take that next step along the path and it is now urgent that we all should choose to enter the strait gate and walk the path to our predestined life of greater refinement and spiritual power. We all have a deep-seated desire for coherence and union with the Divine. If we allow ourselves to trust that this is a possibility, only then will it be possible. We must trust we are on the right path, trust that when we arrive at our place of focused, aligned, unfolded perfection and Divine love, joy and spiritual creative power that the following will be true:

> For verily I say unto you, that whosoever shall say unto this mountain, be thou removed, and be thou cast into the sea; and shall not doubt in his heart, but shall believe that those things which he saith shall come to pass; he shall have whatsoever he saith.
>
> Therefore I say unto you, What things soever ye desire, when ye pray, believe that ye receive them, and ye shall have them.
>
> *— Mark 11:23–24*

Chapter 10
The Golden Strands

> Seek the wisdom that will untie your knot,
> Seek the path that demands your whole being.
> Leave that which is not, but appears to be.
> Seek that which is, but is not apparent.
>
> — *Rumi 68*

The path to great spiritual wisdom, love and power is one of deletion rather than addition. We must peel away all the layers or programs we have accumulated, we must peel away the negativity overlaying our soul, and we must come to the understanding that we actually know very little and that much of what we think we know, we have wrong. One of the central messages of the previous chapters is that if we wish to approach God, we must first let go of many things. We must let go of our judgements and the belief in the absolute rightness of our knowledge. We must let go of our belief in dogma, we must let go of fear and its offspring; indeed, we must let go of a great deal of our mental and emotional programming and we must let go of our ego and our will. In addition, we must let go of our perceived pain and our trauma, as any stored negativity will block our path to God. In short, we must let go of much that we perceive makes our daily reality and who we are. We must also learn how to love unconditionally, and we must, as a natural part of this process, learn how to trust. Having unburdened ourselves and therefore with a greater lightness of being, and in a powerful position of trust and love, we may then journey to the centre of ourselves, to our divine soul. Our soul, once consciously reached is the portal to expanded life, love, spiritual power and the next stage of our journey.

It is easy to write these things, easy to read them, easy to understand them, but how are we to make them a reality? Each step in the early stages is quite difficult. Is it not true, though, that anything worth having is usually hard-won? Nothing of worth is ever accomplished overnight. To get to where we wish, need and must go will take practice, but there are simple and logical steps we can follow which are detailed in the following chapters. For now, let us just assimilate what has gone before. One of the objects of Chapter One was to show how very little science today does know and how often what was once considered absolute and concrete fact is subsequently overturned. True, illumination is dawning within the scientific world: recently many great advances have been made and, when considering the implicate realm, science is starting to emerge from the fog of ignorance. However, there is yet so much more that needs to be understood. Our knowledge of the natural world is still pitifully limited because of our ignorance of the implicate realms, but in our arrogance, we persist in believing we know more than we do. It is these erroneous beliefs that are causing great and increasingly irreparable damage to ourselves and the whole of creation. And it is only when we completely overturn Darwin's paradigm for living of "survival of the fittest" and replace it with a model based upon co-operative relationships in all areas of life, that sanity will be restored, and healing may begin for all and on all levels.

If we take the very little that modern science understands and compare it to the ancient wisdom texts, we see that science is now dimly beginning to understand what has been known since ancient times. Unfortunately, we cannot wait for the scientists to piece together the whole picture, as it is urgent that we all now begin to understand the way of all things. In addition, to rely solely on science as a path to spiritual wisdom, love and spiritual power is a broken reed, as the fruits of science rest primarily upon the evidence of our five physical senses. The path to God can never solely be via the left-brain analytical door of science, and the language of science is not for everyone: not everyone wishes or is able to consume tracts of quantum physics. As we have seen, there are as many paths to God as there are individual fingerprints, so understanding all the ramifications of the little that science knows today is not entirely necessary. It may be illuminating and enormously helpful for some, but not for others. With the limited knowledge that current science has, a wise person will practise the art of discernment, read and understand with the left-brain, then with the right-brain intuition assimilate what feels correct. Do not dismiss the little that is known purely because the final and concrete answer is not available today. We do not have the time to wait until all the T's are crossed and all the I's are dotted. No one has the whole picture and if we wait until it emerges, if it ever does, we will be left behind, or worse miss out altogether on our evolutionary journey.

Both science and multiple religious texts tell us that we are all connected, each to the other and to everything else; that there is no such thing as separation. Therefore, each tiny action and thought on our part will affect and influence the whole web of creation in either a positive or a negative manner. Understanding this will help us to be more careful what we think, as we will need to assess if our thoughts are positive, helpful and life-giving or if they are negative, unhelpful and destructive to the whole. Knowing that each action we take will send a ripple out into the web of life, we will think more before we act. Our actions now will be more intentioned and thus more potent, as we realise that each action whether positive or negative will have a far greater effect than we ever previously imagined possible.

Understanding the law of "what ye sow, so shall ye reap" we will know that in harming others, we are in the final analysis in the most profound way harming ourselves. With this new way of thinking and being, we cannot help but become more conscious.

Believing there is a Divine Presence of whatever form we may imagine inherent within all in the multiverse including ourselves, we can cease to feel as though we are alone; alone and carrying a great load. It will be impossible to feel lonely again, because how could we, knowing we are connected to all that is? Knowing that there is a pattern, a purpose underlying all of life, knowing the multiverse is in its very essence striving towards purity, perfection and unconditional love gives all of us a primary purpose. Knowing we are beings in the process of birthing out of the realms of dark energy – the field of fear – into the realms of light gives greater understanding. We will understand that until we have completed the birthing process, yes, there will be pain, there will be darkness, ugliness and trauma as these are all integral aspects of the creation process. However, these aspects are not deliberately and without reason inflicted upon us by a cruel and uncaring God as is often claimed, but rather they are the necessary equations of the birthing process itself. As light is born from the warp and weft of darkness, apparent chaos and struggle are the initial and intermediate effects. Note the word "apparent", as all depends upon our state of being when engaged in these processes, all depends upon our points of view. It is possible for our birthing to be far less painful and traumatic if we choose to believe this is a possibility and if we choose to place our focus and intent on the light of God while we are negotiating our birth. Once we understand the process, we can then move with greater ease through these painful aspects, even glorying in them as they herald our progress, knowing that it is so often our resistance that causes the chaos and pain. Know also, "what we resist persists". Once we are fully born, the realms of high spin that we will inhabit will contain none of those aspects, as how could they? High spin, pure white light may not contain the opposite within it.

Knowing there is a Divine plan, we can release a great deal of stress and worry. Knowing we are not the Divine with dominion over all, we can stop trying to run everything, stop trying to control everything. We will know that the sensible, intelligent thing to do is to let go, relax, tune in, listen, and start to interact with God the Divine Creative Field. We can seek to know it, to understand it and to hear the grand and glorious symphony that it is playing. We can know that although we are tiny spectators, we are also important integral players in this grand symphony, and we may choose the degree and the quality of our involvement. We can know that once we choose a path to the Divine, once we interact with the Divine, we will be guided in all things large and small always for the highest good, as all outcomes will be aligned with the Divine plan. We can know that once we have found the thread, the pattern, all we have to do is follow it. Our life from then on will flow with ease. Conversely, we will know that while we are trying to run the show, to second-guess everything, to look ahead and to each side (and often behind) to take all the strain, our lives will be in many ways a burden to us. This is not the way it is designed to be, this is an unintelligent way to live. Intelligence is the capacity to select or discriminate, so be intelligent – discriminate, choose another and better way to live. If we have memory programs of whatever kind that are negatively affecting our lives, as we all do, then isn't it an intelligent act to let go of this useless, even harmful baggage that is no longer needed? Would it not be a better thing to function always under the direction and guidance of our divine soul? Does it not make perfect sense for us to choose to function from this clear and pure spark of God than for us to be primarily functioning and creating from corrupted software that is so often not our own? Are you not curious to see what will happen should you choose to delete all that redundant software and live from the pure essence of your divine soul? The fewer programs we have running, the clearer will be our vision in all things, the more freedom will we experience – freedom to be truly ourselves, the unique individuals that we are. While we are functioning from memory programs not our own, we are not living our life, not our authentic life. Indeed, it is almost impossible to be authentic, to know who we truly are.

The more we delete our memory banks (brain and cellular) of all the accumulated and redundant garbage that is retained there, the more will the extremely sophisticated systems we all have, but seldom use, be able to function. The sooner we start using all of the miraculous physical equipment we each possess for something other than the purely basic temporal activities we have up until now been focused on, the sooner will we be able to see, hear, know and love the Divine – as the American surgeon and author Julian Johnson so obviously did when he wrote the following:

> When a man hears the divine audible life stream, he hears God. When he feels it, he feels the power of God. This current must not be understood to be like a river running in one course. It is more like a radio wave flowing out in every direction from the grand central broadcasting station. In fact, it comes from the supreme creative centre of the universe of universes.
>
> This wave has two aspects, a centrifugal flow and a centripetal flow. It moves outward from the central dynamo of all creation, and flows back toward that dynamo. Moving upon that current, all power and all life appear to flow outward to the uttermost bounds of creation, and again upon it all life appears to be returning towards its source. Upon that wave, we have to depend for our return to our original home.
>
> — *The Path of the Masters*

Johnson has almost perfectly described the activity of the spiral form torus of creation forming from Zero Point described in Chapter One. This had not been put forward as a theory when Johnson published his book in 1939.

After reading this book you may decide to take another look at religion, either your own or another that is not so familiar to you. Religion has received much bad press over time, a great deal of it more recently and much of it being well deserved, but do not let that put you off entirely. As we have seen, many contain the same truths and essential messages. Always remember that the promise "seek and you will find" is an absolute and fundamental aspect of the Divine as it intelligently interacts with all in creation; you, however, must take the first step. The only reason we have not until now been aware of this presence is because we have not been listening. We have not been quiet enough to hear, we have not looked, we have not seen and, most important, we have not believed. How may we see, hear and know something we do not wholly believe exists? We are all wired in such a way that this is an impossibility for us. Install the software first, then we may run the program. Our beliefs are an essential and integral part of our evolutionary process. In the temporal world, if we were to try to journey to somewhere we did not believe existed, it is doubtful we would arrive. If we looked for something we did not believe existed, it is doubtful we would find it. If we tried to see something we did not believe existed, we would not be able to see it. Our belief systems in this fluid multiverse are our fixed markers in the physical realms. Without a belief in the validity of our evolutionary journey, without a belief in the Divine, these things do not have any reality for us and so are not a possibility. Without belief, trust and faith no divine evolutionary journey is possible. We would not expect to become an excellent athlete, musician or whatever unless we first believed that it was possible and second, we received the required discipline and training. We know we would need to focus and dedicate ourselves to hours of training in order to accomplish mastery over our chosen activity in the explicate realm. Even the most basic of activities such as speaking, reading and writing require hours of learning. Therefore, why do we think and expect that we should receive the gift of an elevated consciousness or higher vibratory spin with all the consequent benefits such as mental telepathy, pre-cognition, remote viewing, inter multiverse communication, the ability to manifest in the physical and, above all else, conscious loving interaction with God without any particular effort or dedication on our part? Why do we seem to think this is a right and not something to be earned? Why should the accomplishment of our greatest potential, greatest relationship – divine creative and infinite wisdom, unconditional love and power – easily and magically be given to us? Hard work, diligence, practice, focus, desire, trust, commitment and faith to name just a few are what is required, and then the prize may be ours. If we wish to realise God, we have much work to do. We can take heart from the fact that not all of us are designed nor destined to be great athletes or musicians, but all of us are designed and destined – should we choose – to be one with God and to receive all the blessings that this relationship automatically bestows.

A starting point for this work is the recognition of and interaction with our divine soul, as our soul is the direct link to the Divine. With a corrupted soul, we cannot make that connection, cannot approach God unless we first take certain and particular actions. Should we choose not to take those actions, we are a lost soul that cannot progress to immortality. The health of our soul should therefore be of primary importance to us, and as with everything else, if we wish for immortality, we must earn it. Should we believe we are merely a collection of subatomic particles, atoms, molecules and cells all somehow coming into existence by accident and remaining in existence by accident, then to decay and disappear at the end, then there is no further journeying from there, no work to be done. We can rest easy in contemplating our oblivion, in the belief that even if we do have a soul, it will indeed be mortal. A well-known scientist commented recently that atheism is the most logical of belief systems, but for me the belief system of "no soul, no creator God" commits a cardinal sin: as apart from anything else, it is such an extremely boring belief system. What can one do with it?

Still, some may prefer it. However, it is hard to realise such a belief system as the universe is infinitely creative and therefore such a boring, dead-end concept is entirely alien to the eternal process. In addition, from a left and right-brain viewpoint, this limited belief system offers little as one has explored it in all its ramifications in a moment. What use is a belief system such as this? Should we choose to believe – we have the free will to do this – that we are all possessed of a divine soul with the potential of immortality and interaction with God, then our world suddenly expands. Our lives take on great and fundamental purpose. If we are a potentially immortal spiritual being, residing as a temporary inhabitant of a bag of water, which is itself residing in this particular space-time continuum as part of a vast system of multiverses of divine purpose, love and power, then our world expands. We are now living in a world of limitless horizons, with infinite possibilities. There are journeys we may take, new realms to explore, new ways to define and refine ourselves, new relationships, and new ways of being, doing and becoming. With just this one change in our belief system, all else changes. There is suddenly light where there was darkness, hope where there was none, purpose where only purpose-less reigned supreme. Why worry about whether we can concretely right now prove the existence, the reality of our divine soul and God? Why even look beyond the many positive gifts this one belief system will bring?

The time is not here, not right now, that we may see and prove the whole picture. However, the moment we choose to recognise our soul, choose to interact with it, is the moment our soul will immediately register the change of vibration and with the change of vibration will come over time all the proof needed. The higher vibratory field of the soul will immediately start to impact and affect the lower field of the physical body; and even if a deep state of unconsciousness is present, even if a great degree of disconnection exists, change will immediately take place, even if not immediately registered. If these changes are not immediately registered right away, do not worry about it, as the following chapters give exercises and clear instructions on how to accelerate and assist this process so that eventually they may be consciously registered. Therefore, think upon your soul, its existence in your reality and think, "How does it look? What is it like? Can I see it? Can I sense its presence?" (A note of warning: do not become attached to any images that may arise with these thoughts, as they will change over time as evolution takes place. What we may see as our soul now will appear quite different in times to come. Do not fix any images, do not create any images and do not create names for any images, as this will impede the divine flow and consequently progress. Hold only to the belief that you have a soul and allow that thought form its own life).

It is probably appropriate here to say a word about "guides", "angels" and various other entities that come under those headings. If we should establish a relationship with let us say our "guide" and clothe this being in various garments while also naming it, there is a real danger that we may have created it from our imagination for various or particular needs we have. Our imaginations are ever-fertile, and we are skilled at creating within our virtual reality world, even if we are not consciously aware of this. We may then carry on quite an intense relationship with a figment of our imagination. When we conduct a relationship with ourselves in this way, it can be very comforting and it may get us through bad or lonely times, but these constructs will divert us and delay our progress. The entity may in fact be real, but by clothing and naming it we are fixing it in our reality and creating a stuck point of energy. The danger is that instead of killing Buddha when we meet him, we attach ourselves to him, in which case we have ceased to move forward. In all our dealings with the implicate realms at this time, we are not sufficiently skilled or evolved to truly know the reality of what we are apparently seeing, hearing or dealing with. Therefore, wise travelers in these realms, will be extremely discerning and never seek to establish personal relationships with any apparent beings encountered there. Rather, they will accept with thanks what is offered of positive, wise and helpful content and leave it at that. Our guides/angels do not require that we clothe them and name them, nor do they require that we keep them with us throughout our long journey. Indeed, if we are moving at a reasonable rate they will change quite often, and this in itself is an indication of progress made. All that is required is we give thanks and love always for all assistance and care that is extended to us; we should not and must not get caught up in relationship with these beings. Normal human relationships are for this explicate realm. When we attempt to conduct ourselves in the implicate realms using the same methodology we are misunderstanding the realms we are interacting with and may possibly inhibit growth rather than assist it. No attachment is a key here.

If unconditional love is truly the ground of our being, how are we to gain a greater understanding of it? The word "love" is used carelessly and often these days. Many times love is given as the excuse for negative behaviour. So-called love is used as a tool, a weapon, an implement to bind and control. In extreme cases, we may kill the one we profess to love, because we say "we loved them". None of this makes any sense, as if we are in a state of pure love, loving another, it is impossible that we can commit any such acts which spring from the dark fields of fear and its many offspring. In addition, a being of greater light and higher spin may attract another in a so-called loving relationship purely and simply because the being of lesser light is automatically attracted to the greater light. This is more common than one would suppose, and while a positive result may be the outcome, often the desire has simply been to somehow take that which another possesses without the necessary work and evolutionary processes. Often these acts are simply a clear demonstration of a disconnected, fractured and confused being attracted to greater light and frequency, as a moth is to a flame. The instinctive urge to evolve and possess this greater light and love for themselves takes over and confusion reigns supreme. This predatory behaviour can result in extremely negative, destructive and even violent outcomes – all in the name of love. Any destructive behaviour in the name of love is caused by rampant low-vibratory negative influences woven throughout all the major fields of the being (normally excluding the soul field, but sometimes can include a corrupted soul) and it is these influences that are paramount. If our souls are paramount, negative acts in the name of love are impossible. With all the above and more, commonly being enacted, love, its quality and effect has become so confused and twisted that we barely understand what we mean by the word anymore. If we are to invite love in and integrate the energy of unconditional love in our life, we need to know what it feels like and to understand and be familiar with its frequency. We must be able for our own sake to recognise what love is and what it is not.

When we think about love, when we move into it, it has a softening effect upon us. Love is God's great solvent. Love dissolves all hardness, all concretised thought forms, all negativity, all resistance, all blockages. When we are immersed in a field of unconditional love, we dissolve; resistance is difficult if not impossible. All is fluid if we are immersed in this particular vibratory rate, as fluid as the Divine Creative Field. It is impossible to be angry, to hold on to old grudges, old grief, anything that is not positive and of God, because the field of unconditional love cannot contain within it anything that is in opposition, otherwise it is not love. Love is a pure refining vibration: to direct our attention to this vibration is to direct our attention to all that is positive, healing, light, all that is of the soul and of God. The more we love, the more will we be filled with all the virtues and consequently fewer vices. The more we love, the more will we be easily able to forgive and forget, the smaller will life's difficulties appear and we will begin to glide through life with perfect ease and no little glory. Once we know how to become a perfect vessel/channel and to then outflow the vibration of unconditional love at will, we are spiritually powerful indeed. This is because the pure vibratory rate of unconditional love is a unified, harmonious and blazing field of high spin, pure white light and infinite power, holding within itself the symphony of the multiverse – which is the Divine Creative Field expressing itself. God is pure creative unconditional love – nothing else! In a field of unconditional love, we live in a state of grace where all things are ours should we choose, always of course under the caveat "Not my will, but Thine". Conceding that the will of the Divine is paramount in all we do is a vital key to our further evolution as our will must be of necessity the same as the Divine Will if we are to unify. It cannot be any other way. The waves of love are fractal, infinitely repeating, shareable and cascade to the Divine perfection of the golden mean ratio; therefore, love is an infinite dance of Divine creative perfection, which raises the vibration of all it touches. In addition, as we have seen, if love is combined with the vibration of gratitude, its power is greater. If we choose to have as our paramount daily focus and state of being a love of the Divine imbued with gratitude for all that is present in our daily life, whether great or small, if we with focus, intent, and power align ourselves with this, then our lives and all those around us will be transformed over time. All that is negative will be unable to survive in the subsequent vibration; all that is dark will have to move ever further away. So simple, don't you think, and elegant?

The Metta Bhavana described in Chapter Six will powerfully assist in gaining mastery over flowing unconditional love at will. Unconditional love, once recognised and really understood, transforms us all. Once we have mastered the exercise we will know love as the ground of our being, as God in action, as the vibration imbuing all things in the multiverse, and we can become one with this vibration any time at will should we choose. Indeed, it is desirous that we achieve this state as everything rests upon it. Learn how to do this, take instruction, then practice will make perfect. In all our long journeying on our evolutionary path, the vibration of unconditional love must be a daily companion, as without this high spin field ever-expanding from its seed soul, no further advance is possible.

In seeking to learn about love, in seeking to ground this energy and send it forth, we need to practise the noble art of discernment without which we may be led astray. There are false stars that we may follow, there are emotions that masquerade as love but are far from it, and we must learn to tell the difference. Once experienced, the memory of the vibration of pure unconditional love will be burned into all the neural pathways and energy patterns of all our fields, and the acceptance of any lesser substitutes will not be possible. Pure unconditional love makes no demands, it seeks no price for its presence, it illuminates all within its sphere, it raises the frequency of our fields and initiates the greater unfolding of our soul. It is possible for this luminous field to become a greater part of ours; it is possible that the field of unconditional love becomes a simple fact of our life out of which all further events will unfold.

Should we seek for the blessing of pure unconditional love through the medium of another human being at this time, we may be discouraged or demoralised, as few of us are perfect and therefore we have not perfected the art of manifesting pure unconditional love. Know that the love received from another human being will be as perfect or imperfect as the being generating the love. Seeking pure unconditional love from an imperfect blocked being does not make a great deal of sense. However, as long as we are all aware of this fact, none will be too disappointed or discouraged. At this point in our journey most of us are still incoherent and fractured beings with much negativity in our fields: we are not aligned with our divine souls, our souls are not paramount, and so we take little or no instruction from them and therefore little or none from the Divine Creator. However, the moment we engage in any kind of love, no matter the quality, the solvent action will take place; our fixed ways will be worked upon and our negativities removed. The solvent action of love, no matter how imperfect, may create chaos of sometimes epic proportions in beings not fully birthed, which is the action Kahlil Gibran spoke about so eloquently in Chapter Six. It is easy for us at this stage of our development to get lost in the tumult of loving human relationships. Sometimes we may find safe islands within the relationships and often when we do this we cease to grow. We choose perceived fixed points, safety and security, with our needs supposedly met, only to find we have chosen a diversion or a blockage, rather than evolutionary growth.

It is, some may say, easier and safer to primarily access unconditional love directly from the Divine Creative Field through the agency of our individual soul than to navigate the often hazardous world of human loving relationships. Should we choose this pathway, once the Divine is accessed and the connection honoured then unconditional love may outflow from us to others as we choose. In the beginning, this flow will be intermittent and therefore finite, as we will be imperfect channels. The intent of the Divine is that we become perfect channels through which the Divine may express itself. This is our designed destiny and to perfect this art is our primary purpose at this time. When we are coherent, conscious and unified beings, with our divine souls unfolding, then we may with ever-greater facility express perfectly the Divinity of God in action. This is great work; this is part of our evolutionary journey, and understanding the process and gaining mastery over it is our next step. The process is simple and elegant and, once it is understood, practice will result in ever-greater expertise.

Should we choose this path to unconditional love, then, it is more likely that as a result we may attract another of equal experience and ability. Then both may revel in the outpouring of divine unconditional love as before, together with experiencing it flowing through the medium of another human soul, with less risk of becoming embroiled in the pain of love Gibran described. Love outflowing unconditionally brings its own rewards, as all will find. All manner of positive things begin to flow back because "as you give, so shall you receive": the law always works in its full perfection.

To work in direct relationship with God does not mean that human relationships are excluded, but it does mean that with the wisdom, skill, love and spiritual power obtained through this primary relationship, human relationships become more easily navigated and thus more successful. In this way, not only are we able to enhance our own growth, but also, we can assist another to grow. This is meaningful, purposeful work. On our eternal quest for love, we may hold this vision of the quest in our minds. Notice, however, the change to be wrought is always upon our self; it does not work any other way. First, we change ourselves, and *then* we may change the world.

Even if, while fully grounded in the explicate realm, we were all to love as much as we can, in all the ways that we are able, as perfectly as we are able, then we and our planet would be transformed, as all love no matter how imperfect is eventually healing, refining and thus evolutionary. It is for each of us to choose our own individual path, but choose we must. Otherwise, what is certain is that we will be forced and our way will be made even more difficult and painful.

Some may say all this talk of love is fine, but what about the power of evil? Where does that enter the equation? Let us first define it. If we look at evil as an energy, which it must be, then the definition would be "dark, negative, therefore of low vibration – chaotic energy, which is imbued with intent that is inherently unstable", and the source of evil is any intent that is in opposition to God whether individually or collectively. This is why it is inherently unstable, as all aspects in opposition to the Divine are not unified, harmonious and coherent: stability is a quality of God. If we remember how easily individual thoughts and actions can become collective and therefore more powerful and widespread because of the action of morphogenetic resonance, then we can easily understand how great evil may form, spread and appear to have enormous power as well. What we have to remember is that anything that is a negation of God is inherently weak. When evil, even great evil is confronted with the blazing field of pure unconditional love, its seeming power melts away. It can be no other way. In addition, even without being confronted by love, evil will always ultimately destroy itself. This is because the path of evil is an involuntary one, wherein the spiral spin of energy has folded back on itself and is therefore spiraling in decreasing mode – back to nothingness, the field of fear – the primordial sea of all beginnings. This is why we see evil beings become ever more fearful, ever more fractured as they progress in their evil, as the friction resulting from being in opposition to Divine intent causes ultimately fatal stress – a complete and total fracturing of the entire soul field. The result is always destruction, more than likely destruction of not just the physical but also of the divine soul seed. This is death indeed. All stress registered in our soul field is a manifestation of our opposition to Divine intent, whether in large ways or seemingly inconsequential. A being of high spin light and love may stand before great evil and yet remain inviolate. Where we go wrong is in presuming that because physical death has possibly occurred for the being of light, evil has won. This is not so. All that has fundamentally happened is that evil has effected ever-greater destruction upon itself and, with each subsequent evil act, grows ever weaker and more fractured and incoherent until finally the entire field is so damaged that retreat from this state is extremely difficult, if not impossible. We see this downward spiral of evil intent being played out time and again, but the obvious lesson never seems to be learnt. We can, if we choose, each become great blazing fields of pure unconditional love aligned and unified with the Divine Creative Field and therefore utterly fearless before which no evil can stand. It is as simple and as elegant as that.

So here we all are, minute fields of light, like so many tiny glow-worms lighting our own spiral evolutionary journey through time, space and beyond. Even though we are linked to all through the eternal web, essentially our journey is a solitary one. It starts within, which is the only doorway; and this is why there are as many paths to God as there are people. Each unique being is an individual doorway to God. There is no other entrance and so it is essential we know well our travelling companion – our self. The fact that we are currently so filled with fear, so powerless, so patently not what is understood by illumined, wise, unconditionally loving or divine, means we have a great deal of work to do and the work is of course on our self. Many of us spend great amounts of time on our physical bodies and having a well-working physical body is essential, as we will see, but the emphasis on our evolutionary journey is of necessity on the whole being. We need first to understand, then deconstruct, before we can again construct. Think of it as a spring-clean of the whole being. If we think to spiral off the wheel while keeping all in place as it ever was, we will fail. All activities other than this that we engage in while in this particular space-time continuum are merely diversions. Should we fail to undertake this spring-clean, fail to make some progress, then we are condemned to die as we were born – we have wasted our life. Our life is, or should be, an evolutionary spiral dance towards ever-greater refinement, light, and love – nothing else. All that works towards this goal is positive; all that does not is negative or neutral. Should we fail to advance we will be as the caterpillar that fails to construct the chrysalis or, once having created the chrysalis, fails to evolve into the butterfly – thus is a life unfulfilled.

Because our lives have this great overriding purpose does not mean we cannot enjoy the journey. In fact it is a requirement that we should do so, as our attitude is everything. There is no reason our lives cannot be happy, fun and fulfilled. Family, friends, success, money and careers are all part of the warp and weft. Indeed, all these aspects can be vehicles or lessons for growth: the danger lies in getting lost in the outward manifestations, in not understanding the true purpose of all aspects of this plane that may engage our attention. Engaging in these aspects is not primarily why we are here. Underlying all our outward activities should be the inner thought, "Will this action assist my primal journey? Is this a positive way for me to behave? Am I causing any harm with this thought or action? Am I acting from the positive moral conscience of my soul? Is this my soul's true journey?" With this powerful and purposeful intent integral in every thought and action, how could some progression not be made? It would not be possible to die on the evolutionary ladder exactly where born. The chrysalis would be created, the butterfly born.

The evolutionary forces will sweep us all towards a predestined point anyway. If we are active, conscious, knowing and aware participators in this process then we may understand a greater part of the divine plan. In this knowing, we may actively steer our souls, consciously choose a particular thing, place or point of reference. If we are fully aligned with our soul energy, as fully conscious as we are able, as fully interacting with the Divine and the Divine plan as is possible, then we are ensured of a creative, joyous and successful next stage of our journey. What is more, the speed of the journey will be more of our choosing. If, however, we are more unconscious than conscious, we will be swept along like so much flotsam and jetsam; great trauma, grief, rage and distress may then result. The degree to which we are unconscious is the degree to which we are a victim. We choose this position with all its subsequent consequences if we do nothing. Without wisdom, without greater consciousness, without a direct connection to the Divine, we are at the mercy of all that is. We must learn how to evolve successfully, how to reach the divine place of spiritual power, in order that the turbulent waters of evolution will not sweep us away in their wash.

It is said that a little knowledge is a dangerous thing, but no knowledge at all will be devastating. Read and absorb wisdom from the ages, seek the old wisdom that is currently being returned to us. Look with a discerning, critical eye if you wish at the planetary cycles, planetary precession and all the cycles of the sun, moon and other heavenly bodies. Become familiar with our landscape, with the great, complex and wonderful machinery of the celestial clock. This does not mean we have to know all with a detailed left-brain understanding. Once linked into the Divine much wisdom is intuitive, but it is important that we each at this time start to build a relationship with the spiritual (not manifested) elements and beings in our multiverse. The divine beings that inhabit our heavens have much to impart: we need to learn how to listen, hear, see and understand – our very existence depends upon it. The extent that we recognise our position in the whole of the Divine plan is the extent of our humility. The extent of our relationship with the Divine is the extent that we are conscious, rational, discerning and evolved. Should we choose to express that we are masters of the universe, that we are at the pinnacle of our evolution and that we have ultimate free will, we are choosing only to express the level of our arrogance, ignorance, immaturity and lack of grace.

At the museum in the Tuscan hilltop village of Lucignano there is a most beautiful reliquary called *L'albero della vita* (Tree of Life). This venerated religious icon has been the subject of many pilgrimages over the ages. The symbol of a Tree of Life is common throughout the world as it depicts in clear pictorial language the soul journey we all must make. The tree of Lucignano is gilded to symbolise the sun, or light and life, and is decorated with materials and ornaments that have an equally high symbolic value: gold and silver for sun and moon; coral for sacrifice; rock crystal for purifying value; and precious stones for virtue. Numerological symbolism is also present: six pairs of branches make a total of twelve, with a thirteenth element on top for irradiating light; the corals total seventy-two in number (twelve sets of six). Carl Jung, who translated metaphor into psychological language, wrote in *Man and His Symbols* that the dynamics of the tree symbolise "the process of individuation". Or, if you prefer our soul's evolutionary journey in becoming multi-faceted glorious beings of light, fully individuated but not separate. The branches terminate with pictures of various saints or revered beings; the pinnacle of the tree is a pelican. This bird is an ancient symbol of both destruction and creation; it is believed to tear its breast to feed its young therefore it is a self-destroyer, but in giving its own blood it is a preserver and creator of life. The trunk rises strong and straight to the top. The tree is the illumined meeting between heaven and earth – the place of manifestation; it translates the presence of the transcendent into human symbolic language. This is a clear three-dimensional depiction of our journey through physical life. We may deviate, stroll along a branch or two and perhaps stay and worship at the feet of a prophet, or Jesus, who is hanging below the pelican near the top, or we may choose to go straight from the base to the apex. However, we may choose to go, the journey is always from base to apex; we will eventually end where the divine path designates. Our only free will is how long we choose to make the journey last and how many deviations, sacrifices and purifying passages and how much pain we choose along the way.

We may choose not to have a relationship with the Divine Creator, but the only reason for the gift of free will is that we should choose a relationship with the Divine, as relationships have value only if the contact is freely given. Love freely given is the only love worth having. The Divine Creator does not force us to interact with it, does not force us into a relationship: it is always our choice. Our free will is given full play in this regard. When we choose to align with the Divine, choose to become coherent and to interact in full and complete relationship with the Divine Creator then this act has enormous meaning, is the summation of our existence and is full of potential. Should we choose to give up our own free will in this, our most important relationship, our lives will be transformed. Our friendship and love is the one great gift the Divine Creator desires and our coming to the understanding of the real meaning behind our gift of free will is primary. This is the reason for our limited free will: if we choose to use it for other purposes we will be limited or worse in our endeavours. To see the end, we must be able to understand fully the beginning. When the disciples said to Jesus, "Tell us how will our end come?" Jesus said:

> Have you found the beginning, then, that you are looking for the end? You see, the end will be where the beginning is. Congratulations to the one who stands at the beginning: that one will know the end and will not taste death.
>
> — *Gospel of Thomas 18*

The journey is a glorious one. There may be lessons along the way arranged for us all by the Divine, but take heart from the fact that these lessons happen only because we need them. They are always for our learning, our improvement; they are always positive even if they do not appear to be so at the time, often indeed quite the opposite. They happen only because our way is blocked by something within us. If the way is to be cleared, it is necessary for life lessons to happen. We may from time to time perceive that we are suffering solely from external events, but this is never the case. All suffering is only perception, all pain is only perception; when consciously linked to the Divine, the viewpoint shifts, and the pain is no more. As Kahlil Gibran so eloquently says, we may be pruned and threshed, our dreams may be shattered and so on, but take comfort always from knowing the Divine knows and sees the whole; we do not, nor can we at this time. To lighten our journey, though, the Divine always displays a wonderful sense of humour. Often amid high drama, the humour, beauty and absolute perfection of events unfolding, apparently planned to the tiniest detail, will leave us breathless with wonder. Events will work in ways we could never have thought out for ourselves with our small viewpoint; creations of the Divine are always superior to ours, always perfect. As we learn how to rest in the field of Pure Divine Unconditional Love, to dissolve in the field at will and to outflow this

Divine vibration to all, then we will seek only this and all the fruits of this will follow.

Chapter 11
The Physical Body

> You yourself must make the effort.
> The Buddhas are only teachers.
> What you are is what you have done.
> What you will be is what you do now.
>
> — *Buddha*

Having spent quite some time in the more esoteric realms, we now come down to earth a bit. If we are to move forward at all on our evolutionary journey, then any progress must be enacted through all the limitations that the physical realm dictates. The next three chapters deal with three of the primary bodies we each possess. We have no difficulty using the word "body" for our physical body, but it may seem strange to refer to other bodies that are contained within our whole being. All these so-called bodies are energy fields; and while we may find it difficult to call our emotional field a body, we would find it equally difficult were we to term our physical body a field, which of course it is. Therefore, for clarity and simplicity I refer to all three as bodies although they are fields of energy, each with a different frequency. This does not imply separation, as all are intrinsically linked to each other and the multiverse.

Many religions view the human physical body as a temple because it houses (or should do) the soul. The reasons for this reverence of the physical body as a temple are profound and important. Any field that has as its essence and vivifying factor the Divine Creative Field is of itself Divine and therefore viewing the manifested physical container as a temple is easily understandable. Further, if we are to effect the perfect alignment of our soul with our physical and other bodies, it is necessary that the physical body be as healthy and coherent as possible. With the perfect alignment of the soul and physical body comes greater overall coherence, greater conscious awareness, illumination, interaction with the Divine and thus greater possibility of successful unfolded evolution – and therefore greater joy, love and spiritual power. Successful unfolded evolution – enlightenment – means that a multi-faceted, fully conscious, interactive, aligned and powerful soul has evolved to its fullest spiritual potential.

The Bible refers to our body being a temple for the Divine within and goes further to say that because of this, we do not belong to ourselves but to the God within, and so we are not free to do as we wish with our body. Even when considering our physical body, we must at all times function under "not my will, but Thine".

> What? Know Ye not that your body is the temple of the Holy Ghost which is in you, which ye have of God, and ye are not your own? For ye are bought with a price: therefore Glorify God in your body, and in your spirit, which are God's.
>
> — *1 Corinthians 6:19–20*

With this in mind, we can understand that our treatment of our physical body must in all ways be a reflection of Divine intent. We can understand why the house of something as special, fundamental and

Divine as one's soul must be treated with due reverence, respect and care. If we honour, love and respect ourselves because we are conscious of the divinity within, the very essence of which is love, how could we not treat the physical manifestation of our soul the same way? The problem is that we do not for the most part think about our soul and our inherent divine nature in any way at all, and therein lies the source of the abuse of our physical bodies that so many of us engage in. If we look to the source of the physical manifestation, we will find we are unable to continue so many of our incorrect practices. In reality, the state of one's physical body (and all our other bodies) is a direct reflection of the state of one's soul or our relationship with it. In addition, if the tiny seed soul is so marginalised by a dominant will, ego or left-brain, the soul moves out and away for its own protection and stays enfolded, a seed of potentiality. Thus, the soul primarily leaves the physical manifestation in all its forms and fields to its own devices, and what amounts to almost a virtual thought-form entity without true Divine reality being the result. Much of the madness we see around us today is generated from these virtual field entities with little integrated Divine integrity. Also, if we marginalise our soul in all the ways we have devised to do this and our soul then moves as far out of the physical body as it possibly can, while it is way out there, "you" are not really "here". Therefore, it is impossible to be conscious, aware, truly sane, coherent and aligned, and it is also impossible to further evolve.

Without Divine content at play, corruption eventually in one way or another is realised throughout all the fields, and thus ever-greater disconnection occurs, from which it is increasingly difficult to regain any semblance of being whole and aligned. It is only with all aspects in alignment and fueled by the Divine Soul that true health, stability, unity and coherence in all the fields and their manifestations can be realised. It is very logical and simple. It is terribly important that we understand this, as our soul cannot align and begin to unfold while the lower vibratory field of the physical is seriously disconnected and incoherent – dis-eased. This is because the physical manifestation, the temple, is the vehicle the soul must manifest through in this space-time continuum and it is in this space-time continuum that we are called to evolve at this time. Without a properly functioning physical body our soul is powerless and unable to further evolve. (I am not here referring to the natural processes of aging, as this does not in any way impede evolution, in fact it may assist it).

In a later chapter, we will learn a powerful exercise for aligning the three primary body/fields with each other and with the soul. For this exercise to be successful, all bodies/fields need to be in a reasonable state of care. So how do we care for this temple of our soul? How do we ensure it is able to align with our soul? Are there simple practical things we can do? Are there simple commonsense things we can stop doing? Well, everything is really just a matter of commonsense, of love and care, of engaging the mind, being reasonably conscious and walking the path of balance of the Buddhist, then everything will quite naturally fall into place. However, if there has been a great deal of abuse of the physical body over a length of time, then it will take time and effort to correct – but with diligence, focus and a will to succeed, success will come. As a species, we are all suffering a dangerous corruption of our constitutions. We have become debilitated by our disconnection from the Divine, improper diets and a plethora of toxins (both in the chemical form and unnatural man-made energy fields) and with each generation we are dramatically weakening. Disease and a general debilitation are becoming endemic. Good practice, together with vital whole food, are essential to protect the housing of our souls, for if our bodies are allowed to degrade beyond a certain point, our souls will no longer be able to use the human physical bodies as vehicles for evolution. Hippocrates, the father of medicine, said, "Let food be your medicine; let medicine be your food." In our modern world, we have forgotten this injunction and if we are all to heal our bodies and to then maintain good health, the quality and integrity of our food must be paramount. We cannot achieve a perfectly functioning temple unless we address this aspect – and apart from anything else, eating good food is a celebration of physical life and the Divine inherent within.

Together with the neglect of the physical that we see all around us, we have as part of our western culture anyway, a cult of worshipping the physical. We truly are living in strange times indeed when our places of worship are the many gyms dotted about the landscape, here we spend hours at the altar of the end manifestation – the physical. Our focus, often our whole attention, is on our outer physical perfection. We are spending a great part of our time, energy, focus and money on the physical aspect that will shortly fall from us and decay. We spend no or little time at all on the aspect of ourselves that will live on long after the physical manifestation has re-merged with the stardust and water from which it came. This is not health; this is not balanced logical behaviour. To focus on the end manifestation, the least important aspect of our being, and to ignore the source of our being, shows how truly disconnected we have become in all things. We have embraced a culture where youth and physical beauty, the physical finite and truly ephemeral things are worshipped, while wisdom, love and spiritual power are not considered worthwhile aims. Because of this, we shun and fear what should be venerable old age and our passing over from this realm – death. These things are kept as far from our vision as possible. We worship youth and beauty and all the glamour of the physical to the detriment of all else. This is delusional. To be fit and healthy is one thing, but an over-focus on the physical without any focus at all on the spiritual is seriously unbalanced and ill health of one kind or another in all our fields will surely follow.

We need to cultivate a conscious awareness of our physical manifestation in a different way to the one above. A conscious awareness of our body means that we are immediately aware if we are at ease. If we are not, we are able to quickly access the source of our dis-ease and make changes. With a conscious awareness of our physical manifestation, we are at all times finely tuned to our well-being. We are immediately aware if we have entered an environment that has very negative emanations and may be toxic for us.

We are also immediately aware if a person interacting with us, or crossing our path, is emanating angry, predatory or other negative field effects. The opposite is also registered: the kindness, the inherent honesty or the love emanating from other beings we meet throughout the day is fully processed and thus creates stronger connections. Until we are able to instinctively and consciously (this is the key here) register and process all fields as they affect ours, and until we are healthy enough that our fields are so stable under all circumstances and can thus defuse all negative fields as they affect ours, we will remain eternally unstable. This powerfully affects our physical manifestation. We will remain being blown hither and thither by each field effect flowing into ours. We remain at the mercy of all, without any real stability and inherent spiritual power. We remain unable to create anything positive of lasting effect, and we remain unable to evolve as we are eternally unable to align with our soul and thus the Divine Creative Field. In the interim stages on the path to health while we are vulnerable because of our instability, if we should find when we become more conscious that we have a great number of people and situations in our life that are negative and toxic, then the first thing needed to be done is to address this. All situations and people who are to great degrees affecting our fields in negative ways so that perhaps we are in a permanent state of defensive preparedness for war, must be released. Great courage is required to accomplish this, as fear of change and the unknown is one of our greatest fears. However, we have the free will to make the required changes should we choose. All that is toxic in the initial stages must be removed from our lives. I say "in the initial stages", because once we have achieved stability in all our fields under all circumstances, once we are aligned to a degree and the field of love is flowing strongly in all our fields, then we automatically affect all that crosses our path in a positive manner and outside influences/ frequencies affect us not at all. This is great spiritual power indeed.

As we know, it is impossible to say precisely where the boundary of each being lies. This is because each of us stretches into infinity, reaching out and touching all within the multiverse. We affect all without end. So if we have allowed our being to become corrupted or damaged in any way, whether great or small, then we are projecting this damage out into the field and affecting all else with our contamination. The negative elements we have created will affect the whole adversely, therefore in all self-abuse we not only damage ourselves but all others as well – and on a scale we may find hard to imagine as it is in all ways – both great and small. Under the law of "what ye sow so shall ye reap" we cause ourselves far greater problems out into the future than we think when we observe the limited manifested field effects of our actions solely in our physical body. The overall field effect is immense in contrast to the observed dis-ease or breakdown of the physical. We need to meditate on this and if we are able to assimilate this profound knowledge, all self-abuse in whatever form will begin to cease. Conversely, if we are stable and aligned in all our fields with our soul, and if the field of the Divine Creator is strongly part of our field, then we emanate and pulsate out into the infinitely interconnected field of the multiverse all that is positive, all that is healing and all that is loving. The benefits, the flow-back field effects, can only be imagined. Light, wisdom, joy, love and spiritual power will flow out from each of us, touching and raising the vibration of everything and everyone. To live a truly meaningful life, one need do nothing else but this. Having very good health until a great old age is only a matter of sensible practice. If we were all to become more conscious and think before we act, taking responsibility for our own health, many more of us would live to a healthy and active old age. Bad health does not just happen. Good health or bad is a choice, as is everything else. All that manifests as dis-ease or corruption in the physical has its source elsewhere. As we become ever more conscious, we learn to screen out of our lives all that may cause dis-ease or corruption of whatever kind and bring in all that is nurturing and loving. As we learn to "know ourselves", to love ourselves and to know and love the Divine, we begin to respect ourselves together with all of creation and thus we begin to take care in all ways of our Divine physical body the temple of our Divine Soul. When we have learnt how to do this, our body then supports and assists us on our journey in the perfect manner it was designed to do. If we do not make the positive choice, we not only jeopardise our seed soul, but we risk the completion of our epic journey towards immortality.

We are spiritual beings residing temporarily in a physical world and we need a properly functioning physical body that is able to house, support and align with our Divine soul in all of its activities and purpose according to the overarching Divine intent of God. Anything less than this is an insult, an abuse and a negation of the Divine Creative Field and we open ourselves to greater inchoate energy with its subsequent fracturing and corrosion of all our fields. It is only with this profound understanding of the true nature and function of our physical body that unconscious harm may be avoided, and we can thus move forward in conscious relationship with God, revelling in all the joy, wisdom, love and spiritual power this Divinely ordained evolutionary journey brings. Nothing less will do.

We have placed in an addendum further information regarding many aspects that positively and negatively affect the physical body and setting out simple ways to make positive change.

Chapter 12
The Emotional Body

> All the world's a stage,
> And all the men and women merely players;
> They have their exits and their entrances;
> And one man in his time plays many parts,
> His acts being seven ages.
>
> — Shakespeare, *As You Like It*

Emotions, how they rule our lives, in a greater way, some say, than our minds. Is this a desirable state of affairs if we wish to evolve? Do our emotions contribute to our lives in an overall positive manner? Do we have control over the myriad of fleeting emotions as their charge shimmers through all our fields? Can we imagine life without this constant turbulence throughout our fields? Would it even be possible to reach such a state of emotionless being – and if so, is that desirable?

Well, the way we are currently ruled by our emotions is *not* a desirable state of affairs and this is because our emotions are a major contributory factor in the overall instability of all our fields. While the veritable storm of often conflicting emotions surges continuously throughout all our fields, we cannot become stable, coherent, peaceful and aligned and so we cannot further evolve. If we add to this the fact that so many of our emotions carry a negative, even deadly charge, it will become clear that our emotions not only hold us back but may also send us spinning on a path of involution rather than the desired evolution. When we look at the big picture, we can see that our emotions must come under our conscious control before it is possible for us to move forward. Knowing this, we can also know that there must be a way we can accomplish this, as all in the realm of the Divine Creative Field has inherent logic and intent. Evolution appears to be the overriding purpose, so if our uncontrolled emotions are blocking that purpose, there must be a way in which the purpose can be attained. Therefore, we must find a way to delete the negative emotions and gain mastery and control over all else.

Awareness and consciousness are keys here in the work we have to do, because how are we to delete our negative emotions if we are unable to first identify them as they flash through all our fields? Deleting negative emotions will always eventually bring us to fear, as all negative emotions spring from this original inchoate field. Anger, hate, jealousy, envy – all are the offspring of fear. Delete all trace of fear from our emotional body and everything else associated with fear will quite naturally fall away as well. It is as easy and as difficult as that. All positive emotions such as joy, happiness and thankfulness are the offspring of love: since we do not wish to delete love from our fields but enhance it, we do not need to address actively each positive emotion. All that is required is that we delete fear as this automatically increases the vibration of love in all our fields. As the fear leaves, the resulting vacuum is automatically filled by the coherent and loving field of the Divine. All our fields will then quite simply and naturally become more coherent and unified and are thus calm and are more fully under our control. When our emotional body attains the untroubled realms that are of pure love, and the peace that passeth all understanding, we have complete mastery over all our emotions.

How may we in full conscious awareness attain this control and reach this desired sublime state? There are many paths to success. For example, we may seek the help of those skilled in memory (thus emotion) deletion, we may seek the help of powerful spiritual healers, or we may work away quietly on our own, perhaps with prayer or meditation. The more receptive we are to Divine energies, the greater our success. There are quick and simple ways of deleting all negativity from our fields; as we allow in the Divine, this perfect field of love automatically deletes all negativity in whatever form – as long as we are not attached to our demons, they will just fall away quickly, effortlessly and painlessly. The exercise we will learn shortly will greatly assist all to prepare for this kind of work; or, if no extra help is sought from outside sources, it will prove enormously helpful over time, not only in dealing with and deleting emotions but in all other areas of evolutionary advancement. Let us first define exactly what emotions are, their major sources and the hang-ups we have around them. We know that the ultimate source of all negative emotions is the field of fear, but do all negative emotions come to us as a direct consequence of our fear? Do all our emotions actually belong to us, or do they in reality belong to someone else? Finally, do our emotions have a purpose?

The dictionary's definition of emotion is "agitation of mind; excited mental state". That is, emotions agitate the mind, and agitate means; move, shake, disturb, excite, revolve mentally. It all sounds the opposite of quiet, peaceful, prayerful, meditative – which are the attitudes one needs in order to interact and align with God. It would be hard to listen properly to anything while we are revolving mentally and are agitated, hard also to communicate properly. So we begin to see why uncontrolled emotions will block our path to the Divine. A field that is disturbed, chaotic or agitated is the opposite of the Divine Creative Field therefore, it would be impossible to move into and align with it while our fields are experiencing any of the above conditions. We can now understand why we need to address our emotions if we are to accomplish alignment with our soul and hence the Divine.

The Emotional Body

If everything is energy, then presumably emotions are energy vibrating in a particular manner. The problem is that on our evolutionary path moving out of incoherence towards coherence, all emotions (leaving aside love and its offspring) are essentially incoherent in nature and therefore must be deleted from our fields. The many emotions that make up our primary being, the degrees to which they are negative or positive, under our control or not, are the clear markers for our position upon the evolutionary path. If we are to evolve to higher and higher vibratory states of being, the inchoate, lower vibratory rate emotions must fall away. We may judge our position and therefore how much more work we have to do by the type, quality, intensity and frequency of our emotions. As we learn to look with clearer eyes at all things, we will be able to see what we need to tackle next, see what emotions are stopping us from further progress along our evolutionary path to full spiritual power. Emotions arise from a number of sources, the primary one being the field of our origin, the inchoate field of fear. While we are still in the midst of our birthing process, we are ruled to a great degree by what we are trying to leave behind. Once we understand that the intent of the multiverse is that we move away from this field of our beginnings, then we also understand that in moving away from fear, we are in all things and in all ways assisted by God. All we really need to do is to practise the noble art of Wu Wei, give up our tiny will to the Divine Will and go with the flow of the Divine Intent. We know that to move forward we must delete fear from all our fields, so with this fundamental premise established we will now look at some of the other primary triggers of our emotions.

A major source of activation of our emotions, perhaps surprisingly, is the heavenly planetary bodies we discussed in Chapter Five. We live in a system that is positively laden with charge of various kinds. As energy fields interact, i.e. a planet or planets with our own, one effect is an emotional response which we then direct outwards into the manifested realms. As these great beings have an equally great energy field, their fields activate and disturb ours, which includes activating our emotional body. We learn greatly by the ebb and flow of our emotions; an energy surge of a particular emotion carries a particular lesson within it. It could be said that our emotions are vehicles for lessons and therefore they are needed. Once a lesson is learnt that has as its vehicle a primary emotion such as anger, the anger will lose its energy within the primary field. The lesson, once learnt, depletes the charge. There may be many lessons to be learnt around anger, but each lesson assimilated depletes the primary field of charge and thus the start is the hardest part. As progress is made, the going becomes easier, the charge becomes weaker and the darkness of the overall field is lightened. Awareness and greater consciousness are the results, together with all the naturally derived benefits of owning fields depleted of anger.

As the planets are our teachers and guides, they are a primary source of stimulation throughout our entire emotional body. They play their particular and potent energies upon the Earth and us in varying intensities at various times as they progress on their stately journey through the heavens. Each planet has a particular energy field. For instance, Saturn is always denoted as an oppressive, heavy energy representing among other things responsibility and ambition. As our bodies are fields of electromagnetic energy and our physical aspect is predominantly a saline solution (a perfect conductor of energy), then the powerful energy fields of these planetary beings affect us most profoundly. If, for example, Saturn is in a position of primary influence we may feel depressed and so react with anger or impatience to a situation that of itself does not justify such a reaction, thereby creating damage of an emotional nature, which will flow through to all the fields including the physical. This response will not only affect our own fields but all within the multiverse and thus we will have to answer under the law of reaping what we sow. If we are sufficiently aware at such times, we will recognise the pressure, stress or depression as having an external source, so we register that it is not ours and we do not "own" it. It is the internalising of negative charge throughout all our fields that we must stop, and then automatically we will no longer direct negative and harmful charge out into the multiverse.

In becoming familiar with the fields of the planetary beings we begin to intuit and understand the source and the trigger for some of our emotions and we move with the intelligent intent of the planet's field, rather than reacting to it. We come to a full understanding of the role the planets have to play in our evolutionary journey and we begin to work with them, rather than unconsciously reacting to their unperceived potent energies.

The more attuned we consciously become to these great beings, the more we practise the art of Wu Wei and merely flow with their urgings rather than resisting and possibly creating ever-greater negative charge within all our fields. If we are conscious enough to find the thread of the Divine flow and to then follow it, we will be unlikely to make mistakes either large or small, as long as we align ourselves with the Divine Intent. If we are conscious of and receptive to the guidance and teachings of these great divine beings, our emotional body will gradually and easily over time lose all negative charge anyway. Fear, anger, hate, jealousy and the rest will not even be a memory, as memory holds a charge within it and there can be no residue in any of our fields from these emotions if we are to successfully evolve. Because the multiverse abhors a vacuum, as negative emotions lose charge and fall away the field of love inflows, and the field of the Divine Creator becomes ever more ours.

Another source of emotional body disturbance may be the lowest vibrating field of our being – our physical body. If the field of our physical body is out of balance because of mineral depletion, which then cascades into vitamin and hormonal depletion or imbalance, this can profoundly affect our emotions because all are connected. A shortage of zinc may cause depression; a shortage of B vitamins may cause irritability and even anger. The liver, if struggling with toxins or an over consumption of alcohol may cause anger, as it is the seat of anger. However, of themselves, such things do not create negative emotions; they merely bring them to the surface and activate them. If these emotional charges were not held in the primary field they could not manifest in the physical, no matter the state of the physical. In addition, these charges within the emotional body field have a constant and underlying effect upon the physical body field, which can activate and contribute to greater abuse and neglect. It is impossible to have a healthy physical body while maintaining an unhealthy emotional body. Indeed emotions play such a primary role in physical health, that it is now believed over 75% of all ill health is caused by negative mental and emotional charges. We may in fact abuse our physical bodies to a degree with toxic substances/food and not incur subsequent physical ill health if our emotional and mental bodies are healthy. Again, we arrive at the underlying and primary premise that all change for full health in all our fields, all forward movement on our evolutionary journey, must start with focused intent upon those aspects that are inherently of a higher vibration, all that is positive, all that is a natural outflow from the Divine source.

Hormones regulate our moods and emotions, and it can be surprising to learn that after menopause many facets of the being once thought to be intrinsic are found to be merely the results of hormonal activity. Where there was desire, agitation, ambition, excitement, stress and the desire for stimulation, there is now only peace, stillness and joy. What was thought to be integral to the being now appears as ephemeral as all else linked directly with the physical. With this new state of calm, it is much easier to communicate and interact with our soul, as before the cacophony created by the vigorous hormones made achieving stillness and peace more difficult. However, hormones aside, we can only ever manifest that which we have, and hormones of themselves do not create emotions: it is merely that the emotions are given greater charge for expression through the facility of the hormones. With fewer hormones, as in after menopause, just because the emotions are not manifested so greatly in the physical realm does not mean they have been deleted; they merely lie dormant to possibly reappear when one is under pressure at any time. Just because we do not see them, does not mean they are not there, but as we work towards aligning with and unfolding our soul, we will begin to delete their charge even if it is not immediately apparent in the physical.

Another potent and powerful source of emotions may arrive within our fields from an external source. We register them as ours, but they may in fact belong to another. As we interact with others, our energy field moves into and fuses in a greater way (remember, we are all connected anyway) with others around us. The moment we place our attention upon another, whether we feel empathy or antipathy, we deepen this connection. Depending on the kind of person we are, whether we have strong boundaries, whether we are very open or not, we may find we are allowing other's disturbed emotions to enter our fields and remain there as though they were our own. We, in other words, "own them". This is an unhealthy practice as we have enough disturbances in all our fields as it is without choosing to assimilate others along the way. Again we come back to how conscious and aware we are, since if conscious and aware we will immediately register what we have done and release these emotions back to their source where they belong. Nothing of a positive nature may be achieved by taking on another's baggage. This does not mean we cannot sympathise with another. In fact, if we keep our own fields as clear and as healthy as possible we are in a position to help in a far more meaningful and positive way than merely taking on another's negativity, which serves only to further distort our own fields. If by doing this we were clearing them of their disturbing emotions, it would possibly make sense, but the multiverse does not work in this way: we each must deal with our own stuff, we may not just slough it off on to another. That just doubles the negativity. Have you ever gone to a social gathering feeling quite happy, positive and relaxed and within a short time felt quite the opposite? For some, it is very easy to pick up others' negativity. A simple check at such times is to ask, "Who does this belong to?" This will tell us whether the emotion we are now feeling is ours. If it is not, we will find that it has suddenly lifted, maybe only slightly but enough for us to know this emotion is not ours. We may then just release it. Should we find the emotion does indeed belong to us, it is appropriate to ask, "Why am I feeling like this? What has been the trigger?" and to follow on from there to its source. In this way, our awareness increases, and we begin to comprehend our trigger points for activating certain emotions. We thus begin to clear and heal our emotional body.

As we know, the brain with its trillions of cells stores memory, and as emotions are integral aspects of memory, where there is memory there will be emotions. Together with memory stored in the brain, we also have cellular memory – memory from this lifetime and inherited genetic memory passed to us through our DNA from our ancestors. This is a great deal of memory, which is also a great deal of emotion. This entire interconnected and interrelated field of memory holding within it our emotional body is in constant contact with and stimulated by both external and internal fields. The emotions thus held within our fields are activated not only by sensory perception but also from within through imaginary realms that are themselves activated by other disconnected fragments/strings or whole fields of stored memory or emotion. Our emotional body is a vast, complex and highly reactive disturbed field indeed. In other words, we are a veritable seething mass of conflicting emotions, some of which are truly ours and others which are not but we have chosen to own; and all are held within the field known loosely as our emotional body. Rather like a boiling pot of liquid where we are only aware of the large bubbles breaking at the surface of the liquid, so are we in relation to our emotional body. As with the pot of boiling water, we are unaware of the millions of tiny bubbles of emotion existing within and arising from the deep unconscious of our being. This vast and unquiet field is blocking our unity with our soul and thus the Divine Creative Field, as neither of those two fields seethes with turbulent emotion.

We create memory and further emotional baggage on a daily basis until we learn how to experience all, without retaining any residue. We must learn how to be merely players, as Shakespeare put it, or as the *Gospel of Thomas* tells us to be: "Jesus said, 'Be passers-by'." If we are passers-by, this does not mean we are not involved, that we do not give of ourselves and our best to all aspects of life, but it does mean we do all without attachment to the event and its aftermath. We involve ourselves in all, but then move on holding onto nothing of what has just gone before. In this way we begin to free ourselves of all the incoherence caused by emotion and residue in our fields and we move more effortlessly through life, learning from all our experiences but carrying only the wisdom of the learning with us. In the initial stages we observe the way we are feeling, we seek to understand why and then, leaving all grief, pain, misunderstanding and so on, in the hands of the Divine, we pass on. Finally, we gain mastery over our emotional body and events do not trigger emotions at all. In this way, our emotional body gains and maintains full health. The *Gita* as always is eloquent on this subject:

"The disciplined self, moving among sense objects, with the senses free from attraction and repulsion, interested only as a spectator of the passing show, mastered by the self he goeth to Peace."

So, do we need emotions? Most definitely. They teach us as we go along our individual paths. Without emotions, how would we learn when we are relatively unconscious and unaware? However, as we become more conscious and aware, emotions begin to hold us back. We no longer need them, and we must find ways to let them go. We have probably all experienced the entire gamut of negative emotions over time and we know that they are not enjoyable; life would certainly be more pleasant without them. Knowing that all negative emotions, such as hate, anger, jealousy, greed, lust and so on, stem from fear enables us to feel compassion for anyone immersed in such emotions, because how may we be angry with, dislike or even hate someone who is afraid? If we do, it is because their fear is triggering ours. If we are in any way aligned with our soul, all we may do is feel sorry for them and have compassion for them. Just as we cannot give love unless we already possess it, so we cannot inflict pain unless we are ourselves in pain. The degree of pain that we inflict upon another is the degree we have within us. We are merely projecting out into the multiverse, that which is held within We cannot give what we do not have; this applies to the negative as well as the positive. Once we understand the way of the multiverse then we understand that truly unconditional love and compassion can be the only response to all emotionally charged situations.

To be afraid is a terrible thing, as it is fear of the primeval fundamental darkness in which we instinctively know we may be annihilated in the inchoate field of our beginning and therefore we cease to exist in individual form. This is why fear is so terrible, why it is the summation of all negative emotions and why it is the most difficult emotion to defeat. However, responding to a violent abuser only with love, compassion and forgiveness is inappropriate, as the system in which we have our being, while being one of love, is most definitely one of "Tough Love". The fundamental law of "as ye sow, so shall ye reap" confirms this. It does not mean that we set out on personal vendettas, but that, what we put out we will receive back, and it may well be that the ultimate punishment is inflicted by the system itself over time, even another time altogether than this, and may not ever be of human origin. If we should allow a violent person to be at liberty (when we had the responsibility to contain them) so that they were able to inflict harm upon another, then we also have thus sown and so shall we reap. All confused libertarians need to contemplate this, particularly as now with the dramatic shifts in energy that are taking place, we have vast numbers of frightened, angry beings causing mayhem and carnage around us. This phase will lessen over time, but until we all gain more wisdom and thus truly understand the situation and can assist healing, greater protective measures need to be considered, rather than less as we have right now.

One of our immediate tasks is to become emotionally healthy, so let us look at some of the common areas where emotional ill health arises. We know that anger, whether buried deep within or raging on the surface at regular intervals, is a block to all progress on the evolutionary path. Indeed, anger is a block to almost all positive activities that we may attempt to perform in this physical realm; it is certainly a block to creating loving and successful relationships. Anger contaminates and fractures all it touches; nothing of a positive nature can ever be built while this chaotic and destructive energy is present.

Many of us have learnt that anger will get us what we want. Like spoilt children we use it to bully and beat our way to what we in our deluded darkness think is success. Anger may get us more material goodies; however, unity with our soul and God can never be accomplished with anger. All anger must be released from our emotional body if we are to become emotionally healthy and successfully evolve. There are many ways to do this: what is important is that a way is chosen, as with anger in our emotional body our fields will be fractured to a great degree and unity and wholeness can never be attained. All anger must be released, ownership of it let go, no matter the seeming justification for holding onto it. Anger harms not only ourselves but all those close to us, it also surges out into the entire multiverse, touching and distorting all and it will eventually, one way or another, flow back to us and cause us much harm. By allowing this energy's existence, we harm the entire web of the multiverse, and this situation will not be left unresolved.

Many times, we hold onto old emotions, perceived hurts, because we are unable to bring ourselves to forgive the perceived originator of our hurt and pain. We nourish our pain; we develop it and nurture it until it grows and becomes ever more meaningful in our life; until the pain and the events around the pain become almost a virtual being in itself. We are masters of creation, but we do not realise this, do not realise our own power. In refusing to forgive, we are refusing to let go, and while we hold onto it, it remains ours. So, our pain, anger, hurt and resentment that we originally created (these emotions were not imposed upon us by an outside agency, even though we keep telling ourselves they were) continues and even grows with each passing year. Unless we can learn to forgive and let go, we will never be emotionally healthy. The first time we choose to let go is the hardest, but when we see that it didn't hurt much, if at all, we wonder why we made such a big deal of it. Our subsequent lighter sense of being is all the immediate reward we will need. The real rewards reveal themselves with time as the art of forgiveness sets us free from negative field effects and thus heals all our fields, empowers us and initiates the process of alignment. This is why Jesus among many other great spiritual teachers made much of this ability:

> But if ye do not forgive, neither will your Father which is in heaven forgive your trespasses.
>
> — *Mark 11:26*

As with all else in this wonderful system, the law of forgiveness is perfect. If we do not forgive, we cannot be healed: if we hold chaotic energy within our fields that has arrived there under the law of reaping what we sow, and if we are unable to allow the similar actions of others to delete from our field, how may the results of our negative actions be deleted? Both are intrinsically linked: if we forgive – let go, the actions of others, this action on our part, automatically deletes all in our field under the law of self-similarity. One cannot be dealt with while the other remains. Here again we find we must take the first step. If we first are able to forgive, this will create of itself forgiveness for our own transgressions. If we refuse to forgive, we are blocked in all our fields, therefore how may we lose the charge of our own transgressions? The one condition holds both in place.

Attachment causes much emotional trauma. Delete attachment from our life and much of our emotional pain will cease. If we wish to be emotionally healthy, giving up our habit of attachment is a big part of the equation and until we gain mastery over this, our emotional body will be constantly disturbed. Giving up attachment and "not my will but Thine" go hand in hand. If we choose to surrender our will to the greater will of the Divine, then we automatically give up all attachment – it is as simple and as difficult as that. However, it is a hard thing to do so it will not be accomplished overnight, but it is possible just as soon as we choose to believe it is so. On this subject, let us look at some of the wise words of Buddha:

> If a person is to avoid being caught in the current of his desires, he must learn at the very beginning not to grasp at things lest he should become accustomed to them and attached to them. He must not become attached to existence nor to non-existence, to anything inside or outside, neither to good things nor to bad things, neither to right nor to wrong. If he becomes attached to things, just at that moment, all at once, the life of delusion begins. The one who follows the Noble Path to enlightenment will not maintain regrets, neither will he cherish anticipations, but, with an equitable and peaceful mind, will meet what comes.

Finally, another great source of surging emotions is resistance. One could even say that in the final analysis, all pain and suffering comes from resistance. The degree to which we resist an event is the degree that we will suffer. Resistance to change, resistance to all of life's events that we perceive as unwanted or negative, resistance to letting go when we should, in short resistance to all of the Divine Creator's great ebbs and flows is a primary source of our emotional ill health. (Remember, what we resist, persists). While we feel we are masters of the universe we resist so much and thus the resulting turmoil, pain and anger continues. What we must realise is that it is neither the event nor the subsequent emotion that caused our suffering; it is only ever our reaction to the original event. Resisting life's slings and arrows as they come at us is foolish, for if we allow them to pass and stay in the calm quiet centre we each have in our midst – residing in the field of our soul, in the field of the Divine, then there is no trauma. Once we learn how to do this, we may suffer horrific events yet can calmly and peacefully move on; taking no negativity in whatever form with us, in the quiet knowledge that ultimately, we are loved, protected and safe. We can then pass on to the next scene in this great play, with the same quiet confidence that all is well and only then will we begin to become emotionally healthy and align all our fields with the field of the Divine.

There is a simple exercise one can perform that shows clearly, because it is in the physical realm – that our resistance causes us pain, not the event itself. When next in physical pain, when it first hits, relax and move into it instead of tensing, stressing and pulling away. You will find the pain immediately lessens and will quite quickly disappear altogether. The pain comes from our resisting the physical sensation; once we cease to resist, the pain is no more. The wisdom of no resistance applies to all levels of being and all fields of our being. All perceived pain and trauma comes from our initial resistance to an event. The accomplishment of this exercise requires a focused intent and a relaxed, peaceful trust. In the initial stages, it is difficult but as with everything else practice brings success. Once accomplished, this ability may be applied to all negative (as we perceive them to be) events. If we, in loving allowance, accept each event, move into our pain and grief then let all go, holding no residue and trusting in the healing love, wisdom and power of God, we heal and empower, rather than harm ourselves.

We have seen what an impermanent, constantly changing, vital living system we live in. Yet we fear and resist change. We desire permanency, fixed points, walls around us that are indestructible. Any change engenders blind panic, fear and anger, leaving our emotional body in a turmoil. This is a strange software program we are running. How may we live in a system that is in a state of permanent flux and yet only be happy if we have no changes? Therein surely madness lies. We must come not only to accept change but also to go with it and flow with it. If we then observe what is created next with the trust and wisdom that flows from conscious relationship with our own soul and the Divine, we may glide through all with perfect ease and no little serenity knowing that all is well, all is as it should be.

Now let us contemplate Shakespeare's words above, as they give a clear picture of how things truly are. We are all merely players on a stage: the emotions that so churn us up, cause us to seethe and writhe, do not have any real substance. They are merely the ebb and flow of certain energies that do not have anything to do with us unless we choose to own them, and we have the free will to choose *not* to own them! We are not victims of a powerful and cruel world; we are ourselves beautiful, powerful and Divine spiritual beings should we choose to recognise this. If we do not, this state of being is not then a reality for us. It is as simple and as difficult as that.

The exercise I give in Chapter Fourteen helps us to view what is going on as a play. When we are able to stand back a little we see more clearly, as with the ground so close to our face, as it is at present, true vision is impossible. When we are not immersed in raging emotion, we find the scene is removed somewhat, and with the perspective that distance brings we are able to understand more and can see our true role in the play as it unfolds before our eyes. We are then able to participate in the play with calmness and serenity, rather than reacting amid a sea of emotions to perceived events. Note the word "perceived", as without distance our view is necessarily distorted. When we are bound up in raging emotion, our thought processes are impeded, and we cannot be logical. With the help of perspective, we will find ourselves saying calmly in response to almost all dramatic, even life-threatening events, "That is interesting. I wonder what will happen next." We begin to develop a childlike wonder at it all; we become as small children, fearless, safe in the knowledge we are loved and protected. When we have arrived at this stage after much diligent work, we will find we are not reacting emotionally any more to all events. We will find the pulse isn't racing, we dwell in a calm, even place and our mind is quite clear and undisturbed in the midst of all. It is then we know that we are well on our way to becoming master of our emotional body instead of a slave to the ebb and flow of our emotions. We see and think more clearly and are far more effective in all we do. What is more, the strain upon the physical body is dramatically lessened and thus greater overall health of all the fields begins to prevail.

He who hates not light, nor busy activity, nor even darkness, when they are near, neither longs for them when they are far;

Who unperturbed by changing conditions sits apart and watches and says "the powers of nature go round", and remains firm and shakes not;

Who dwells in his inner self, and is the same in pleasure and pain; to whom gold or stones or earth are one, and what is pleasing or displeasing leave him in peace; who is beyond praise and blame, and whose mind is steady and quiet;

When a man of vision sees that the powers of nature are the only actors of this vast drama, and he beholds THAT which is beyond the power of nature then he comes into my Being.

— *Bhagavad Gita 14:22-24, 19*

It is with the arising of emotions that so cloud and confuse the mind that we commit the worst sin of all: we confuse and deceive ourselves. When our emotional body is as a still, illuminating lake, we see all clearly and calmly, and reflect back all perfectly. We retain power instead of leaking it; all that is not ours is sent automatically back to its source. Thus, we are also automatically protected and are more powerfull. The degree to which we react emotionally in an unconscious manner is the degree to which we have evolved. If we are to align with our soul and thus reconnect with all those inherent energies, if we are to then align and interact with the Divine Creative Field, we must arrive at the point where all our fields are as calm, luminous, unified and coherent as the Divine Field of Love. In other words, we must in all our fields become the same as the field of love, which is God. Anything that is of love, any emotion, action, thought or word that springs from the field of love will help to bring us to the required place. Anything not of love, and we are going in the wrong direction.

A friend once went to a clairvoyant and said, "Please tell me about my future." The clairvoyant, a wise man who knew that my friend was not one for personal change, replied, "Look at your past, as your future will be the same as your past." Or:

> "If you want to know your past life, look into your present condition; if you want to know your future life, look to your present actions".
>
> — *Padmasambhava*

The choice as always is ours, and the Bhagavad Gita so eloquently encapsulates this chapter simply describing the vision:

> Hear now how he then reaches Brahman, the highest vision of Light.
>
> When the vision of reason is clear, and in steadiness the soul is in harmony; when the world of sound and other senses is gone, and the spirit has risen above passion and hate;
>
> When a man dwells in the solitude of silence, and meditation and contemplation are ever with him; when too much food does not disturb his health, and his thoughts and words and body are in peace; when freedom from passion is his constant will;
>
> And his selfishness and violence and pride are gone; when lust and anger and greediness are no more, and he is free from the thought 'this is mine'; then this man has risen on the mountain of the Highest: he is worthy to be one with God.
>
> — *Bhagavad Gita 18: 50–53*

Chapter 13
The Mental Body

Man's life lies all within this present, as 'twere but a hair's breadth of time. As for the rest, the past is gone, the future yet unseen.

— *Marcus Aurelius*

Everything within the multiverse is imbued with consciousness and thus intelligence and the mental body is the field through which we consciously interact with both the explicate and the implicate realms. It is through the faculty of our mental aspect that we may discriminate, interact with, organise and direct all the forces within the natural world. In addition, the mental aspect is the mechanism whereby all comes into manifestation in the physical realms. Utilising the mental body with aligned, focused and powerful attention, the form is made manifest from the implicate order. The source of mind's energy flow is the Divine Creative Field via the soul, the mental body and thence the physical brain. Therefore, mind's energy has the potential to be infinite and full of spiritual power. Most importantly the mental body is the field through which the incarnate soul interacts with God – the Divine Creative Field – so if our mental body is fractured and incoherent, contact with God is impossible.

> We belong to a living Earth in an intelligent universe.
>   Intelligence is not a human monopoly.
> The universe is made of intelligence and consciousness.
> Planet Earth is a self-organising, self-managing and
>   self-correcting living organism.
> Wherever there is life there is intelligence and
>   consciousness.
>
> — *Satish Kumar*

If we understand the nature of the mental body and, with this knowledge, control and direct our mind with focus and intent, we can bring into manifestation, organise and direct all. In other words, we are co-creators with God; always bearing in mind that any co-creating must work under the immutable law of "not my will but Thine". It is only possible to become a co-creator if we are first aligned with the Divine Field as, while aligned, all work is automatically performed under the law, will and creative intent of the Divine. We are acting as conscious willing servants of God. It is not possible at this time for us to become unfettered creators, working solely from our own limited free will, particularly if our will is not in accord with or is in opposition to the Divine will. Also, our creative power is limited by the degree of our alignment/evolution. Because our mental body plays such a pivotal role in all our activities and consequently in our evolutionary progress, if we wish to advance, we must address its overall health and alignment. Our mental body must become fully aligned with all our fields, our soul and the Divine Creative Field.

Guru Nanak Dev, the founder of Sikhism, said, "Conquer the mind and you conquer the world." One could say the greatest instrument of torture ever devised was the human mind. Oh, how we love to torture ourselves with our fecund imagination. In our mind, we dwell in the past and the future, rarely in the present. We seize upon the most fleeting of thoughts that have no basis in reality and grow them until they take us over, thereby creating yet more powerful thought forms =

emotions, and thus turbulence in all our fields. The mental body is the most powerful force in the explicate realm, after the Divine of course, but it is ephemeral and is not to be found anywhere in the physical body. Many believe that the seat of the mind is the brain, but if we are aligned, the field of mind is infused throughout the soul field, an all-enveloping field in which the physical being resides. If we are not aligned, the field of mind may be as disconnected and fractured as all our other fields: it may be way out there while you are over here. An incarnate being's field of mind, no matter where it is hanging out at any particular time, must use the physical brain as its apparatus if it is to project into this space-time continuum. This is why many of the materialist mind set have become confused and think that the brain (which is mostly fat and water) itself creates thought, intelligent mental activity and consciousness.

So, what is mind? Are *you* your mind? Are you the sum total of your mind, as some would have it – Richard Dawkins, for instance. Are our thoughts that come from the field of the mental body through our brain created by us in the mental body field, or is it the brain, mind's servant, that creates thoughts? Many who dwell primarily in the physical as the only logical reality are convinced that our physical brain is the creator of all our thoughts. Is there another possibility? As all in the multiverse is actively intelligent and connected, all is one; is it possible that mind is an information web linked to all and therefore linked to all mental activity in the multiple fields of the multiverse? Indeed, we now know that information controls and regulates – even non-locally, all functions within the multiverse. Information is a key to life. Thus, our so-called thoughts are compositions of universal thoughts/information which are processed and coloured through the filters of our individual fields of inherent emotion and memory, which are themselves held in the totality of our being, to be then birthed as personal mental activity by the projection of our physical brain into this space-time reality. Mental activity in its totality arises from our universal interconnectedness, planetary fields, inherited genetic memory, physical body stimuli, outside stimuli (actions, words, sights and sounds), the external energy fields of other people, morphogenetic resonance, together with all the many subtle interactions our fields experience moment by moment. This multiplicity of sources together with our imagination will keep our mental body overcharged and fractured unless we take steps to halt much of this activity. Why we need to halt it we will shortly see. The dictionary defines imagination as "mental faculty forming images of external objects not present to the senses – creative faculty of the mind". As our mental body does not create thoughts as such, but sticks fragments of charge together, we have no problems creating the virtual fields represented by imagination. In this teeming intelligent soup of the multiverse, random strings of charge are processed and combined with others to create a seemingly individual thought-form from combinations, according to our prism and focused intent. Now focused intent is the key here, as this process may be conscious or unconscious and herein lies the problem. If unconscious and we dwell much in our imagination, the creativity of the mental field can become very intense. We will mix and match to suit our points of view, our fear and our level of evolution and thus we create great turbulent mental fields that have no basis in reality and these fields will serve to fracture further all our fields. The more fractured all our fields are, the more this process increases – and if it increases to the point of total overload, the field of our mental body blows a fuse and we experience complete mental breakdown. If we are in any way aligned, centred and unified with our soul, we do not stick fragments of charge together – mindlessly – unconsciously.

There is a further source and process of mental activity, which is direct Divine communication, this is the path of the Prophets, Mystics and Sages. This mental activity arrives via the mental body and the mechanism of our brain as pure original thoughts, not the usual mix-and-match we project on a daily basis, but as single shining strings imbued in their totality with Divine truth, wisdom, joy, love and spiritual power. This mental activity is projected into this plane of reality as a direct and original stream of energy – consciousness, from

God, via the agency of our right-brain, which means they arrive via a completely different aspect of the physical brain than all other activity. Few of us are aligned enough and quiet enough to receive information in this direct way; most of our mental activity is processed through our chaotic fields and thus our mental activity is coloured and skewed by our inherent software program and our emotions, so:

> For now we see through a glass, darkly; now we know in part; but then face to face shall I know, even as also I am known.
>
> — *1 Corinthians 13:12*

Our dark glass may well be that we tell lies and cheat. If this is the predominant characteristic of our mental processes, our software program, we would view the world through this lens and believe that the rest of the world operated through this same lens. We would make the error of basing all our decisions, all our judgements, all our actions on this false premise. Curiously, because like is attracted to like, we would also draw towards us others operating in a similar vein. In this way our belief would be constantly reaffirmed and soon we would come to believe that all people are liars and cheats, the whole world is crooked, and our actions and words would reflect this belief in ever-greater ways. This is an extreme example, but this process is going on for all of us all the time, in small ways and large. Once we are aware that this process is happening, we can begin to observe ourselves, identify the exact nature and origin of each particular prism of the dark glass, and see the light of the real and the true shining behind the dark glass. Once we understand that it is our inner vision that colours our external reality, we can begin to dwell more in reality. While we all see through a glass darkly, our reality is constantly shifting to accommodate all programs, judgements and points of view, and thus the explicate realm is a hazardous field to navigate. In this chimerical darkness, our only compass is the unerring true north of our divine soul and God.

Now let us look at the physical structure of our brain. Scientists have analysed various parts of it and determined that certain parts perform certain functions, but in many ways the brain is the last frontier, as we know so little about it. There have been cases where we thought that particular parts could only perform particular functions, but when those parts have been damaged through accident, other parts of the brain would kick in and take over. We have divided the brain very broadly into three aspects, commonly known as the left-brain, the right-brain and the reptilian or old brain (which is at the base of our skull). We know memory is stored in the brain, but it is also stored throughout all our physical body. The left-brain is viewed as the analytical, logical, no-nonsense side of reason; its functions assist us to work effectively through this physical space-time reality. The energy field of the left-brain is considered to be masculine: positive, aggressive and outgoing.

The right-brain is the source of all intuition, creativity and inspiration and is the channel through which initially all interaction with God is facilitated. The right-brain is feminine: negative, passive, reflective. In our modern society, many products of right-brain function are dismissed as nonsense or imaginary. Our western school systems are based primarily upon developing left-brain function, which is why indigenous people often do not do well in our schools. This primary focus on the left-brain also explains why we no longer create much great art, music or architecture and most of what we do create is very ugly, beauty being an attribute of the right-brain. The left-brain has no concept of harmony, balance or beauty. Dwelling primarily in the left-brain also explains why we no longer create so-called miracles, it is also why many of us believe there is no God, as if we primarily dwell there, we dwell in a finite and God-less realm. The left-brain is the realm of the atheists. The god of atheists is the logic, reason and concrete deduction of the left-brain. When we dwell primarily in the cold and lonely regions of the left-brain, depression and even suicide may well be a direct result. The left-brain is the seat of the ego, the "I". If both regions of the brain are not equally respected and balanced, if the "I" of the left-brain is not moderated by the spiritual dimensions of the right-brain, then classic projections of mental thought-form entities may result. When primarily focused in the left-brain, disassociated from our divine soul we can and do create virtual mental entities of considerable independence, power and force. Much that is unbalanced, incoherent or even malign in human nature and events at this time; emanates from such entities. These are in effect virtual beings, and we are seeing ever more of this phenomenon as we move towards the end of the age of darkness. The instinctive intuition of the soul is projected through the right-brain, and as we develop the alignment of all our fields with our soul and God, we begin to increase greatly the activity of the right-brain until we are using it in its fullness, as quickly and as easily as we now use the left-brain. We develop the ability to use the two hemispheres simultaneously with increasing competence and speed, which makes us more effective in all ways and we begin to speed our evolutionary progression towards greater spiritual power.

As we saw in Chapter Five, we have arrived at a critical point and the balancing of brain function is one of the primary aspects we must address. We are urged to use all aspects of our brain with fluency and mastery, as this together with aligning all our fields with the field of our divine soul will accelerate our evolutionary progress and bring us to a place of great creative spiritual power. If all our fields are aligned with our divine soul and thus by implication the Divine Creative Field, the aligned mental body working through a fully functional whole brain then naturally functions directly under the guidance and intent of God and to its greatest potential. Right now, we only know how to utilise a very small percentage of our miraculous equipment. The mental body activated and infused by the Divine is the greatest power at play in the manifested explicate realm, as it is in the implicate. The mental body activated and infused by the Divine is a field of high spin: excluding the pure fields of soul and the Divine, it is the highest vibratory field in the explicate realm. To gain control over all forces in nature, one has only to gain control over the mind. If we are to gain control over our physical and emotional bodies, if we are to further evolve and align all our fields with our soul field and thus the Divine, then we must gain control over our mind. If we are not in full control of our own mind, we are out of control in all our fields: instead of being powerful creators, we are fractured, incoherent victims.

How do we arrive at a state of full health of our mental body? It is misleading to separate our being into parts, i.e. mental health and physical health, as both are locked into such a close and interdependent relationship, with all aspects affecting all else and we need to hold this in mind while examining our mental body because we have split the mind into two. We have decided that it consists of two parts, the conscious and the subconscious. We are so immersed in the idea of separation that we are not happy unless, like a mechanic, we can break the engine down into its smallest component parts. Any slight difference anywhere and we say, "Let's break it down here and look at each part separately. That will tell us more about the whole." While this works to help us understand more on one level, we must always be aware of the dangers of this practice, because we run the risk of losing sight of the whole picture. The glory of the Divine plan may be lost to us in the minutiae. This breaking down into component parts gives us the illusion of control; we have reduced the whole to small enough pieces that we, small as we are, can assimilate. This makes the explicate realm a less frightening place – the smaller the bits, the more control we have. Or so we think.

The so-called conscious mind and its activities are the froth on the top of the whole field of the mental body, the bubbles that break upon the surface much like boiling water: the most obvious are the ones we pay the most attention to. The depths of the field, the aspects closest to the source of the charge, the creative force and reason for the charge, is ninety-eight per cent of the time ignored. As a Tibetan monk I saw being interviewed on television said, "You in the West have all things turpsy–toppy." I loved that and agree: we are often upside down in our thinking. So, we have it that the so-called conscious mind is generally quite sublimely unconscious, while the subconscious is always aware, more knowing and awake at all times.

We generally think of the subconscious mind as the dictionary defines it: "not aware, not knowing, not aware of external factors, mental faculties not awake". However, the subconscious mind is in far greater aware and close relationship with all the fields of the multiverse, both implicate and explicate including the field of our soul and the Divine, than our conscious mind. What we really have is a complete misunderstanding of the whole. It is the so-called conscious mind, the froth on the top, that is "not aware, not knowing, not awake" and the subconscious mind that is all of these things. The conscious mind is the less wise and less knowing aspect of the mental body because it is less aligned with the soul and with the Divine. What we must do first is to realise the error in our thinking and then understand that there is only one mind – mental body, and that the charge furthest from the source is just that. We then need to learn how to access easily the deeper recesses of our whole mind at will; to pay close attention to it, interact with it, and by doing this – heal it. Because our so-called conscious mind is more embedded in the physical, it is more distracted and abstracted by things of the senses, and there is more activity on the surface. If the surface is where our primary focus is, then we are easily overwhelmed by all things of sense perception. As Julian Johnson says: "Desire may draw us to objects of sense... The senses overwhelm the mind, and the mind enslaves the soul." Thus, we eternally wander, with our souls enslaved, confused and confounded, through the chimerical landscape of our current evolutionary epoch. While we persist in addressing only the outer fringes of our whole mind, we will remain unconscious.

Further, to label aspects of the mind as subconscious is unhelpful, as this gives us the idea we are not able to access and or use this part of our mind in our day-to-day affairs. Nothing could be further from the truth. By dividing the mind in this way, great harm has been done, as we view the most potent active part of our mind as being out of reach to us. If we are to "know ourselves", we must access our whole mind.

We must interact with, listen to and use our whole mind in all our affairs and in all our ways. We must begin to develop a relationship with the deepest part of our mental body. It is only then that we may begin to know the full depths of our being. While we persist in focusing and functioning primarily on the surface of our mental body, we will remain deeply unconscious.

If we are afraid to venture into our own depths because our fear is controlling us, we will remain stuck and unable to evolve further. So, we must plunge bravely into the depths, fearlessly looking in the face each aspect we find there. When we dive deep into this pool, passing through layer after layer surprisingly, we find that unlike the busy surface of our mental body, where all the sources of mental activity discussed above are frenziedly flashing across the field, there are comparatively few here. Admittedly, these few are sometimes frightening demons and entities that we have refused to deal with in the past – we have thrust them deep into our depths hoping that if we ignore them, they will go away. But they do not, as they are in fact our old enemy, fear. Our first task, then, on the path to mental health is to plunge into the depths to slay these illusory foes. I say "illusory", because as soon as we direct the brilliant light of our clear focused and divinely inspired intent upon fear, it vanishes in a cloud of fragmented dark energy, and if we refuse to have anything more to do with it we will never see it again. It is as easy and as difficult as that. With a little clearing, we will find that aside from those seemingly terrifying foes, calm reigns supreme. Instead of more mental activity, we find less. Once clear, our mental body is a unified, mercurial and reflective field of consciousness of beautiful light and potentially infinite power. It is our fears, dark imaginings, residual demons of past happenings, programming inherited and otherwise, that have changed the field of our mental body into the murky and blocked field we find when we first investigate it. On mind and consciousness, the *Bhagavad Gita* has this to say:

> Of the Vedas I am the Veda of songs, and I am Indra, the chief of gods. Above man's senses I am the mind, and in all living beings I am the light of consciousness.
>
> — *Bhagavad Gita 10:22*

It is a sad fact that we are not taught at home, at school or anywhere else how to access and use our whole mind; in fact, in many ways we are deterred from doing so. Ignoring such a vital aspect of our being as though it does not exist is unhealthy and hard to understand. The refusal or inability to recognise and engage in any daily meaningful way with our whole mind is why we behave as though we are deeply unconscious and disconnected – because we are. Our mental body is the vital field through which our soul manifests in the explicate realms, without the full use of this field in this realm, our soul languishes ignored, a potentiality but nothing more. However, the evolutionary thrust is such that we desire to be whole, we know we can be so much more than we are right now, we instinctively know we are fractured, incoherent and incomplete, and instinctively we seek to address this and to heal.

The degree we are conscious is the degree of our mental health and the more conscious we are the greater our rate of spin – the higher our frequency, because with consciousness comes alignment and with alignment comes refinement. When we move into all these states of being, we experience greater freedom and creative power than hitherto known. When we are aligned and conscious, it is impossible that we may commit unkind, greedy, violent or cruel acts as we see and hear more clearly and thus understand more: when conscious and aligned with the Divine, we become more like the Divine. As our ever more unified fields move into greater alignment with the Divine field, all properties of the Divine field become ours to the degree of our alignment. In this higher spin state, we know that those who do commit such acts are in all ways unconscious and disconnected – their fields have a relatively lower spin rate, therefore greater incoherence, which results in greater darkness, as lower vibration means less light as the fuel required to spin is light, the light/life of the Divine Creative Field. Because they are unconscious and disconnected, they cannot comprehend all the ramifications of their acts. It is then that we can fully understand the true meaning of Jesus's injunction, "Forgive them for they know not what they do."

When we seek and begin to attain consciousness and alignment with the Divine, we do not act in ways that are out of alignment with the Divine Field; we do not act in ways that are a negation of all the Divine represents. When standing in our achieved place of higher spin light and spiritual power we can clearly see more of the greater picture and we know there is no other possible path for us. In this enhanced position, our response to all in trouble and misalignment can only be with unconditional love and compassion.

If we wish to assess the health of our mental body and how conscious we are, there is only one place to start – within. A little self-examination is necessary. One of the first questions we might ask is, "Am I living an authentic life?" which means is it my life I am living or someone else's. Have we given our power away and perhaps not realised it? It is very easy to do this, as this condition can creep upon us so slowly that we do not see each turn of the wheel; we just wake up one day and realise that to all intents and purposes, we have vanished. We may have given our power to things, situations or other people (this is the most common – other people seemed to take it, but actually we allowed them to). When we lose ourselves, when we give our power away, we become scattered, unhappy, maybe constantly angry, irritable or depressed and thus leak ever more power in all directions. Our life may not feel like our own, we are not fulfilled, not realising our true potential, but we may console ourselves by attempting to become the greatest martyr there ever was. We perhaps tell ourselves we are really leading a valuable full life, because we are sacrificing ourselves for the noble cause of that other person or situation, but the funny thing is, we do not feel good about it. We all have a particular soul journey we should be on, we all have particular abilities special to us, and if we have not yet found and followed our individual star, our being will reflect this neglect in all our fields. We are all very clever at playing mind games with ourselves, if we allow it. Our capacity for self-deception is great, hence the need for the inward journey of knowing ourselves. When we engage in any negative mental body activities, we set ourselves on the path to self-immolation, the end of which can only be massive disconnection from the soul and thus the Divine.

So how do we become authentic and with a healthy mental body? As with all else, with focus, intent, trust and above all practice. When we first set out to conquer our own mind, we encounter formidable foes in the many thought-form entities and programming embedded within the mental body. We need to change the software and use the delete button relentlessly. Old habits die hard and we must choose to police our every thought, as without this constant attention to the activity of our mental body we will fail. In policing our thoughts, we must constantly bring our mind back to the present, always back to right now, as the thoughts we follow down the primrose paths of the past, the future and "what if" help keep us unconscious. We may require help deleting some of these programs and there are excellent workers in many different modalities, some of which are working with the powerful new energies that are now available. These new energies make our task of becoming whole, healthy and aligned more rapid, effortless and painless. The new energies quickly wipe all deleterious cellular memory from our fields; this facilitates all the other work to be done. Again we have a Catch-22 situation here, because if we are aligned with God all obsolete memory programming, all negativity, is automatically deleted. However, until we do some preparatory work it is difficult if not impossible to align with God. The beginning is the hardest, but as our fields clear and we become more conscious and aligned, the inflowing Divine energies directly assist us. Remember we can and should always ask for help in these activities – we must knock on the door. There is much besides that we can ourselves do: our thoughts are electrical charges of energy and therefore powerful. If our mental body is flooded with negative thoughts, the work is made harder and success more difficult. With every negative thought we take a step back and move from evolution to involution – away from the Divine. If we wish to become co-creators, just one negative thought does us much harm and impedes our progress. It is because of this that mental hygiene is one of the first and most important things to monitor. It cannot be said too often, watch every thought, do not allow the negative full birth, and do not follow a negative thought down its chosen path. Refuse to go there.

Another important aspect of mental health is the diet we feed our mind. Do we digest a regular diet of violence, ugliness and negativity in whatever form? If this is the case, then we are working against ourselves as we try to align our bodies and interact with our soul, as all these negative vibrations are anathema to the soul's energies. As we have seen, the soul will move away and misalign even more if these violent ugly frequencies are invited into our fields. Our mental body, like our physical body, requires a healthy diet. If we respect our mental body and ourselves, we will have regard for our mental health and will feed ourselves a diet of only that which is positive, uplifting, nurturing, beautiful, harmonious and loving.

If we should find ourselves thinking such things as "I am no good", "Life is difficult" and "I will never get what I want", just choose not to go there. Remember, if we cannot control and master our own mind, we will be unable to master anything else worthwhile. This is one of the great keys. In this multiverse of energy, thoughts of any kind have enormous creative power. We will manifest that which we think, even if it is in a limited and negative way. It may be helpful here, if we consider a useful Buddhist precept: before speaking we should ask ourselves: "Is it true? Is it necessary? Is it kind?" This is a positive discipline to adopt, for if what we say is always the truth as we see it, we will be more likely "to say what we mean and to mean what we say". How are we to communicate with each other if we are unable to do this one fundamental thing? We must also commit to dealing with what follows from the changes we make: we must commit to being brave and resolute, then with focused intent on the Divine success is not only possible, but also assured.

When considering mental hygiene, it is not possible to overlook that popular activity – worry. Worrying is the greatest waste of energy and power, and the stress produced from our wild imaginings is guaranteed to hold us in our current stuck position. Worrying, as with negative thinking, is a habit. We must choose to delete the program and change the habit. Think, "I will not think such things." Do not examine whether these thoughts might actually be true: we do not want to know. Just hit the delete button. Think the opposite more positive thought, if that helps, although it is always better to work towards clearing the field of thought forms altogether. Then we may rest in the space of no thought and our mental body can have the long-desired and much-needed rest. It is only when we clear a space that we may hear our own divine soul and the field of the Divine Creator.

Which brings us to silence. How may we have a healthy mental body, how may we interact with our own soul, let alone God, if our days are filled with sound, the cacophony of which will drive out all resonances from the high-vibratory fields? Why is it that in our modern world we are so afraid of silence?

> Why are you so afraid of silence, silence is the root of
> everything.
> If you spiral into its void a hundred voices will thunder
> messages you long to hear.
>
> *— Rumi*

If we are addicted to sound, we do not have a hope of contacting God. Constant sound, no matter its quality, will over time fracture all our fields and thus make it impossible to align with the Divine. The young, permanently plugged into literally soul-shattering sound, are endangering their immortal soul. This may sound overly dramatic, but once the soul fragments, negativity from diverse sources flow into the now incoherent soul field, and a spiral descent towards involution is activated in all the fields. To many, silence is scary; for some, to be alone with only themselves in the space of no one and no sound is one of the most frightening things. Nevertheless, if this is the case what is being expressed loud and clearly is that we do not like our own company and we certainly do not love ourselves. What is more, we have absolutely no desire whatsoever to get to know ourselves. It hardly needs saying that with this situation, without the desire to unify with oneself, it is not possible to unify with anything else. The reason silence is so frightening is that the moment the silence descends, the moment our fields are not vibrated by the constant field effects of sound, all the demons, all the negativity, all that we are avoiding by using constant sound, comes rising rapidly to the surface to be confronted. So, we turn on the sound again. Our old friend fear again needs to be confronted so we can dwell happily within a field of perfect, blissful silence, in happy communion with ourselves: if we are not able to this, no further evolutionary advancement is possible, and the danger is ever-present that we may regress.

A review of a recent film gave a wonderful description of religious people as "nutters who need to get out more". This amused me greatly, as the reporter was quite correct in a way. If we "get out more" and surround ourselves with diversions, immerse ourselves in materiality, then the things of the spirit will be lost in the resultant clamour, glitz, glamour and rush of the modern explicate realm. Conversely, if we are to evolve, if we are to align ourselves with our divine soul and thus the Divine, we need to stay in more, in the quiet and the stillness, where we may hear, see and come to understand, know and love the ineffable mysteries.

> The more and more you listen, the more and more you hear; the more and more you hear, the deeper and deeper your understanding becomes.
>
> — *Dilgo Khyentse Rinpoche*

If we are to progress to the next step and become powerful spiritually aligned creators in our own right, then our mental body must become a calm and reflective field of consciousness. It can no longer be the turbulent, fractured field it currently is; a field that surges with the minute-by-minute flow-on field effects from an immature emotional body and all the other negative vibrations we allow into our whole being. The harmonising and deleting of the emotional with the mental must be done in tandem as they work so closely together. It is not possible to arrive at the health of one field while ignoring the other. What is the vision of a healthy mental body that we may hold in our mind? Is there one major quality we must attain? All the great spiritual writings are quite clear on this; our mental body must be stable. The *Bhagavad Gita* says, "He whose mind is free from anxiety amid pains, indifferent amid pleasures, loosed from passion, fear and anger is called a sage of stable mind."

The energy field of our mental body must be stable. It must be calm and reflective and at all times under our control. When we control our mind, we will never be heard to say, "I have no choice" or "I had to do this or that". We will know that at all times we have choice because we are acting from the calm centre of our physical, emotional and mental bodies, which are themselves always under the stable, unified and harmonising powerful field of our divine soul. If we are to project (in Sanskrit the word commonly translated as "creation" is literally "projection") our consciousness in the act of creation with power and intent, our mental body cannot be destabilised by waves of emotions or an overload of conflicting, meaningless or negative thoughts. This does not mean we are unfeeling or indifferent, but that we have reached a higher vibratory level of coherence and unity whereby we are able to observe pains and pleasures without becoming enmeshed in or attached to them either emotionally or mentally. We are able to view all as being under the overarching control and protection of God.

Is there one simple way to attain a stable mental body? The *Bhagavad Gita* as always is helpful:

The Mental Body

> The mind is restless, Krishna, impetuous, self-willed, hard to train: to master the mind seems as difficult as to master the mighty winds.
>
> Krishna: The mind is indeed restless Arjuna; it is indeed hard to train. But by constant practice and by freedom from passions the mind in truth can be trained. When the mind is not in harmony, this divine communion is hard to attain; but the man whose mind is in harmony attains it, if he knows and if he strives.
>
> — *Bhagavad Gita 6:34–36*

So in order to become stable, our mental body must be in harmony, which the dictionary tells us means "agreement pre-established between body and soul before their creation". Therefore, we must be in agreement with our soul, which as we know also means in agreement with the Divine. That sounds easy, doesn't it? Move into agreement with our soul and we have our mental body under our control.

> When all desires are in peace and the mind, withdrawing within, gathers the multitudinous straying senses into the harmony of recollection.
>
> Then, with reason armed with resolution, let the seeker quietly lead the mind into the Spirit, and let all his thoughts be silence.
>
> And whenever the mind unsteady and restless strays away from the Spirit, let him ever and for ever lead it again to the Spirit.
>
> Thus joy supreme comes to one whose heart is still, whose passions are peace, who is pure from sin, who is one with God.
>
> The one who pure from sin ever prays in this harmony of soul, soon feels the joy of Eternity, the infinite joy of union with God.
>
> He sees himself in the heart of all beings and he sees all beings in his heart. This is the vision of the Yogi of harmony, a vision which is ever one.

And when he sees me in all and he sees all in me, then I never leave him and he never leaves me.

— *Bhagavad Gita 6:24–30*

The directions are very clear, are they not? It is beginning to look as though if we wish to be stable, to heal and be in harmony and thus evolve to our predestined place of full spiritual power, all we need to do is to align and agree with our soul, which will automatically bring us to alignment and agreement with the Divine. Simple, and extremely elegant.

Leaving aside for the moment the goal of evolution and spiritual power, if we just look at what is required for us on a simple level to be able to interact directly with the Divine, we will see that if our mental body is not stable, is not in harmony with our soul, there can be little or no interaction. This is because, our soul projects through the vehicle of the mental body of consciousness when we directly contact God. If our mental body is fractured, incoherent and therefore unstable, we are unable to use it as a vehicle for projection. Not only are we unable to project with power and intent, but we are also unable to receive – hear, as the internal cacophony drowns out all else.

If our mental body is cluttered with inconsequential thoughts, desires and baggage real or imagined, how are we to utilise it efficiently, or utilise it at all when it comes to interacting with dimensions outside this space-time continuum? It is not possible. It is not even possible for us to function properly in the most ordinary of ways in the manifested realm if we are in this state, so how could we project and interact with other realms? For our mental body to project effectively out of this explicate realm and into the implicate ones, it must be aligned, stable and in harmony with all our other fields. If we are not in this state of being, interaction and union with the Divine is not possible. All those people rushing around saying "God does not exist" are merely telling us the state of their mental body among many other things.

When we have arrived at the point where our mental body is a calm, luminous field of pure stable consciousness, we find that for much of the time we are peacefully blank, dwelling naturally and easily in the now, at one with all that is. Then, when we are required to perform a mental function, our mind is rested and focused and thus even more powerful than it ever was before. You may wonder how you could function normally in the world with this preferred blank and peaceful mind – it does not seem possible that you could be effective. In fact, it makes everything easier and it makes us much more potent, focused and powerful. The passage from Marcus Aurelius at the beginning of the chapter is a great key: the first step to achieving a healthy mental body is to discipline ourselves to be only in the now. To be in the finite and tiny moment of time that is *right now*. How do we learn to live in the moment? As with everything else, it is just practice. Our minds may be in the habit of darting hither and thither with thousands of thoughts happening almost simultaneously. We may be in the habit of imagining all sorts of possibilities for the future, many of them dire; we may be in the habit of clinging onto thoughts stemming from past events. If we are to gain a stable, lucid and blank mind, we now have the keys and must determine to police *every* thought and use the delete button relentlessly. Once we start on the path to a healthy mental body, we will be amazed at all the unnecessary thoughts we have been accustomed to. These thoughts clog our mental body and exhaust our brain and thus our physical body, as our brain uses the greater percentage of our physical energy for its electrical activity than the rest of our body combined. When we still and calm our mind, when we have become sages of stable mind, we have so much more energy for all the other aspects of physical life.

In what may well prove a titanic struggle, all is merely habit, all is merely programming, change the software and the result must be different. Once we clear to a degree, once we have a few glimmers of a blank screen, we may work with greater focus on allowing ourselves only thoughts that deal with the here and now. The moment we notice that our mind is straying off into the past or the future, we must pull it back and delete the thought. A quiet mental body is healthy; a blank screen when we do not need to use it is healthy. It is the beginning of wisdom, the beginning of serenity, alignment and harmony.

> When the mind of the Sage is in harmony and finds rest in the spirit within, all restless desires gone, then he is one with God.
>
> — *Bhagavad Gita 6:18*

Many ancient races practised, as some in Africa do today, powerful rites calculated to violently catapult the whole being into a stable, harmonious and greater spiritual state. These rites of passage were undertaken by aspiring spiritual leaders and involved subjecting the being to extreme mental conditions, such as poisoning to induce a catatonic state and then incarceration in a sarcophagus with a number of beetles for a specified period of time, or being buried in an anthill for a proscribed period. The aspiring spiritual leader under these conditions either went mad – fractured his mental body and/or other fields completely – or the extreme state experienced on all levels and in all fields had the effect of deleting fear, stored memory and all inconsequential activity that was cluttering the fields. If he went mad, he was deemed unfit for high spiritual office, if he didn't, he was now a great spiritual leader as he had been catapulted into another state and other realms altogether, cleansed in all his fields and had survived intact. Now we do not practise such rites, which is possibly just as well as they are extremely dangerous, even if effective. We are lucky, however, in that the new energies playing upon the Earth are here to effect the same result as being incarcerated in a sarcophagus with beetles. The process is longer and at this time gentler, though we cannot presume that all will stay this way.

If our mental body is incoherent and unstable, we cannot function as a pure clear channel for God. Rather than owning a mental body that is like a wild untamed creature over which we are powerless, if we rest our mind in the perfect peace of the Divine Creative Field, we will own a mind that is a perfectly honed, stable and powerful instrument under our full control.

> Those who know all, but are lacking in themselves, are utterly lacking.
>
> *— Gospel of Thomas 67*

The universe is in a constant state of flux: nothing lasts forever, the so-called good things and the bad all have their time and move on. If we allow ourselves to watch the play of events, allow ourselves to observe the dance, only ever seeking to further align with the Divine, then practising the noble art of Wu Wei, we may weave the Divine like a golden thread throughout our day and rest in the stable field of the pure luminous consciousness of our powerful mental body.

> Give me thy mind and give me thy heart, give me thy offerings and thy adoration; and thus with thy soul in harmony, and making me thy goal supreme, thou shalt in truth come to me.
>
> *— Bhagavad Gita 9:34*

Chapter 14
Passage to Spiritual Power With All Its Many Gifts

Pilgrims why are you turning round in circles, what are you looking for?
The Beloved is here, why search in the desert?
If you look deep in your heart you will find Him within yourself.
You have made the pilgrimage and trod the path to Mecca many times.
You rave about the holy place and say you've visited God's garden but where is your bunch of flowers?
There is some merit in the suffering you have endured but what a pity you have not discovered the Mecca that's inside.

— *Rumi*

After all these many words, there are in truth only three simple things we need to do if we are to achieve union with the Divine, spiritual power and all its many gifts. The first is to acknowledge our soul and align our being in all its many facets with the field of our soul. The second is to submit our will to the Divine Will. From these two simple yet difficult acts, the third will naturally follow: we will come to know and love the Divine – we will have found the beloved deep within our heart – and ever more align with God. All that is of the Divine will quite simply and naturally become ours. To assist in accomplishing these three essential acts, an ancient exercise will be of great help. Before we look at that, however, let us reflect again on a few important points.

The same truth shines from religious spiritual beliefs and our current scientific thought. We can also see that the evolutionary process is an inherent process of the multiverse; indeed, that evolution is God in action. We are an individuated and integral part of the whole and thus we are evolving through time and space with all else. As we have limited free will, we may speed up or slow down our evolution, subject always to the confines of the system and governed by its immutable laws. We know that we are relatively unevolved beings; the current state of our planet, our predominant cultures and the ultimate fruits of our labours show that there is very little of a high vibration taking place anywhere.

We can understand from the many ancient scripts that the future illumined perfection of our yet relatively unevolved souls is the meaning and purpose of our existence. In other words, we are here to grow and perfect the unfolding of our souls into the pure multi-faceted diamond that is its inherent potential. This is our primary task on this physical plane of existence. God is inherent within his own creation, and we are destined to evolve through time and space in order to become through this evolutionary process in ever-greater similarity with God. Should we choose to accelerate the evolutionary process towards higher resolution and greater refinement, we will then quite naturally enjoy closer interaction with God, as we are moving into self-similarity and therefore greater communion with the Divine. It follows that we would also unfold to greater wisdom, vision, creativity, joy and love, together with the power to consciously navigate in other realms, even at the point of so-called death and beyond. In addition, we would also find we are able to control and organise all that is vibrating at a lower rate than we are, i.e. all physical matter and all aspects that have a lesser vibratory rate. In other words, in our greater alignment with the Divine, we will begin to become truly creatively spiritually powerful, all of course under the caveat of Divine Will.

The direct passage to powerful illumined life is according our Divine soul primacy in our life, thus aligning with it and thence God – the Divine Creative Field. The following simple but powerful exercise will greatly assist and accelerate this work. It is quite well-known, although there are various adaptations.

It is unwise to start this exercise unless we have first completely committed to continuing it every day, no matter what. If this exercise is started then stopped after only a few months, all the fields of the being may fracture to a greater degree than existed before starting. This is a very serious warning.

Set aside time every day for this exercise. It need only be twenty minutes per day, but it must be every day without fail. It is better if the twenty minutes are at the beginning of the day rather than the end, for reasons which will become clear as we go on. It is also important to perform the exercise on an empty stomach, as we are withdrawing all the vital energy of the body to one point for this work, and the body does not take kindly to endeavouring to digest food while this other activity is attempted. Get up twenty minutes earlier: we can all find twenty minutes a day. It is just a question of priorities and this, because of all the benefits it will confer, should be the greatest priority. The exercise is like a meditation or prayer, so somewhere quiet is needed, particularly to start with. After a time, it is possible to perform it in the middle of the noisiest place with equanimity. In the initial days, it is preferable to make a ritual of always using the same place, sitting on a cushion on the floor in a semi-lotus position with the hands resting on the knees, the thumb and forefingers touching in a closed circle. This position is all about energy flows of the body; it contains and circles the energy flows, which assists in making a concentrated focus easier, more powerful and with fewer energy leaks. In the beginning:

When you meditate, there should be no effort to control, and no attempt to be peaceful. Don't be overly solemn or feel that you are taking part in some special ritual; let go even of the idea that you are meditating. Let your body remain as it is, and your breath as you find it.

— *Sogyal Rinpoche*

Now close your eyes. After some years you will be able to work just as simply with your eyes open, but to start with this will help. Next, the key to all energy work in this realm, the key to knowing thyself, the key to the doorway to other realms, is a one-pointedness of attention: using the mind, the energy focal point is directed at the third eye. This is the point between the two physical eyes in the centre of the forehead. With a concentrated mind, focus on this one point – detaching yourself from the outer world of the senses to enter your inner world and all other worlds, in a highly focused, super-conscious state of being. The key to going within is to hold powerfully and clearly the mind and thus all vital energy of the body at that one point of entry within, that one point of power. Using faculties that are not physical, we learn to look with our inner sight, hear with our inner hearing and to sense all with our inner senses.

The first time you try this will not be easy; it may even seem impossible. The way to success is, as with all else, repetition and practice. The first time you try it, the left-brain, the will, the emotions, the ego all take fright and begin vociferously asserting their previous primary positions within the being, as this exercise if successful will result in their assuming their rightful quiescent and subservient role within the whole. Approach this exercise as you would approach attempting to discipline and teach a spoilt child – with persistence, patience and love.

Now, sitting comfortably, silently express the intent to look at your physical body. With your inner sight bring all your attention to this one task. How does your body feel? Is it relaxed, uncomfortable,

comfortable, tension in some places? Stay with your physical body, resting, observing all and allowing all that arises to arise. We know what our physical body looks like when looking with our physical eyes, but when we observe it with our inner eye, another image may arise. It may be enormously different from the usual one you have of your physical body. That is fine: whatever arises is fine. From now on, you may find the same image will always arise when you do this exercise. The same will happen with the other bodies; different images may arise for each one. Just allow that to happen. Do not become attached to any of these images, as they will change over time as you evolve, and if you become attached to any of them you will impede your progress. Just watch and feel your physical body with your mind. One by one let the tensions go and relax. Try to breathe as deeply down into the abdomen as possible. Let go and relax. When you feel you have reached a measure of relaxation and comfort, then move your focus onto your emotional body. Now your first thought is probably I have no idea what my emotional body looks like. It is best not to have any preconceived ideas, the position is one of openness and stillness, accepting all that arises without judgement. The emotional body is the energy field created by the multiplicity of emotions that surge through our fields at the given moment. The field of the emotions is distinctly different from the physical body. When one elderly lady tried this exercise for the first time, upon being asked to focus on her emotional body she burst into tears and cried off and on for three days. She had spent the greater part of her life never dealing with her emotions in a healthy manner; she had suppressed everything, kept a stiff upper lip and carried on. By the time she attempted this exercise, the moment she allowed her attention to focus upon this vital field of her being it had a dramatic result. Her emotional body was such an overloaded field and the mere act of attention acts as a conduit, so that all stored emotions, mostly negative in vibration (that was why they were not dealt with in the first place), surged through the conduit. Releasing the lid from the dustbin of her emotional field was a very healthy thing to do, although dramatic. So be aware that if you feel emotional or tearful after starting this exercise that is healthy. Stick with it and focus on

Passage to Spiritual Power With All Its Many Gifts 275

clearing all the fields. Keep the focus on your emotional body until you have a measure of calm and clarity. In all this work, all that is required of you in the initial stages is to focus and observe, then let go. Observe your rising emotions, make no judgements, do not follow them with your thoughts, do not hook onto them, just observe them and then let them drift away. Once you have reached a relatively peaceful stage, move on to your mental body, remembering that the whole exercise takes only approximately twenty minutes each day.

The mental body is the hardest aspect for left-brain people to work with because the left-brain's dominance constantly interferes with any work undertaken. However, without control of the mental body and all its latent powers, no evolution is possible. So again, focus on the mental body. A different image will arise in the mind for this: allow it. It is possible that no images of any kind arise at first, which is fine also. Whatever happens is okay. Let your thoughts flow up and off, keep clearing the screen, and as before do not follow your thoughts, do not become attached to them, just observe. Breathe deeply and allow, without judgements of any kind.

You may find that the first five minutes of the entire exercise is spent clearing garbage from the day before – events, words spoken that you did not realise had stuck with you, will clearly be seen front and centre. It is a good idea just as a single exercise to have these five minutes of daily clearing, hitting the delete button on all angry, negative thoughts, as we then start each day with a cleared and peaceful field. Entering each new day without any negativity caught within any of our fields means each new day really is that, a completely new day and we are therefore much more effective and powerful in all we do. Once you feel you have reached a measure of a calm, controlled and ordered mental body, move onto the next step.

This next step is most important. Breathe again deeply, make sure you are comfortable, then bring to your mind again the image you saw of your physical body. Hold it there, then bring to the fore also the image of your emotional body, then your mental body. Possibly you only saw a dark blank screen, a strange shape or symbol, or just a colour – whatever, all is okay. Even if all the body images appear to be the same, do not worry, just bring each to mind with the different words, physical, emotional, mental. Now that you have all three images before you, visualise bringing all three together into one – stay with that image of the three in one with as much focus as possible for as long as possible. It may be only a second or two.

Now we move on to the soul. With all your attention, focus on your soul. (From this one small act on our part – the moment we direct our attention to our soul, great changes will occur in the whole being.) Again, allow any image to arise. It will change dramatically over time, and it does not matter what it is at this stage. Do not create an image; do not fantasise what you would like to think your soul looks like. We must work only with what is. If you attempt to work with a creation of your mind, no progress will be made. If you allow an image to arise without any mental help on your part, without interference from you, the images will be accurate. Should you start interfering with the images because they do not suit your conception of yourself, the exercise will not be the relatively quick and powerful tool it is. Honesty with oneself is at all times crucial, even more so with an exercise such as this. Once you have an image of your soul, or if no image just darkness, move on and again bring to the centre the vision of the three previous bodies as one, then visualise – with the power of your focused mind – bringing the three in one together with your soul. Stay with this fusion of all four fundamental aspects of your being as one, in as focused a way for as long as possible. Again, it will not be long. Then end the exercise with gratitude and thanks to yourself and all else as you see fit.

The point of this exercise is threefold. One, we are clearing our fields of accumulated garbage and therefore we calm and heal fractures. Two, we are centering and aligning all our fields in order to function as a unified and harmonious, soul centred being. Three, we are paying attention to our soul. We are recognising our soul and interacting with it as we invite it to align with our other fields.

This process of alignment is of necessity a slow one, depending on the original state of all fields. As our fields begin by gentle degrees to align with our seed soul, the soul begins to unfold; much like the bud of a flower opening and the energies of the soul begin to influence all the other fields. When complete alignment has taken place all fields are working under agreed and acknowledged Divine laws – the Will and intent of the Divine Creative Field.

This exercise creates a combined and centred field of the physical, emotional and mental bodies. We become centred and aligned in these three and the soul is then able to inhabit this newly unified and more coherent field. As the soul moves closer, its field will affect the others; as they are affected, the soul is able to mover ever closer and so on. The soul automatically moves closer as our physical, emotional and mental fields are now more similar to the field of our soul, and our soul is therefore attracted by this. Once our four fields are self-similar, our soul may then begin to move to the position it is designed to inhabit, which is the very centre of all our various energy fields – and then we may start to work under our soul's direct guidance and authority our soul then begins to fully unfold. Thus, we begin to work under the direct guidance of God. It is in this way, and only this way, that we can become truly coherent, harmonious and spiritually power-full in all our fields.

All power originates from the Divine, and the path to the Divine is through the agency of our own Divine soul. While our soul is out there in left field somewhere, we have no real power. We cannot evolve, we cannot accomplish anything that is real, and we will never attain spiritual power. It goes without saying that this powerful process will change all aspects of the life, both inner and outer, physical and metaphysical. The whole process may take many years for some, less for others. We all start at a different place, and we all work with a different focus and effectiveness. There is one essential thing we must not do – we must not start this exercise with an expectation in mind. In other words, it is not wise to become attached to the outcome because then we will try to control the process. We may then begin to create in order to imagine it is moving as we feel it should. If we think the entire course of events is too slow, we may become frustrated and disillusioned, so it is best to start without attachment to the outcome or time frame, but merely with a resolve to proceed no matter what. Just choose to walk this path in a spirit of enquiry because we wish to actively, intelligently and above all consciously take part in our own evolutionary progress. The *Bhagavad Gita* outlines the procedure for basic meditation as well as the reward:

> Day after day, let the Yogi practise the harmony of soul: in a secret place, in deep solitude, master of his mind, hoping for nothing, desiring nothing.
>
> Let him find a place that is pure and a seat that is restful, neither too high nor too low.
>
> On that seat let him rest and practise yoga for the purification of the soul: with the life of his body and mind in peace; his soul in silence before the One. With upright body, head and neck, which rest still and move not; with inner gaze which is not restless, but rests still between the eyebrows;
>
> When all desires are in peace and the mind, withdrawing within, gathers the multitudinous straying senses into the harmony of recollection.
>
> Then with reason armed with resolution, let the seeker quietly lead the mind into the Spirit, and let all his thoughts be silence.
>
> And whenever the mind unsteady and restless strays away from the Spirit, let him ever and for ever lead it again to the Spirit.
>
> With soul in peace, and all fear gone and strong in the vow of holiness, let him rest with mind in harmony, his soul on me, his God supreme.
>
> When the mind is resting in the stillness of the prayer of yoga, and by the grace of the Spirit sees the Spirit and therein finds fulfilment;

Then the seeker knows the joy of Eternity: a vision seen by reason far beyond what senses can see. He abides therein and moves not from Truth.

He has found joy and Truth, a vision for him supreme. He is therein steady: the greatest pain moves him not.

He sees himself in the heart of all beings and he sees all beings in his heart. This is the vision of the Yogi of harmony, a vision which is ever one.

And when he sees me in all and he sees all in me, then I never leave him and he never leaves me.

> — *Bhagavad Gita 6:10–30 (order of some verses are altered; not all are included)*

If we do this exercise every day, if we pay attention to all our fields in a way we never have before, out of this new attention and focus will arise new self-knowledge, new care, love and respect from "knowing thyself". From this may arise the desire to know more generally in a conscious and active manner and you may therefore embark on one or more of the many modalities that abound in the fields of self-awareness, spirituality, energy balancing, healing, meditation, genetic memory erasure and so on. As we begin to align, to heal on all levels, as our fields become clearer and more coherent, we become more intuitive and will know instinctively the most appropriate next step to take.

One of the first and most helpful results of this exercise is that as we become more centered and whole, we begin to observe events that are happening around us in a more detached manner. All events appear to move back and thus instead of being immersed in the events where we are too close to see clearly, too emotionally involved, with the new dimension of distance the whole is more apparent. We see the big picture; we now merely find all interesting instead of stressful or alarming etc. With our new view of the whole comes understanding, wisdom and a new calm. Where before we might have reached for a sedative or alcohol, now there is no need, as all has the appearance more of a play we are observing than a drama in which we are enmeshed. What was puzzling before is now understood; in the midst of chaos there is calm; in drama, reason and clarity prevails. We inhabit a field of unified and harmonious energy and within this field we experience only a calm, contemplative view of tumultuous events. If sometimes events do get too much, all we need to do is sit down, go into the exercise and almost instantly all the drama falls away and peace is restored. With greater practice, even merely to visualise going into the exercise while events are raging around is often enough to induce calm. If nothing other than this ability comes out of the exercise it is a powerful and useful tool indeed.

> The sense of observing what is going on in the mind and emotions and the sensing of the external world, without being caught up in these processes, is an indication that your experience of awareness in the observation mode is making progress. The happening of a "peak experience" in which there is a sense of oneness with all existence, a sense of deep peace, a sense of overwhelming joy, a sense of great humbleness or thankfulness, a sense of great Power in a state of peace, are all indications that the attunement to the inherent excellence and perfection in all existence is making progress.
>
> — Ashton Wylie, *Power to the People*

To understand that all of life's events are lessons for further evolution is to understand that once the lesson has been learnt, the universe will never repeat it. Once we are able to trust that this is how things are, then whenever trouble or drama strikes, instead of being traumatised we can ask, "What is it I am to learn from this? What is right about this I am not getting? How am I supposed to respond to this situation?" If there is no death, only the eternal immortal life of our soul on its journey through all the dimensions in its constant spiral of increasing perfection, then the question can only be, "How may I assist my evolutionary process?"

Another curious aspect of the spiritual path is that we do not need to experience death in order to be reborn. During our physical life we grow in spurts. When young we suddenly shoot up, plateau, and then grow again. The same happens with ageing: we age suddenly, wrinkles appear almost overnight it seems, then for quite some time nothing happens. As we grow in spirit, the process follows the same pattern. Great progress is made and then we plateau. Sometimes there is much spiritual activity and help, then all is silent and quiet as though we imagined it. We must learn in these times to hold fast to our focus and trust and know that all is well. All in life ebbs and flows, waxes and wanes. This walk along the conscious spiritual path is no exception.

Sometimes our growth spurts are so great that another process altogether takes place. If we are able to see in ways other than the physical, at these times the entire incorporeal energy fields that are "you" enter a chrysalis stage. For days, sometimes weeks, the fields of the whole being as represented by the various images you see when you focus on them will appear to be dormant and in a chrysalis-like state. After the required period, and it appears to vary with each particular stage and each person, we emerge with our fields ever more aligned, harmonious and lovingly spiritual power-full. Each time this happens we can know we have advanced and are thus in a way born again through this process without having to experience physical death. It is important to understand this process, as during the dormant time we need to take special care of ourselves. We may find the normal things we liked to do no longer attract us, or most often we find we have little or no physical energy as our ultimate energy source is almost completely, but temporarily, shut down. At these times, it may be difficult to perform the exercise: the images may not arise anymore, we may find all has changed and we are immersed in complete darkness, with no energy running. Do not worry about this. Be calm and wait; proceed always with the exercise no matter what until this dormant period is over. Once the leap in evolution is accomplished, a greater degree of alignment, higher vibration with subsequent focus and spiritual power, will be realised. Each new power surge is locked into place with the result that the new stability in all the fields, the coherence and alignment is semi-permanent. I say "semi" as nothing is set in concrete, and we can all fall back again should we choose. (That is until we reach the stage whereby falling back is no longer a possibility). This is why until a certain stage has been reached, we must not stop the exercise: until a particular degree of alignment has been locked in, it is reckless to stop.

All of this is a natural process. The only difference now is that we are actively and in a state of full awareness participating in and therefore accelerating the process. At a particular stage our soul will instantaneously align with each cell in our physical body as the system is holographic: our physical, emotional and mental bodies together with our soul are all exactly replicated in each cell under the law of "as above, so below". If we could see our soul and, with our inner sight, see our entire being we would see as many representations of our soul as there are cells in our body. This is a beautiful and breathtaking sight. This process will reveal that our soul is now beginning to consciously interact with the whole being and is taking authority over all the fields. This is an essential element in our continual refinement and is to be celebrated and actively participated in. We will thereafter notice changes in the manifested aspect of our being, the physical body. This will be confirmation that our work is bearing fruit.

Once we are fully engaged in this ever-evolving process we will find that our intuition increases enormously. We must learn to respect this useful and fundamental aspect of our being. Our intuition, if listened to without questioning, is never wrong and we will always be acting from right motives, since intuition is a fruit of our divine soul and is thus aligned with God. It is guidance given from the higher vibratory realms and we ignore it at our peril.

As we progress along the spiritual evolutionary path, our natural and dormant clairvoyant and clairaudient faculties (the faculty to see with inner sight, or hear with inner hearing, what is happening within the explicate or the implicate realms) begins to develop. All of us have the necessary faculties to employ these arts should we choose. Indeed, it is desirous that we should do so. These abilities develop quite easily without any conscious action on our part other than the desire to walk the path to spiritual union with the Divine. The ability to experience pre-cognition and mental telepathy are also hardwired within our being. It is just that we are for the most part so incoherent, so fractured, so full of clamour and noise that we have never experienced these things, so we say they are not a possibility for us, they do not exist. But they do and they are our birthright. Once we have reached the stage when these faculties are in use every day, then we are near the truly exciting part.

At a particular stage of our progress along the path, we will hear the glorious and Divine music of the spheres, the music of the multiverse. As we begin to interact with the Divine, the ability to access this whenever we wish is ours. This Divine symphony is a sound so wonderful, so complex and yet simple, so perfect and so profound – there are no adequate words to describe it fully. It will create so great an impression that once heard, it is never forgotten, but remains always as a glorious background to each minute of each day. The music of the spheres, of the multiverse, will move to tears all who hear it: the beauty is so overwhelming as to dissolve all our senses and emotions into it in a moment. Every particle, every cell in the whole being responds by dancing and dissolving in the love, peace, light and indescribable beauty of the Divine Creative Field's whole vibration. It thereafter remains always with us as a constant, glorious memory, a reminder of the creator's presence that no one can ever take away. You will know it when you first hear it, and you will be so moved by it that you will never be the same again. You will also, once you are relatively well aligned, hear your own celestial sound; this will also be a moment most profound as this is "you" sounding throughout the universe in your beautiful and individual manner. This sounding is how we are heard and recognised throughout the multiverse.

Know also, one of our primary tasks:

> We are here to turn darkness to light.
>
> — *Sefer Yetzirah 60 – Zohar 154*

In other words, we are becoming co-creators with the Divine, assisting in spinning light – creating, within the fields of darkness, and in this process we ourselves are being refined.

> For this reason I say, if one is whole, one will be filled with light, but if one is divided, one will be filled with darkness.
>
> — *Gospel of Thomas 61*

It is so simple when we know how, so simple when the codes are broken. If we are aligned with our Divine soul, if our fields are coherent and unified, then we will be filled with the light of God under the law of self-similarity. However, if we are misaligned, fractured and incoherent, we will be filled with darkness. There are of course all the degrees between the two.

We can become an illuminated field of high spin, a field that is vibrating at the same rate as love. Our field will be extremely fine and dense; light-filled, intelligent, coherent, self-regulating, infinite, creative and power-packed. As the field of the Divine is also the field of love, this then is the ground of all: "God is love" is an accurate statement. We can begin to become gods in our own right, working under the law of "not my will but Thine" interacting in full conscious and loving relationship with God.

> I am the sceptre of the rulers of men; and I am the wise policy of those who seek victory. I am the silence of hidden mysteries; and I am the knowledge of those who know.

And know, that I am the seed of all things that are; and that no being that moves or moves not can ever be without me.

There is no end of my divine greatness. What I have spoken here to thee shows only a small part of my infinity.

Know thou that whatever is beautiful and good, whatever has glory and power is only a portion of my own radiance.

But of what help is it to thee to know this diversity? Know that with one single fraction of my Being I pervade and support the Universe, and know that I AM.

— *Bhagavad Gita 10:38–42*

On that glorious note, we come back to earth, back to the explicate realm, as that is where we must start.

If we all start from the ground of the Divine in all aspects of our life, if we seek spiritual not temporal power, not for our own physical ends in the physical world but as the path to union with God, if we seek not to have control and dominion over others but only to have control and dominion over ourselves, if we seek only "not my will but Thine" in all things as in doing this we are seeking to surrender ourselves in the ultimate act of loving humility and grace, if we seek to advance only our own evolutionary journey as to do to this we also automatically assist the evolution of all, we cannot go astray. It is in any event foolish to seek power over others when we have little or no power and authority over ourselves. Power is and can only be aligning oneself in totality with God, the source of all, as then the fundamental law of the multiverse is acknowledged – higher vibratory fields direct and control the lower. It is imperative that we find our way back to the creative centre of the multiverse, to the point of oneness, the point of no resistance within the unified field of the Divine Creator.

We need to choose our own way, thinking for ourselves, as this is a uniquely personal journey. Socrates said: "To find yourself, think for yourself."

So many do not think for themselves. We need to change our belief systems to beliefs that are holistic and infused with wisdom, love and the Divine, in order that we may become more conscious and enlightened, as without the Divine Creator interwoven in every aspect of our daily lives, we are all in trouble.

> Jesus said: "I took my stand in the midst of the world, and in flesh I appeared to them. I found them all drunk, and I did not find any of them thirsty. My soul ached for the children of humanity, because they are blind in their hearts and do not see, for they came into the world empty, and they also seek to depart from the world empty."
>
> *— Gospel of Thomas 28*

These powerful words were spoken 2000 years ago, and so little has changed.

There is a very simple path to the Divine, to assuming spiritual power, should we prove capable of making the leap. Our belief systems are who we are, as energy always follows thought. What we believe in, what we focus upon, is who and what we become. Some say, "I do not believe in anything", but this is not possible as to believe in nothing is just as much a belief system as to believe in something. Those who claim to believe in nothing are liable to bend with each passing breeze or break with a passing storm. They possess little or no moral compass and dwell primarily in the explicate realm of illusion. If we have not built our belief systems on strong foundations, if we have not created a strong principled, ethical and spiritual foundation for ourselves, how may we steer ourselves through and beyond this mortal plane and, more importantly, how may we evolve to a higher state of being? We are all fallible human beings at a relatively early stage of our evolution, so how important is it that we recognise our Divine inner being, our soul? How may we successfully evolve if we recognise no authority, no higher source of light, creativity and power than our own? How may we successfully evolve if we do not believe in anything?

Often the highly educated rely solely upon their left-brain to navigate this world. They speak to and listen to only that aspect of their being and are blind and deaf to all else. They use the so-called superior equipment of their left-brain to supply all their answers. They never feel the need to look elsewhere. This is sad and crippling for them and for the world at large. We have come to revere left-brain thought as the only compass by which to steer ourselves. More often than not, it is those who dwell primarily in the left-brain who govern us and create the world in which we live. This has negatively affected the multiverse at large and has had enormous detrimental effect on all. We must look outside our limited left-brains, use *all* our God-given aspects, not just one tiny part, so that we may begin to understand and see the whole picture, the great and glorious creative symphony that is the multiverse of God.

I recently came across a wonderful small book containing the letters of a seventeenth-century monk called Brother Lawrence. He did not bother himself with very much on an intellectual level, as he found a simple, efficient and direct path to God. He decided at the outset that the foundation of his spiritual life was to be faith. Once he had decided upon this course of action, he tried no other and he called the methodology he used "The Practice of the Presence of God". This involved bringing God into everything he did, acknowledging God, thanking God, having conversations with God. In short, he created a close and loving daily contact with God every bit as real as one would with a corporeal friend in the explicate realm.

> The Practice of the Presence of God he said, "must stem from the heart, from love, rather than from understanding and speech. In the way of

God, thought counts for little. Love does everything and it is not needful to have great things to do".

We know from previous chapters that this would have produced definite and concrete results, and it did. Brother Lawrence found his life overflowed with such abundance that he appeared to spend much time thinking he was not worthy of all the rewards he was reaping:

He expected to have in the course of time some great affliction of body or mind, and that the worst that could happen to him would be to lose that sense of God which he had so long had, but the loving kindness of God assured him that he would not completely abandon him, and that he would give him strength to bear such evil as he might allow to befall him. With that, he feared nothing, and had no need to consult anyone about his soul. When he had desired to do so, he had always come away more perplexed. Being willing to die and lose himself for the love of God, he had no foreboding. Complete abandonment to God was the sure way, and one on which there was always light to travel. It was needful at the beginning to act faithfully and renounce self, but after that there were only unutterable joys.

— *The Practice of the Presence of God*

Brother Lawrence engaged in an unbroken conversation with God, without mystery or artificiality. It is only necessary to realise that God – the Divine Creative Field is intimately present within us and all things, to turn at every moment to this presence and ask for help, recognise his will in all things, do well all that which we clearly see is required of us, offering what we do to God before we do it, and giving thanks for having done it afterwards. It is as easy and as difficult as that. It will quite simply be a straight path to coherence and union with the Divine and the assumption of spiritual power should we choose to take it.

Passage to Spiritual Power With All Its Many Gifts

Abide in me, and I in you. As the branch cannot bear fruit of itself, except it abide in the vine; no more can ye, except ye abide in me.

I am the vine, ye are the branches: He that abideth in me, and I in him, the same bringeth forth much fruit: for without me ye can do nothing.

If a man abideth not in me, he is cast forth as a branch, and is withered; and men gather them, and cast them into the fire, and they are burned.

If ye abide in me, and my words abide in you, ye shall ask what ye will, and it shall be done unto you. Herein is my father glorified, that ye bear much fruit.

— *John 15:4–8*

The benefits of relationship with the Divine and the fruits of real power are countless, but I will list a few here:

- You have opened your mind, not closed it.
- You have adopted a logical point of view rather than an illogical one.
- You look at yourself with different, more positive eyes.
- You look at others on this plane of existence with different, more positive eyes.
- You are now no longer alone, and never can be; you never actually have been, but now you know it, therefore you will never again know loneliness.
- Knowing you are not alone, knowing you are supported, guided and empowered, you lose your ever-present fear and all its offspring.
- Once you lose your fear, the vacuum you have created is filled with the high frequency field of the Divine Creative Field – God, which is love. Therefore, instead of being fear-full, you are filled with love.
- You are supported, guided and empowered in all you do.

- The support, guidance and empowerment comes from the highest vibratory realms, therefore the vision, the wisdom, the knowledge and power is greater and more true than any from this manifested plane. You are always working under the direct, divine loving guidance of your soul, and as your soul is a spark of the Divine you are therefore always working under Divine guidance without thought or effort, so the results are always perfect.
- You now know there is no such thing as "death", only a changing of form and a moving from one realm to another. This knowledge removes the residual fear, allows greater wisdom and courage, and so greatly assists in times of trouble and trauma.
- Knowing that it is impossible for anyone to die, you view loss in a wiser, more positive, healthy and holistic manner.
- You know there are boundaries you may not cross; there are acts you may not commit; and therefore, like a child, with boundaries in place you feel safer.
- Conscious focus on the further unfolding of your own soul and its evolution gives an integral and primary purpose to your life.
- Knowing that as you evolve to ever-greater alignment, coherence, refinement and therefore higher spin rates, greater light, you are helping not only yourself but others and the planet, in fact all in the multiverse, also to evolve. How can there be greater meaning to life than this?
- With greater alignment comes greater wisdom and therefore understanding, and with greater understanding greater compassion and love arises. With a wise and open mind, fearless, full of courage, with boundaries in place and primary meaning underlying all; always assisted and guided in all you do and, above all, in direct communication and loving relationship with God, how could your field not be a harmonious and unified field of love itself?

. . .

With the Lord in thy heart, with all thy being, with his grace thou shalt attain to the supreme peace and the eternal status. Further, hear the most secret, the supreme word that I shall speak to thee – "Become my minded" "Let this mind be in you".

— *Mahavakya, The Song Celestial*

In other words, keep the energy field of the Divine in your heart, your mind and your being, you become "my minded" – the same field as the Divine. Become aligned and unified, vibrating at the same rate as God, and you will attain peace and immortality for your soul will live on through its destined evolutionary cycles. Always balanced between this world and the spiritual realms; always conscious that the here and now is not all there is; with all your energy fields clear, coherent, integrated and aligned; always working under the guidance and direction of God via the individual agency of your divine soul; with your physical, emotional and mental fields powerfully pulsating, attuned to their source and clear of all negative aspects – how could you not be Divine Power?

> Krishna – I have given thee words of vision and wisdom more secret than hidden mysteries. Ponder them in the silence of thy soul, and then in freedom do thy will.
>
> Hear again my Word supreme, the deepest secret of silence. Because I love thee well, I will speak to thee words of salvation.
>
> Give thy mind to me, and give me thy heart, and thy sacrifice, and thy adoration. This is my Word of promise: thou shalt in truth come to me, for thou art dear to me.
>
> Leave all things behind, and come to me for thy salvation. I will make thee free from the bondage of sins. Fear no more.

These things must never be spoken to one who lacks self-discipline, or who has no love, or who does not want to hear or who argues against me.

But he who will teach this secret doctrine to those who have love for me, and who himself has supreme love, he in truth shall come unto me.

For there can be no man among men who does greater work for me, nor can there be a man on earth who is dearer to me than he is.

He who learns in contemplation the holy words of our discourse, the light of his vision is his adoration. This is my truth.

And he who only hears but has faith, and in his heart he has no doubts, he also attains liberation and the worlds of joy of righteous men.

Hast thou heard these words, in the silent communion of thy soul? Has the darkness of thy delusion been dispelled by thine inner Light?

Arjuna – By thy grace I remember my Light, and now gone is my delusion. My doubts are no more, my faith is firm; and now I can say "Thy will be done".

— *Bhagavad Gita 18:63–73*

Addendum: The Physical Body

We are energy beings therefore to function properly our bodies need to maintain their electromagnetic fields. These need to be functioning in all their glory, without breaks or stagnant energy points. If our energy fields are unbalanced, depleted or blocked our physical body will reflect this, often quite dramatically. As an electrical energy being, our body in all its fields requires full and balanced mineralization to fire coherently. Minerals are the essential fuel for health in all aspects of our being. In addition, if we are missing key minerals, we will not be able to manufacture the essential vitamins our body needs, not to mention all the many and powerful hormones. If we remember "as above so below", everything is interconnected – reflexing to and affecting all else; and our physical body is no different. We cannot deplete one part or aspect without affecting the whole.

The ideal is that we should receive all the essential mineral elements from our diet, but some soils are now so depleted that this is not possible, and supplements are required. New Zealand's soil, for example, has a shortage of selenium, an element that is essential if we do not wish to suffer from cancer. We have one of the highest rates of cancer in the world, and a correspondingly low level of selenium. Zinc is another essential mineral for, among many other things, brain function. Depression and suicidal tendencies are many times a direct result of a shortage of this mineral. Administer zinc supplements and the dark clouds dramatically roll away without any dangerous or debilitating side-effects. All this is just commonsense, practical stuff. If we all take a little time to think for ourselves, be aware – conscious, look for information on the internet, read books on the subject, take responsibility for our own bodies and understand how they function and, more importantly what they need to function properly; then diseased bodies will begin to be a thing of the past. In this time of readily available information, there is no excuse for ignorance. Indeed, ignorance can and does increasingly kill. To attempt to heal by breaking our body down into separate component physical parts and to then treat the effects rather than the cause with unnatural toxic pharmaceutical drugs, as modern mechanistic medicine does, is madness. All is one, our bodies need to be diagnosed, treated, and healed with this fundamental philosophy in mind. Any other approach is the result of a belief in separation and of being disconnected from the Divine source of all.

To achieve optimum health and balance of our physical bodies we need to eat a variety of fresh natural whole foods, fruits, vegetables, nuts, grains, and meats, these together with all consumption being in balance, i.e. not too much of any one thing is the sensible path to follow. Make sure the source of the food is a good one: organic produce is better than non-organic, as the mineral and vitamin content is higher. Choose only very fresh food and eat it fresh. This means no processed food of any kind, no pre-prepared food. There are innumerable recipes for simple, elegant, nutritious meals, so lack of time and tiredness are no excuse to abuse our bodies with bad food, junk food or even no food at all. All food should be eaten either raw, or cooked in a healthy way, not microwaved as this deletes almost all its inherent goodness and vitality – we should have more respect for our food and not treat it in this way. Equally importantly, using microwaves to cook our food dramatically changes its vibratory field.

The field is now an unnatural one, and all our fields must expend a great amount of energy changing the unnatural energy field of the microwaved food into the normal natural one of the earth's pulse. Therefore, microwaving what we eat is really quite stupid and the time it saves is something of an illusion, as it is possible to prepare healthy, tasty food quite quickly without nearly destroying it in the process. In addition to good food, we all know we should drink lots of good fresh water, as water is the primary physical aspect of our physical bodies. This needs to be water without any chemicals in it, particularly fluoride, which is a known carcinogenic. It has been estimated that over sixty-five per cent of all ill health is simply a case of severe dehydration with all the flow-on effects that this creates.

We are all spiritual beings on a spiritual path and if this is a conscious path, it will naturally evolve into a journey of inquiry, and learning how best to care for our physical body is a vital part of the journey. I do not believe we have to become a vegetarian, nor do we have to eat some boring ghastly diet that we hate for the good of our body and soul. Many spiritual teachers of the eastern religions teach that austerities are a waste of time and energy as they more often than not lead to little else than increased vanity. If some are worried about eating meat and feel perhaps they should be vegetarians but cannot quite bring themselves to do this, then they may find it helpful if they were to give thanks to the animal, bird or fish that gave its life in order that they could eat. Indeed, it is always a good idea to gives thanks for all we receive. Remember how gratitude ramped up the power of love. If we thank whatever has given its life so that we may live and bless it for the gift it has given us, then in this act we are displaying humility, gratitude and love, which is an act of grace and therefore of higher spin.

The Divine has provided throughout the natural world a veritable banquet of all manner of foods – including all our medicine as well. All we need to heal ourselves is found within nature; there is a cure for every complaint if we only remember how and where to look. Many of us do not have enough respect, knowledge and understanding of food. We look upon it in the same way we view the gasoline we put in our cars, as something we have to do to keep going. Good food however is one of the great joys of this material plane. There is nothing quite like a truly superb meal, accompanied with fine wine, to make one feel sublime, in a "God is in his heaven, and all is right with the world" mood. If we must eat, let us do it well and enjoy it. We should always eat a breakfast of good whole food and fresh fruit (vitamin supplements are no replacement for food and may in time do us harm). We all need to have breaks during the day for refueling and we need to be very conscious while choosing this fuel. Our meal in the evening should be the relaxing and nurturing one after our hard day of work. We in the west are extremely lucky as we have an abundance of food to choose from: there are literally thousands of fruits and vegetables from which we may take our pick, and all are good for us. A selection every day (a minimum of six different ones) is necessary for a healthy body. Meat or fish cooked simply, perhaps with herbs, is not difficult and need not take long: chicken breasts seared in butter, steamed with tarragon and deglazed with say Calvados takes thirty minutes to cook; lamb chops with rock salt and pepper, seared with garlic and red wine to deglaze; or just simply a white bean stew with tomatoes, herbs, onion and garlic, served with a salad or spinach. A simple steak with a large green salad including avocado, onion, tomatoes or whatever. Eggs lightly scrambled with a herbed salad, and good crusty organic bread made the traditional way with any flour other than soy. Home-made soup with bread and cheese is half an hour's work at the most: throw in all the vegetables you have, season with herbs, pepper and salt – be imaginative. There is no excuse for not eating well. Half an hour is all that is needed to prepare a good, healthy and exciting meal. Include herbs as much as possible as they are full of minerals and are medicines in themselves. The seventeenth-century herbalist Nicholas Culpepper says in his *Complete Herbal* that "no one need ever grow old while they have sage in their garden". A fresh, wholesome, healthy meal, a beautiful wine in moderation, good conversation, good music or simply silence; this is all nourishment for the soul as well as the body. After all, they are both inextricably linked and our life and health depend upon our care.

You may say, "That is all very well, but I live alone and I wouldn't go to all that bother just for me. If I had someone here to cook for that would be different." Think for a moment what is being said here: "I don't really matter. It is not worth making an effort just for me. I don't matter enough for that. My life and heath don't really matter." Here again, we have the problem of no self-love and respect. If we do not love and respect the Divine, then we do not love and respect the Divine's creation – ourselves. We therefore abuse the creation, perhaps not intentionally but that is the result. Once we love the Divine and ourselves then this abuse is impossible and we can then love and celebrate our life and ourselves and start simply by cooking ourselves a nurturing, solitary, healthy and whole meal. Anyway, we are never in the final analysis alone – we need to understand this, to know this. Eating alone, one notices the food more, its quality, taste and the euphoria good food and wine brings. Once you get used to this and really enjoy it, you will find you can take yourself out to fine restaurants and can eat your way enjoyably through many courses while drinking, in moderation, some wonderful wine, and then wend your way home, happy, contented and fulfilled. You have taken care of and loved yourself. This is showing respect for and gratitude to the Divine and its creation and, in this act, for all of creation. This way of behaving will also have opened the door to greater freedom, less fear and therefore greater power.

Others may say, "That is all very well, but I cannot afford to eat good food as it is all so expensive." This is a common misunderstanding as the expensive food is the junk food; the expensive food is any food that has been highly processed, fancily packaged and expensively marketed. Whole grains, oats, rice, dried beans and potatoes are all inexpensive staple foods that are quick and easy to prepare. Fresh fruit and vegetables in season are always cheaper. Eat as the French do, only what is in season. We do not really want to eat peaches or cherries in winter because then they are not special in summer when they *are* in season. Also, out-of-season fruits never have any taste. Why waste money in this way? As a test, go shopping for one week and do not buy anything processed, in a packet or tin, anything frozen, no cakes, soft drinks, packaged meals, nothing that has been pre-prepared. Shopping in this way is a great deal cheaper and healthier too. The meals will also be more enjoyable as all fresh, whole products have greater flavour and vitality than dead food without inherent life. And eating in this way lessens the toxic load on the physical body.

Rituals are wonderful, powerful things that for the most part are a lost art in our present-day, mad-rush world. We need to return to making a ritual of some meals, no matter how short or where. If we choose our food carefully, rejecting all that is false, all that is dead (as in over-processed and full of chemicals) and all that lacks vitality and inherent life, this will be a start. Further, if we then give thanks for the food and if in the consuming and digesting, we acknowledge that we are celebrating our life, our health and the Divine inherent in all, then this will become a powerful, satisfying and life-giving ritual that can only heal and balance our temple of the soul together with the rest of our being.

Some may say to this, "I couldn't possibly do that. I work such long hours; I am a very busy and important person. I can't take time out for myself in that self-indulgent way." What exactly is going on here? It is apparent that the ego and the will are in control, because the soul knows that care, love and respect for itself and its manifestations should be paramount. It is only the soulless will and ego that acts in this rash and destructive manner. Abuse, disrespect and lack of care are all negations of the Divine Creative Field, therefore if we are aligned with our soul and hence aligned with the Divine, we will in all things act with respect, care, love and gratitude. This way of being will as a matter of course always include ourselves; it can be no other way. By not eating or eating incorrectly, we are stating loud and clear that we have no time, love, respect or care for the divine being that we are, we are stating that God and its manifestations do not matter. We are stating that money, power, ego, position and all the glamour of the material plane does. We are focusing our intent on the ephemeral and ignoring the eternal. This is illogical, is never going to create a positive and one can only ask, "What is the end game?" Some may answer to this, "I am only going to live like this for a short while, and then when I have enough I will stop and live a more sensible life." My answer to that is: fine, as long as we make sure we know before we start how much is enough, set a date for stopping and stick to it. Otherwise, the goal posts have a habit of moving and before we know where we are, we are trapped in a self-destructive, material spiral going nowhere but down to an ignorant death, having lived a wasted life – dying as we were born.

I do not want to go on at length and boringly about good food as opposed to bad – if we were to use our common sense and think a little, most of the worst assaults on our bodies would cease. We need to be more aware of what it is exactly we are putting into our bodies and with this the question arises again – just how conscious are we? We don't really need anyone to lecture us on this as instinctively we all know, it is just that we are not thinking, not paying attention, not listening to our inner selves. We need to stop to think and look, not to mention smell (it is always a good idea to smell food before we buy it, particularly fruit, as if it has no smell, it usually doesn't have much taste and if does not have either of those it will also lack essential elements) and it is no fun to eat. Logical, isn't it? We must learn to know good food from bad, to love buying it, preparing it, cooking it and eating it. We need to understand that if we eat bad food, junk food, overly processed food, we are saying we do not respect ourselves, we do not value ourselves and we certainly do not love ourselves. Further, we are exhibiting a mental and physical laziness that if kept up will stop us journeying anywhere at all from our present position. How are we to change our lives if we cannot even be bothered to take care with the kind of fuel we give ourselves? How can we have respect for ourselves if every time we eat we are insulting ourselves? How can we love ourselves if every time we eat, we are systematically destroying ourselves? Be aware, be conscious, take small steps at first and always remember if it has taken fifteen years, for example, to get in a state of ill health, it will take quite a long time to rectify. Always take courage from the fact that the body will always want to heal itself, will always want to be the perfect temple for the soul that it was designed to be. The moment we change our thoughts, our focus in this regard, is the moment our body will subtly and positively begin to align and assist us in our endeavours.

Let us look at a few very common and **toxic so-called food products** that we ingest at our peril. Margarine is not a health product, quite the contrary. The body is unable to properly assimilate this totally artificial product. Butter is healthy and a good source of Vitamin C – just don't eat too much of it. Canola oil as an ingredient in anything at all is to be avoided as this highly processed oil was first created to be cheap machine oil; it was never intended for human consumption. The manufacturers say they have processed all the toxic aspects out of it, but why ingest such a product when there are so many other completely natural and vital unprocessed oils to choose from? Simply never eat anything highly processed, anything that contains a string of chemical ingredients, anything that is not a recognisable food, anything with any of the following in it: artificial colouring, artificial flavouring, preservatives or artificial chemicals. All these products are about money, not food or health. Canola oil, for instance, is very cheap, which is why it is an ingredient in so many pre-prepared foods. More money is made; your health is of no consequence to the manufacturers.

Another product that has found its way into nearly everything on the supermarket shelves is soy. Soy products are cheap: soy flour is much cheaper than wheat, so nearly all breads are now laced with this toxic product. America has planted vast tracts of land with soy, some of it genetically modified, and it is causing all manner of health problems, many of them currently undiagnosed by the medical profession. Soy beans are toxic to the body: the Chinese only ever used soy as a condiment or when fermented. Their ancient texts record that soy was considered unfit for human consumption. Modern producers again say that they have processed out all toxic substances; but we do not need to eat such products – so don't. Despite the product's inherent toxicity and lack of merit as a food, a large American corporation attempted to initially market soy to the poor of America as a meat substitute. The poor in their wisdom refused to have anything to do with it. The corporation tried again, this time marketing soy as a health product (their annual marketing budget for soy is in excess of $US80 million) and what a success it has been – for the corporation anyway.

Soy is loaded with phytoestrogens (plant estrogens) which can cause massive hormonal imbalance while damaging, sometimes permanently, major glands of the body, in particular the thyroid. Phytoestrogens can cause allergies, rashes and hormonal problems; they adversely affect the entire endocrine system, which is the powerhouse that keeps the body in chemical and electrical balance. The United Kingdom's Chief Medical Officer, the British Dietetic Association and the Israeli Health Ministry have all issued warnings regarding soy products. For some reason this is being kept under wraps, possibly because the business generated from soy is now worth billions of dollars and soy contaminates so many food products. Even though we have an epidemic of allergic conditions, a common indicator of soy contamination, no one appears to wish to join up the dots.

All meals should include a reasonable amount of salt, our bodies are primarily saline, and we need salt to maintain health. Natural sea salt with good mineral content is better than table salt, however, we need to be aware always of our iodine intake as iodine above all else protects us from heightened radiation. With our current heightened solar activity, (see notes on WIFI etc.,) we are all receiving increasing amounts of radiation and our thyroid gland is not able to function normally if we are depleted of iodine. We also need a regular intake of good fats, (not highly processed unnatural products). our brain is mostly fat,

While on the subject of food, I recommend all readers to go to the Slow Food website, www.slowfood.com, and check out what they are doing and what they have to say about food, its production and its preparation. Slow Food was started in 1989 by an Italian who rose up in righteous indignation at the McDonald's hamburger chain's invasion of his country. He rightly viewed this cheap, dangerously unhealthy food as an anathema, so he started Slow Food in opposition to fast food. It is now an enormous and growing world movement which has expanded to preserving seeds and the traditional ways of growing and preparing food. There are now many Slow Food-rated restaurants around the world in which you will be guaranteed a spectacular meal. Fast food is all about money; it has little to do with food. If one is passionate about food in any way whether growing, preparing or eating it, fast food never enters the equation. Fast food is not whole food, it is usually highly processed and contains a veritable compilation of toxic artificial chemicals; at the very best, it is the poorest quality unprocessed food. If one is in any way conscious, aware and aligned, it is impossible to insult the body with such dead and dangerous products. The Slow Food organisation is helping to restore sanity where our food is concerned which can only be a good thing for us all. It is taking us back to what we all need to know if we are to survive and evolve.

Other contaminants we need to consider are as follows. First, because they can and do inflict enormous and often permanent damage or death, are pharmaceutical drugs. Now I am aware that pharmaceutical drugs have protected us from many diseases and have saved many lives. It is their proliferation, overuse and our lack of understanding and respect for these inherently artificial (and therefore without Divine Intent) substances that is the problem. These legal drugs are extremely harmful to the delicately balanced manifestation that is our physical body. Almost all are artificial substances created to mimic natural chemicals, they are foreign to the body and without exception, all have a plethora of negative side-effects ranging from the potentially fatal to permanent degradation of the body to irritating small side-effects. Remember, "all is energy". The energy fields generated from these noxious substances are all in opposition to the natural fields not only of the physical body, but the entire being. All are void of divine intent and are therefore, almost without exception, a negation of the Divine. Again, pharmaceutical drugs are about money, not good health – quite the opposite. Almost all pharmaceutical drugs were created to treat effects rather than causes: they have been created to mask and suppress rather than to heal. Most importantly, they have all been created with the belief system of separation as the fundamental underlying the equation, and therefore most dangerously they are never tested for the subsequent effects when mixed with each other or any one of the plethora of toxic substances we are all exposed to in our whole modern and polluted world. The memory field/resonance of a pharmaceutical drug can and does permanently lie seemingly dormant within the body, without any account ever being taken of these field effects when prescribing more. These are dangerous practices indeed. Sometimes, with the effect subdued or masked (which is the most these drugs do, as they do not heal), we may feel more at ease and then our body begins to heal itself. However, for any sensible person, the rule should be that unless all else has failed, pharmaceutical drugs are taken only ever as the very, very last resort.

Anyone on pharmaceutical drugs will be unable to properly align themselves with their soul. Of particular concern are the mind-altering drugs given to control or alter emotional or mental behaviour as these are particularly deadly (they are being given indiscriminately to children) and will cause permanent damage that is possibly generational. In all situations of supposed mental illness or behavioural problems, always consider first the possibility of the cause being a simple one of mineral or vitamin depletion, or hormonal disruption. This can have as its source either a shortage of essential elements in the food intake or an emotional crisis. If the cause is not from these origins, then it may simply be that the system is overloaded with toxins from artificial food additives – particularly colourings, chemical pollution, sugar substitutes – Aspartame – a known neuro toxin, or the like. Always look first to the logical, commonsense cause of ill health. In diagnosing illness, whatever its kind, we must examine the whole. Ill health does not just happen; there will always be a reason. It may well be an incorrect memory program, whether generational or not, but once identified, the software is easily deleted. First, always, find the cause. The rest is a matter of common sense and focus.

It may be, particularly with mental disturbances, that the cause is spiritually based: holes or distortions may have formed in some or all of the primary energy fields caused by using drugs, either legal or illegal, or the excessive use of alcohol. The intake of anything not of Divine intent must have the opposite held within it and will therefore be of a lesser vibration than the natural fields generated from the divine soul. All substances that are a negation of the Divine Field will cause damage to the primary fields. In addition, what is excessive for one may not be for another: for example, one person may drink to oblivion and do no damage to their field at that particular time (note "at that particular time"), while another may have three drinks, one or two of which were too many for them, and cause quite major damage.

This is another reason why "knowing thyself" and becoming aware is so very important, as the health of our entire being continually fluctuates. This is because all our fields are inherently unstable and we move between all the degrees of balanced and unbalanced states that birthing beings would expect to experience. Because we are all at this time in a continual state of unstable flux; where we are in the spectrum always needs to be taken into account when we seek healing. The holes or distortions we may create in our fields due to improper practices may attract or allow in alien entangled and incoherent virtual fields that are devoid of divine aspect and are therefore harmful. These alien fields may overlay, unbalance and distort our entire field. Sometimes these alien fields are so powerful in their own right they may result in overlaying us and controlling us almost completely, to the degree that our physical being and personality is almost unrecognisably changed. Unless we are reasonably conscious and aware we will not realise what is causing our whole-body distress, and in our modern left-brain world, we rarely seek spiritual healing which is what is required in this instance. (Spiritual healing is in its essence the directing of the higher vibratory unified and coherent energy of God into the fields of a fractured, incoherent or otherwise disturbed patient. The effects of spiritual healing if correctly performed can be profound and long-lasting, leaving the patient with the powerful experience of having made contact with the Divine Field if only for a short time and in an incomplete manner.

During a spiritual healing, the direction of a powerful and focused Divine Creative Field effect channeled by one or more individuals into the damaged field will effect some degree of repair resulting in degrees of coherence being returned. The only caveat is that the patient must themselves seek the healing; they must first have the desire for change. Without this initial external energy healing, most other treatments will prove to be ineffective because the root cause of the problem is not addressed.) The current mainstream medical model under many such circumstances will administer powerful narcotic drugs, which will naturally only make matters worse. The rapid downward spiral movement into the void of all beginnings is then assured and may well be ultimately permanent if the fields are damaged beyond help. Always, in all things, think holistically – go first to the cause, bring the reality of the Divine Creative Field – the unity of all, into everyday conscious thinking and with this holistic and benign conscious awareness we can begin to take more direct and personal control of our health and thus our lives.

Microwave and other field effects need also to be considered when thinking about the health of our energy fields that make up our being, as how could we not? Cell phone towers in close proximity, Smart Meters with their unnatural fields constantly pulsing into the home, 5 G Towers with their hugely damaging fields, and constant WIFI in the home will do untold damage, sometimes quickly, sometimes slowly over time, so that you do not make the connection between those sources and your recently discovered cancer.

Let us pause here and think about the reality of our Divine soul in relation to our modern attitude to and practice of abortion. If we visualise all the fields of our being and then visualise in the centre the smaller field of the being about to manifest in the physical realms with its own tiny soul seed centred perfectly within its tiny field, and if we then imagine that we, with violence and force unconsciously choose (if we were truly conscious this act would be impossible for us) to destroy the physical manifestation of the seed soul without attending to the soul seed itself in any way, we will understand that we have created a situation that can have only powerful ongoing negative field effects. Quite apart from the act of murder we have just committed, which under the law of "as ye sow, so shall ye reap" will one day bring its own cost, we have not taken any account or care of the divine soul itself. What do we think has happened to it? Do we ask, do we think about it? Are there any rites of passage performed for its onward journey? In our very clever modern world where we do not allow the reality of the implicate field or a spiritual presence in our lives much if at all; we do not hold the spiritual rites of passage that would assist these fields to move on, as the reality and importance of them are not part of our worldview. Nevertheless, these aspects are real and powerful. With the death of a being birthed into the physical realm, we all generally perform a rite of passage no matter our religion. However, for some reason in the instance of abortion where the rite of passage is much more critically needed as the tiny soul seed is trapped within the field of its mother and therefore often cannot move on at all, we do nothing. Perhaps we are ashamed of our act, and we think that if we ignore it then it has not happened. However, without assistance, the soul seed may stay trapped within the mother's field, entangled, overlaying, distorting, misaligning and detrimentally influencing all the mother's fields. This manifests eventually in the physical field as chronic ill health. There are thousands, quite possibly hundreds of thousands of women around the world today suffering emotional, mental and often serious physical ill health as the result of an uncompleted abortion. Spiritual healing for both the tiny soul seed and the mother is what is required here, without which good health cannot be regained. We ignore the spiritual aspects in all things at our peril.

Another major cause of damage to our beings at this time are vaccinations. Their composition and overuse should be called into question. The really damaging and frightening aspect is that they can permanently alter and damage our DNA. It is now casually accepted that our constitutions have changed, we are not the well and strong humans our grandparents were, and with each generation we are becoming ever more debilitated. This appears not to alarm anyone or even to trigger any questions. Why? Are we all asleep? How conscious are we? I will not go into this subject any more than that: suffice it to say that there is no excuse for ignorance on this – or any – subject as with the internet all information on all subjects is there for the looking. It is easy to find the exact ingredients of drugs we are thinking of taking, easy to check all the side-effects against the possible positive aspects. We can all look to see how vaccinations are made. If we do not understand all the ingredients, it is easy to look these up. It does not take long, and our life and the lives of our loved ones out into the future may well depend upon it. Children can do this as a project: they love cruising the Net, so encourage them to become involved and to take responsibility for their own health. Knowledge is power; ignorance can and does kill.

There are many substances that some say are bad for our health, but often the problem lies not with the substance itself but our overuse of it. We are not balanced in our approach; if we consume too much of a positive, it becomes a negative. This applies to everything. Alcohol falls into this category: a little good (i.e. with as few chemical additives as possible) beer, a little good wine (red is better than white) is a positive, as it will enhance our life, our meals and our general well-being. That which has been traditionally fermented or brewed is always superior to products that are produced by rushing the natural lengthy process, because this forced process requires that a great many chemicals must be added in order to mask and preserve. It is the chemicals and preservatives that so harm the field of our physical body. Again, these practices are primarily about money, with the lesser focus being the actual product. Once we have adopted a life-giving belief system, once we are more truly aligned with our soul and thus God, we will quite naturally only drink alcohol in moderation anyway, as we will not need to dull or obliterate our pain. The desire to use alcohol to numb and blur the drama of life in this space-time continuum of physical manifestation leaves us. The blurring of life with alcohol is usually accompanied by a dead-end belief system – change the belief system and the behaviour quite naturally follows. With a more positive belief system, we do not get stressed as we did before, so we no longer need alcohol as a relaxant. In addition, as we increase our vibratory rate, we will find that alcohol, which is of a low vibration, begins to dramatically disagree with us. It will so disturb all our fields and create a state of dis-ease that we willingly choose to moderate our intake. Of our own free will we choose moderation and balance, as this engenders greater feelings of unity, harmony, peace and well–being, and each time we unbalance this new state, we like it less and less. We become used to feeling happy, healthy, uplifted, harmonious and joyful and seek only those things that engender that state of being of all our fields.

We all know smoking damages our health. However again, a great part of the problem lies in the chemicals and their derivatives used in the filters and in all the processes of modern manufacture. I am not advocating smoking, but pure organic tobacco leaf, rolled in a leaf, is far less damaging than modern cigarettes. It is possible to smoke and to live a long and healthy life, as there are so many other factors that damage our health and shorten our lives, and if one is happy, positive, eating well and not stressed, then smoking may not harm at all. However, smoking generally is used as a relaxant and a prop in dealing with physical life. It is a crutch, is addictive and as such it cannot properly be an ingredient in a conscious spiritual journey of alignment with our soul and God. All the aspects cigarettes represent are the ones that will quite naturally fall away with greater alignment. On a more mundane level, if we smoke, our taste buds become numbed and we thus are unable to experience fully all the joys of glorious food, which is one of the great positives of being in the physical.

Addendum: The Physical Body

One of the greatest crimes we may commit against our body is the ingestion of illegal drugs. Some are worse than others, but all permanently alter or damage our physical body, in particular our brain. It is true that by partaking of drugs we may apparently easily access realms beyond this one; we may more easily channel divine inspiration in the form of music, art or literature. However, accessing these realms in this abrupt manner, before we have evolved to the point that we can perform these functions naturally and at will, we are engaging in dangerous practices indeed. By ingesting potent drugs, we literally blow pathways and open portals not only through our metaphysical energy fields but also through the wonderful, delicate and complex piece of equipment that is our physical brain, our primary – at the moment – sending and receiving station. By violently assaulting our brain in this manner we risk permanent damage of the physical in this lifetime and possibly enduring damage of our other fields thereafter. We have entered other realms before we are coherent and aligned and thus protected, and so also may others enter into our fields without our consent. If we engage in such practices when we in all our fields are unstable (as we must be to engage in such practices in the first place), we run the very real risk of fracturing all our fields in ways that are beyond our limited physical comprehension at this time. We may also permanently damage our soul so that further evolution is no longer a possibility. If we are lucky in these practices, the worst we will manage to create is permanent damage of the physical manifestation. The ingestion of drugs is a major abuse of all our fields and can only ever be practised by a being without self-love and, as in the overuse of alcohol, abuse in this manner is usually accompanied by a dead-end belief system. All that is a negation of the Divine is usually in place to a greater or lesser degree in the drug user's life. Drug abuse will never be stopped until we address the source of the problem, which are our belief systems which = lack of self-knowledge, lack of love – self and all else, lack of relationship and alignment with our soul and thus the Divine Creative Field. It is as simple and as difficult as that.

Once addicted, the soul becomes far removed from the being and the physical manifestation becomes damaged, or the soul itself becomes contaminated, which also means the physical is in equal state – and so it becomes extremely hard to retrieve the situation. With a being in this condition, who are we to contact, who are we to engage with? Powerful spiritual healing and cleansing must be the first step, after which other help may possibly prevail. Without this first fundamental step, success is difficult if not impossible.

As everything is interconnected and interactive, we need to consider our dental health when considering physical health. Some of our modern dental practices are potential killers; heavy metals such as mercury being used in our mouths, keeping dead teeth in our being (root canals), are causing physical and mental body ill health on a massive scale, as yet for the most part undiagnosed. Again, do your own research in this regard.

There is another deadly source of pollution and damage to our physical body that until recently has not been at all regarded and this source is noise. Remember in Chapter One we saw how Masaru Emoto found that discordant music created ugly, distorted crystals in frozen water; and remember also that sound is integral to creation. Accordingly, we cannot constantly subject all our fields to sound, some harmonious but some not, without creating profound field effects. Our soul resides happiest within silence, all our fields become calmer as they are not resonating to the constant sound. If we subject our bodies to constant noise, whether considered positive noise or not, we damage and fracture all our fields over time. We all need silence for a great part of each day in order to be well, and as constant sound stresses all the fields, this multiple field stress is eventually manifested in the physical. The World Health Organisation's research has shown, belatedly some might say, "the striking contribution of noise to premature deaths from disease. Noise is linked to heart attack and stroke because it creates chronic stress that keeps our bodies in a state of constant alert". Well, common sense should have told us that long before this, and research should not have been needed to discover such an obvious truth. What field effects are being created in the many people we see walking around who are almost permanently plugged into sound – sound directed with force straight into the delicate fields of the brain? We are truly so far removed from the Divine in all our ways that we are becoming mad indeed on a monumental scale, or we could say we are clearly manifesting the degree of our unconsciousness.

Let Balance, Wisdom, Common Sense and the Divine be your guide in all things.

About the Author

Adonia Wylie is a successful businesswoman, author, spiritual counsellor, Reiki master, and clairvoyant. Throughout her career, she has navigated the complexities of spiritual growth, discovering the transformative power of a committed relationship with the Divine. Through her own experiences, she learned that true spiritual transformation occurs when one listens, loves, and aligns with the omniscient intelligence of creation, especially in times of challenge. Adonia's experiences and wisdom have shaped her work, and she now shares her insights in her book Passage to Spiritual Power. She aims to guide others on their own journey toward spiritual love, healing, and empowerment, helping them to unlock the magic that unfolds when they commit to listening, loving, and embracing their connection to the Divine.

Contact Adonia: monastere.publishing@gmail.com

www.ingramcontent.com/pod-product-compliance
Lightning Source LLC
Chambersburg PA
CBHW032335300426
44109CB00041B/852